NEW YORK WORKERS' COMPENSATION LAW

2019 Edition Handbook

Gregory Lois, Esq.

Partner, Lois Law Firm LLC
405 Lexington Avenue, 26th Floor
New York, NY 10174
T. 201-880-7213
F. 201-880-7176
glois@loisllc.com
www.loisllc.com

ISBN-13: 9781728690179

2019 Ed. First Printing November 1, 2018
2018 Ed. First Printing: Nov. 1, 2017
2017 Ed. First Printing: September 1, 2016
2016 Ed. First Printing: December 5, 2015
2015 2nd. Ed. First Printing: November 2014
2015 Ed. First Printing: Sept. 2014
2014 Ed. First Printing: Sept. 2013
2013 Ed. First Printing: Nov. 2012
2012 Ed. First Printing: Nov. 2011
2011 Ed. First Printing: Sept. 2010
Vers. 11/14/18, 3:55 PM

Author: Gregory Lois

This Book is available for Kindle and iBooks.
Educational discounts are available.

Nonfiction. Law. New York.
319 Pages.

Library of Congress Cataloging-in-Publication Data is available upon request. KB1270-1278

Please report errata to: glois@lois-llc.com

DISCLAIMER
This book is not legal advice!

The materials presented in this book are for informational purposes only and are not offered as legal advice as to any particular matter. No reader should act on the basis of these materials without seeking appropriate professional advice as to the particular facts and applicable law involved. While we try to keep this handbook as updated as possible, the materials are not represented to be correct, complete, or up-to-date.

Any websites referred to in this book (or hyperlinks out of these materials if accessed via http or e-reader such as Kindle/iBooks) are for informational purposes only and are not offered as legal advice as to any particular matter. Neither the use of this book or any linked site nor the transfer of information to or from any linked site shall create or constitute an attorney-client relationship between Greg Lois and/or Lois Law Firm LLC and any person. You should not send any confidential information to any web site until after you have entered into a written agreement for the performance of legal services.

ACKNOWLEDGMENT

The author wishes to acknowledge the work of Law Clerk Bailey Ott in copyediting and shepardizing this edition.

CHAPTER LIST

DETAILED TABLE OF CONTENTS

Detailed Table of Contents

INTRODUCTION

History

It is hard to imagine it today, walking down Broadway towards Times Square, but from the late 1800's until the middle of the twentieth century the garment trade was the largest industry in New York City. In fact, more people worked making clothes in New York than anything else, and more clothes were manufactured in New York than in any other city in the world. You can still see the buildings – big ten- and fifteen-story industrial warehouses – in the twenty blocks below Times Square and into SoHo and Tribeca – almost all built to house garment makers.

To visit those factories was to see vast rooms of men and women hunched over sewing machines. Children, too.

It was this miserable working environment that led to the establishment of the first "Workmen's Compensation" laws in America.

There was a fire at the Triangle Shirt Waist Company located on lower Broadway in Manhattan on March 25, 1911. More than 600 men, women, and children were employed there, bent over their sewing machines for twelve hours a day. At approximately 5:00PM, a fire on the eighth floor spread rapidly to the ninth and tenth floors. The doors, which opened inwards, trapped some workers inside. The elevators didn't work and some of the exit doors had been locked shut.

At least 145 workers died that day, some leaping to their deaths to avoid the choking smoke and flames as the factory burned.

Public opinion and organized labor (along with a generous helping of yellow journalism) set the stage for the politicians to enact (and for the courts to subsequently uphold) a system of compulsory insurance providing benefits to injured workers and their dependents.

Since its enactment, the New York Workmen's Compensation Law has undergone more than 1,000 amendments (the most wide-reaching of those very recently, which changes phasing in 2007 (capped weeks of PPD benefits, indemnity pegged to AWW), 2012 (Disability Duration Guidelines), 2014 (Medical Treatment Guidelines) and 2018 (Scheduled Loss of Use among others) and in 1978 was "politically corrected" by being re-named the non-gender-specific "Workers' Compensation Law."

1

In March 2007, New York adopted major reforms to its Workers' Compensation Law including an increase in available temporary disability payments for injured workers with the trade-off being that lifetime permanent partial disability benefits are no longer available. The reforms have spawned significant litigation to clarify the meaning of many of the changed statutory sections. The Workers' Compensation Board has also attempted to resolve many more cases administratively.

In March 2009, a series of articles was published by the New York Times about New York Workers' Compensation. With article titles like "Meatball Justice" and "A World of Hurt," the editorial slant was clear: the workers' compensation system "serves no one well and is arguably the most adversarial of any state in the nation."[1]

In April 2013, the Workers' Compensation Law was changed by the *Business Relief Act* which closed the Fund for Re-Opened Cases, increased the minimum benefit rate, and made other changes to the Law.

In April 2017 the Law was updated to eliminate the defense of attachment for permanent partial disability claims, to revise the "extreme hardship" threshold, and to require the Board to revise the method for computing scheduled loss of use injuries, among other changes.

In October 2018 the Board made permanent the "virtual Hearings" pilot program. The virtual hearing program allows parties to appear in court via web conference.

New York Workers' Compensation Law remains in a state of change with new case law decisions, new regulations, and new Board filing requirements changing the way workers' compensation claims are brought, developed, and defended.

---

[1] http://topics.nytimes.com/top/reference/timestopics/subjects/w/workers_compensation_insurance/index.html, accessed August 30, 2013.

A Brief Overview of New York's Workers' Compensation System.

The workers' compensation system guarantees both medical care and weekly cash benefits to people who are injured on the job. Weekly cash benefits and medical care are paid by the employer's insurance carrier, as directed by the Workers' Compensation Board. Employers pay for this insurance (employees do not contribute).

Nearly 8 million workers are covered by the New York Workers' Compensation Law. In 2017, the Board assembled 176,167 new claims and reopened 313,223 claims when new issues arose. In the same period, 11,742 claims were controverted (or "denied") by the employer/carrier.[2]

The Board maintains 11 district offices across New York, located in:

*   Albany;
*   Binghamton;
*   Brooklyn;
*   Buffalo;
*   Hauppauge;
*   Hempstead;
*   Manhattan;
*   Peekskill;
*   Queens;
*   Rochester; and
*   Syracuse.

The Board also maintains many more hearing points where hearings take place. In 2017, Workers' Compensation Law Judges held 283,411 hearings. Nearly all hearing points were "virtual hearing" capable as this handbook goes to print in November 2018. The Board reports that

About this Book

This book is designed for employers, risk managers, and adjusters who need an easy-to-read plain English reference to the New York Workers' Compensation Law. Each chapter discusses a different topic in detail.

---

[2] These are the most recent figures available, taken from the Board's 2017 Annual Report.

CHAPTER 1: CLAIM OVERVIEW

PART I: CHAPTER OVERVIEW

§1.01   The Four Types of Benefits

Under the New York Workers' Compensation Law, four (4) types of benefits are available to injured workers:

1. **Medical treatment** – emergency and follow-up treatment for their injuries.
2. **Wage compensation for earnings** – lost time while they recover from the immediate effects of their injury.

    * When the claimant is 100% totally temporarily disabled (cannot work at all) this wage compensation is called "temporary total" and compensates the claimant for two-thirds of her pre-injury earnings (tax free) **OR**

    * "Partial temporary" when the claimant can do some work but is not earning their prior level of wages (usually because they can only work part time or have to work at a job that pays less than the work they were doing at the time of the accident). This is calculated as two-thirds of the difference between old wages and post-accident wages.
3. **Death benefits** – payable to the dependents of a worker killed during the course of employment. This is two-thirds of their average weekly wage at the time of injury, subject to maximums and minimums, paid to the survivor for life.
4. **"Permanency" benefits** – payments of money to injured workers to compensate them for the "permanent effects" of an accident.

§1.02   Timeline of the "Typical Case": Admitted Traumatic Accident with Lost Time

1. Initial investigation to confirm loss.
2. If there is medical and lost time, begin benefits.
3. File FROI-00 (Electronic Data Interchange, "EDI").
4. File update EDI documents as the case progresses.

§ 1.03   Immediate Steps for Employee

An injured employee should immediately tell his or her employer or supervisor:

- When she was injured (the temporal);
- Where she was injured;
- How she was injured; and then
- Obtain medical treatment.

In addition, an employee must submit written notice to his or her employer within 30 days.[3] In real life, it often does not work out this neatly – often employees finish their shifts, go home, and get medical treatment without alerting the supervisor to an injury or reporting an accident. More commonly, they do not "remember" they had a workplace accident until after they are terminated, after an adverse workplace decision takes place (like a layoff or reduction in force), or after the employer's internal surveillance tapes are routinely erased (for example, where internal surveillance is only kept for a specific number of days). In these cases, and even where there is no eyewitness to the loss besides form the employee, the workers' compensation Board will routinely rule in favor of the claimant regarding notice despite the obvious prejudice to the employer in defending such late-reported claims.

§1.04   Medical Treatment

Employers may not direct their employees to a particular health care provider unless the employer participates in a Preferred Provider Program ("PPO"). Even where the employer has a PPO, they can only force employees to utilize it for the first 30 days of their medical treatment. Employers can recommend care providing they inform employees of their rights to choose providers of their choice (Form C-3.1).

Self-insured employers, insurance carriers, and the State Insurance Fund are authorized to require employees to obtain diagnostic tests from approved and contract providers who are part of a network selected by the employer or carrier.[4] Employers may require employees to obtain prescriptions from a

---

[3] WCL § 18.

[4] WCL § 13(a)(7)(c).

pharmacy with which they contract.[5] In both situations, notice must be provided to the employee.

§1.05   Investigation and Communication.

All accidents should be investigated fully. The employer should contact the insurance carrier and maintain those communications throughout the claim. The investigation's results should be copied to your defense attorney in the case of a controverted claim.

Any written contact with the claimant's health care provider should be copied to the claimant and the claimant's legal representative, if any. Any attempt to influence the health care provider in any way may be considered interference with the claimant's treatment, which is a misdemeanor.[6]

§1.06   Minor Injuries

For minor injuries, defined as "requiring two or fewer treatments by a person rendering first aid, and with lost time of less than one day beyond the end of the working shift on which the accident occurred," the employer may pay for the first aid treatments directly (instead of referring the incident to the workers' compensation carrier and the Board). Instead, the employer completes a Form C-2F "Employer's Report of Work-Related Injury/Illness" but does not send it to the Board or the insurance carrier – they hold the form in their files for the statutory 18-year period.[7]

§1.07   Responsibilities of the Insurance Carrier

The insurance carrier has 18 days from the date of disability or 10 days after the employer first has knowledge of the alleged accident or within 10 days after the carrier receives Form C-2, whichever is greater, to determine whether to pay benefits or controvert all or part of a claim. Until such controversy is resolved, the carrier does not have to pay indemnity or medical benefits, although the health care provider must continue to treat during this period.

---

[5] WCL § 13(i).

[6] This is referred to as "undue influence."

[7] WCL § 110.

If the insurance carrier agrees with the claim, payment of benefits must begin within 10 days of receiving the C-2 form, or 18 days after the date of disability or 10 days after the employer first has knowledge of the alleged accident.

PART II: REPORTING INJURIES AND DENIALS

§1.08   Injury Reporting

New York Workers' Compensation Law §110 states that an accident must be reported when it:

> will cause a loss of time from regular duties of one day beyond the working day or shift on which the accident occurred, or which has required or will require medical treatment beyond ordinary first aid or more than two treatments by a person rendering first aid.

Information regarding any injury or illness that does not meet the reporting requirements as set forth in WCL §110 must nonetheless be maintained by the employer for at least 18 years and shall be subject to review by the chair of the Board at any time. Even if an injury or illness is not reported, it must be monitored to determine if it meets the reporting requirements at a later date (for example, the claimant obtains more than two first aid treatments).

To be reportable, the injury must:

- Cause the worker to lose one day of work in addition to the date of loss; OR
- Require more than ordinary first aid; OR
- Require at least three "first aid" visits.

The Workers' Compensation Board has an official form for reporting injuries (Form C-2F "Employer's Report of Work-Related Injury/Illness").[8] The form must be provided to the injured worker upon request and has to be maintained (held) by the employer for at least 18 years.

The C-2F report must be filed with the Workers' Compensation Board within 10 days after the occurrence of the accident. Failure to file the report subjects the employer to potential misdemeanor criminal liability, punishable by a fine of not more than $1000. A second penalty – not to exceed $2,500 – can be imposed by the Board.[9]

---

[8] The Form C-2F is available for download here: http://www.wcb.ny.gov/content/main/forms/c2F.pdf

[9] See § 110(4)

9

All injuries other than "minor injuries" (see above for definition of *minor injuries*) must be reported to the Board and insurance carrier **within 10 days**. Failure to file within 10 days after the occurrence of the accident is a misdemeanor and punishable by a fine. In addition, the Board may impose a penalty of up to $2,500.[10]

Statements made on the C-2 form may be legally binding. Questionable claims and claims where the employer suspects fraud on the part of the claimant should be noted on the C-2. The insurance carrier can also be contacted for assistance with completing the form. The C-2 can be filed by a third party designated by the employer, however the employer is ultimately responsible for making sure it is filed.

Filing the C-2F is not necessarily an admission that you agree with the facts of an accident. It is a statement that an employee reported a work-related injury or illness to the employer.

A Board claims examiner may issue an Administrative Decision and impose a penalty of $50 for failure to file a form.[11] The Board may impose a penalty up to $2,500 against an employer who refuses or neglects to file a C-2F.[12]

Given these penalties, employers should make every effort to fully complete the Form C-2F. In recognition of the fact that employers may not have the information to answer all of the questions on the Form C-2 within 10 days of the date of accident, the Board allows for filing of incomplete forms. When this occurs, the employer should complete the form to the best of its ability, indicate where it does not have the information, and timely file the form. However, if the Board receives a Form C-2F that is deficient because a significant number of the questions are unanswered, the employer may be penalized for not filing the form. The decision as to whether a form is deficient will be made by a Workers' Compensation Law Judge or Conciliator.

---

[10] WCL § 110 and 12 NYCRR § 310.2. Also, *see* Chapter 19 ("Penalties").

[11] WCL § 25(3)(e).

[12] WCL § 10(4)

[1]   A word of caution regarding Form C-2F.

As discussed above, filing this report (the report of accident) should not be treated lightly by the employer. Although filing this report seems like a simple clerical task, the statements in the employer's report of accident may be used by the claimant as an admission against interest, even if the information in the report is hearsay. Additionally, in cases where the employee dies before testimony is taken, the first report may be used to corroborate the claimant's version of events.

§ 1.09   Timelines for Denying ("The 18/10 Rule")

A decision by the carrier to deny the compensability of an alleged injury (other than "minor injuries" discussed above) must be reported to the Board and insurance carrier by filing an eClaims form.

There are two different timelines that apply. Th Board will allow for the greater of:

- **18 days:** On or before the 18th day after lost time ("the disability event"); or Require at least three "first aid" visits
- **10 days:** within 10 days after the employer has knowledge of the lost time ("disability event").

The Compliance Unit is measuring Timeliness of Controversy on only lost time claims. The timelines they are checking are (a) 18 days from Date of Accident, (b) 10 days from Date Employer had Knowledge of Injury, and/or (c) 10 days from Initial Date of Disability, whichever period is greater.

To determine the date that the employer had knowledge the Board will use the earliest date of "Date Employer Had Knowledge of the Injury" (DN0040), "Date Employer Had Knowledge of Disability" (DN0281), Board's Assembly Notice Date, and/or the Indexing Notice Date.

To determine the initial Date Disability Began/Current Date Disability Began the Board will look to the filings to see Initial Date Disability Began (DN0056) and Current Date Disability Began (DN0144) are present, and the Initial Return to Work Date (DN0068) is less than or equal to 7 days then Current Date of Disability (DN0041) is used.

PART III: WAGE REPLACEMENT

§1.10   Reimbursement

If an employer continues to pay an employee wages or advances the employee compensation payments following a work-related injury or illness, the employer may seek reimbursement for those wage payments out of any subsequent compensation awards so long as the employer has made a claim for reimbursement prior to the award of compensation.[13]

The claim for reimbursement should be in writing, although it may be made at a Board hearing where a hearing reporter is present to transcribe the proceedings and thus make a record of the request.[14]

The employer may be entitled to reimbursement whether the payments were made voluntarily or as a negotiated benefit (like a collective bargaining agreement).

§1.11   How to Report "No Lost Time" or "Medical Only"

When lost time does not exceed seven days, the claim administrator should file the FROI accepting liability for the medical portion of the claim.[15] An Employer's First Report of Injury Form FROI-00 should be filed; the claim administrator may later file a denial if lost time is claimed (SROI-04). This can also be used when there is no evidence regarding the claim.

---

[13] WCL § 25(4).

[14] The employer forfeits the right to reimbursement for advance wage payments if the claim for reimbursement is not made before the Board makes an award of compensation.

[15] Why seven days? That is the "waiting period" for indemnity benefits in New York.

§1.12   Reporting Lost Time with no Medical.

In an abrupt change from prior practice where no lost time benefits were issued until medical showed a causally-related disability, the Board is now instructing carriers to begin issuing lost time benefits at the minimum rate once
lost time is alleged by the claimant despite the lack of any correlating medical
narrative.[16]

A medical only filing is not appropriate when the employer reports that there
is compensable lost time. For example, a worker was injured at work, went to
the doctor, and called the employer to say that the doctor told him to come
back in ten days with no work until then. In that example, an Initial Payment
(SROI-Initial Payment) indicating payment to the injured worker should be filed
as described in the next paragraph.

[1]   Practical Impact of "Payor Compliance."

There is no requirement that an employer or carrier begin payment absent
medical proof of a disability. The action suggested by the Board will doubtless
lead to claimant being paid unnecessarily. Board Subject Numbers and Bulle-
tins do not have the force or effect of law. To the contrary, the Board is specifically precluded from rendering opinions on disability without supporting medical evidence.

[2]   The 18/10 Rules.

As will be discussed below (Section 1.13[6]), the first benefit check is to be
mailed on or before the 18thday of disability or within 10 days after the employer has knowledge of the accident, whichever is later. WCL § 25(1)(b).

---

[16] See WCB Subject No. 046-808, Dated October 22, 2015 and "Proper eClaims Filing,"
slide 4 of 25, WCB training webinar, September 8, 2015. Link here:
http://www.wcb.ny.gov/content/main/Monitoring/Controversy.pptx

PART IV: REPORTING AND FILING TIMELINE

§1.13   When a Loss Occurs.

[1]   At the time of the accident.

First, the worker gets medical treatment and notifies her supervisor about the accident and how it occurred.

- The employee notifies the employer of the accident in writing, as soon as possible, but within 30 days. The Board may excuse the lack of notice if notice could not be given (for example: the claimant was taken to the hospital and could not inform her employer), the employer had knowledge, or if the employer is not harmed by lack of notice.[17]

- The employee may file a claim with the Board by filing a Form C-3. This must be done within two years of the accident or within two years after the employee knew, or should have known, that the injury was related to employment.[18]

[2]   Within 48 hours of the first medical treatment.

The doctor completes a preliminary medical report on a Form C-4 and mails it to the appropriate District Office. Copies of the Form C-4 must also be sent to the employer or its insurance carrier, the injured worker, and her representative (if any).[19]

[3]   Within 10 days of the accident.

- The employer or its third-party designee reports the injury to the Board and the insurance company with a Form C-2F.[20]

---

[17] WCL § 18.

[18] WCL § 28.

[19] WCL § 13-(a)(4)(a).

[20] WCL § 110 (2).

[4]   Within 14 days of receipt of Form C-2F.

The insurer provides the injured worker with a written statement of his/her rights under the law (Form C-430S). This must be done within 14 days after receipt of the C-2F from the employer or with the first check, whichever is earlier.[21] If the insurer requires the injured worker to use a provider within a network for diagnostic tests, it must provide the injured worker with the name and contact information for the network.[22]

[5]   Within 15 days of initial treatment.

- The doctor completes a 15-day report of the injury and treatment on a Form C-4 and mails it to the District Office of the WCB.[23]

[6]   Within 18 days after the first day of disability, or 10 days after the employer first has knowledge of the alleged accident, or within 10 days after the carrier receives the Form C-2F as per WCL § 25(4).

- The insurer begins the payment of benefits if lost time exceeds seven days. If the claim is being disputed, the insurer must inform the Workers' Compensation Board (and the claimant and his/her representative, if any) by filing an electronic data interchange form FROI-04. If the claim is not disputed, but payment is not being made for specific reasons stated on the notice (e.g., that there is no lost time or that the duration of the disability is less than the 7-day waiting period), the insurer must also notify all of the parties.[24]

- The insurer files a FROI-00 or FROI-04 with the Board indicating either that payment has begun or the reasons why payments are not being made. A copy of the FROI must be transmitted to the claimant and his/her attorney/licensed representative, if any, within one business day of the electronic filing with the Board.[25] If the employee does not

---

[21] WCL § 110 (2).

[22] WCL § 13-a(7)(b).

[23] WCL § 13-a(4)(a).

[24] WCL § 25 (1) *and* 12 NYCRR § 300.22.

[25] 12 NYCRR § 300.22(c).

timely notify the employer, this notice may be filed within 10 days after the employer learns of the accident.[26]

§1.14   Controverting a Claim

A case may be disputed because:

- The employer alleges that proper notice was not timely given; or

- The claim was not properly filed; or

- A lack of causal connection is alleged between the alleged injury and the accident; or

- The employer-employee relationship is denied (*see* Chapter 4); or

- The accident is alleged not to have occurred at work; or

- Any other reason for denying the claim (*see* Chapter 8).

All of these grounds are discussed at length in this book.[27] A dispute will create an adversarial proceeding. The forum will be the Workers' Compensation Board, and a Workers' Compensation Law Judge will hear the dispute.

§1.15   Timelines for Denials

As per Workers' Compensation Law Section 25-2(a), a denial must be filed "on or before the eighteenth day after disability or within ten days after it has knowledge of the accident, whichever period is greater." Failure to file a denial within this time period can result in a $300 penalty assessed against the carrier (but defenses are not stripped). Under Section 25-2(b), a denial may be filed "within 25 days from the date of mailing of a notice that the case has been indexed." If the denial is not filed (by filing FROI-04 or SROI-04), then all defenses (substantive or legal) are barred.

In practice, the Board rarely assesses the $300 penalty for late filing under Section 25-2(a) and instead rigorously enforces the preclusion of witnesses or defenses under Section 25-2(b).

---

[26] For more specifics on when to pay (and how to pay) wage compensation, *see* Chapter 7 ("Indemnity Benefits") in this book.

[27] *See* Chapter 2 ("Fighting Frivolous Claims") and Chapter 5 ("Defenses").

§1.16   Completing the FROI-04 (Denying the Claim)

eClaims Denial Code	Translation
1A: No Compensable Accident (Coming and Going)	No Accident Arising Out of and In the Course of Employment
1B: No Compensable Accident (Horse-play)	No Accident Arising Out of and In the Course of Employment
1C: No Compensable Accident (Willful Intent to Injure Oneself)	No Accident Arising Out of and In the Course of Employment
1D: No Compensable Accident (Not WCL Definition of Accident)	No Accident Within Meaning of WCL
1E: No Compensable Accident (Deviation from Employment)	No Accident Arising Out of and In the Course of Employment
1F: No Compensable Accident (Recreational/Social Activity)	No Accident Within Meaning of WCL
1I: Presumption Does Not Apply	No Accident/Occupational Disease Arising Out of and In the Course of Employment
2C: No Causal Relationship (Stress non-work related)	No Accident Arising Out of and In the Course of Employment
2D: No Causal Relationship (No Medical Evidence of Injury)	No Prima Facie Medical Evidence
2E: No Causal Relationship (No Injury Per Statutory Definition)	No Causally Related Accident or Occupational Disease
3A: No Employer-Employee Relationship	No Employer-Employee Relationship
3B: Independent Contractor	No Employer-Employee Relationship
3C: Not WCL Definition of Employee	No Employer-Employee Relationship
3D: No Jurisdiction	No Subject Matter Jurisdiction
3E: No Coverage (No policy in Effect on Date of Accident)	Cancellation of Coverage
3F: Statute of Limitations Expire	Timely Filing (Section 28)
3G: Statute Exempts Claimant	Employer-Employee Relationship
5A: Failure to Report Timely	Notice (Section 18)

§1.17   Within 25 Days of the Notice Indexing

After the Board notifies the employer (or its insurance carrier) that a workers' compensation case has been indexed against the employer, the employer may file a notice of controversy (FROI-04) within 25 days from the date of mailing of the notice of indexing. Failure to file the notice of controversy within the prescribed 25-day time limit could bar the employer and its carrier from pleading certain defenses to the claim.[28]

Where the employer is **not** controverting (challenging) the claim – If payment has not begun because no compensation is presently due, a FROI-00 must be filed with the Board within 25 days after the Board has transmitted a notice of indexing.

§1.18   Waiting to Index Before Controverting

A common question for adjusters is whether to wait for the Board to formally "index" a claim before filing the Notice of Controversy/FROI-04 (disputing the compensability of the claim). Strategically, if the claimant does not file the appropriate forms or if medical is not submitted to the Board, there is a possibility that the case will not be indexed - in which case, the employer/carrier may not have to file any formal notice disputing the case.

Generally, if a claim is going to be controverted, the FROI-04 and Pre-hearing Conference Statement should be filed *regardless of the state of Board indexing*. Simply put, the potential for a missed Notice of Indexing, tight timelines for filing the Notice of Controversy, etc., make the "waiting" strategy risky.

§1.19   Serving the Denial on the Claimant

The Regulations require that the claimant and her attorney be served with a paper copy of the denial. However, as of May 23, 2014, the Board is no longer accepting paper denial forms. The Board has issued new regulations which provide that the claimant and her attorney can be served with a paper copy of the denial "within one business day" of the electronic filing being issued, The Board

---

[28] WCL § 25(2)(b).

has also issued a statement that the Board will generate these paper denial forms[29] and place them in the Electronic Case Folder "within one day."

The Board has mandated service on the parties of a paper form in the following situations:

- FROI 00 - Original (Mailing to parties is optional)
- FROI 01 - Cancel
- FROI 02 - Change
- **FROI 04 - Denial**
- FROI AQ - Acquired Claim (Mailing to parties is optional)
- FROI AU - Acquired/Unallocated (Mailing to parties is optional)
- FROI UR - Upon Request (Mailing to parties is optional)
- SROI 02 - Change
- SROI 04 - Denial
- SROI AP - Acquired/Payment
- SROI CA - Change in Benefit Amount
- SROI CB - Change in Benefit Type
- SROI CD - Compensable Death
- SROI EP - Employer Paid
- SROI ER - Employer Reinstatement
- SROI IP - Initial Payment
- SROI PD - Partial Denial
- SROI PY - Payment Report
- SROI RB - Reinstatement of Benefit
- SROI RE - Reduced Earnings
- SROI S1 - Suspension, RTW or Medically Determined/Qualified to RTW
- SROI S2 - Suspension, Medical Non-Compliance
- SROI S4 - Suspension, Claimant Death
- SROI S5 - Suspension, Incarceration
- SROI S7 - Suspension, Benefits Exhausted
- SROI SD - Suspension, Directed By Jurisdiction

---

[29] Called a "transaction report" by the Board. http://www.wcb.ny.gov/content/main/SubjectNos/sn046_522.jsp

- SROI SJ - Suspended Pending Appeal or Judicial Review
- SROI SA - Sub-Annual (Mailing to parties is optional)
- SROI UR - Upon Request (Mailing to parties is optional)

So, when a denial is made, the FROI-04 must be printed out and mailed to the claimant and her attorney within one business day (12 NYCRR 300.22[2][b][1][ii]). If the defense attorney did not also prepare and serve a paper C-7 (paper only on the claimant and her attorney) then defense should prepare and file a Form OC-400.5 certifying the controversy.[30]

If the Board finds that the denial was "interposed without just cause," the law allows for a penalty of $300 to be paid to the claimant. This $300 is in addition to any amount found payable under the award.

§1.20   Reporting Every Two Weeks
The insurer makes payments of benefits to the injured employee (if the case is not being disputed).

§1.21   Reporting to the Board

The carrier must notify the Board by filing the correct SROI form (see below) when compensation is stopped or modified, within 16 days after the date on which payments were stopped or modified.[31] The carrier/employer then must transmit the electronic form generated by the Board to the claimant and her attorney (if any) within one business day of the filing.[32]

§1.22   Mailing Documents to the Board

The centralized mailing address is:
New York State Workers' Compensation Board
Centralized Mailing Address
PO Box 5205
Binghamton, NY 13902-5205

---

[30] See 12 NYCRR 300.38. Form OC-400.5 is available at http://www.wcb.ny.gov/content/main/forms/oc400_5.pdf

[31] WCL § 25 (1)(d).

[32] 12 NYCRR 300.22(f).

§1.23   Electronic Document Submission

The WCB allows certain forms to be attached to emails and sent to wcbclaimsfiling@wcb.ny.gov.

Please note that a separate email is required for each claimant. You must put the case number (the WCB case number) in the subject line of the email. Forms that cannot be emailed include those forms that require a verification of original signature.

The received date for all documents emailed to the above address will be recorded by a stamp on the document that indicates the complete date and time the email was received; e.g., "Received by WCB Email on 11/13/2017 9:41:16 AM".

[1]   Forms that Should not be Emailed

- Forms and other documents not related to a specific workers' compensation injury should not be emailed to this address.
- Non-claims forms and documents should be sent by mail to the appropriate Board office or department.
- Forms that require verification of the original signature, Form C-3S, Form C-3.3, Form C-32.1, Form OC-110A, Form MD-3, Form MD-1, Form WTC-12, AFF series, WTC-AFF series, and 110A correspondence with a notary stamp, should not be emailed.

[2]   EDI Replacement for Deprecated Forms

The following forms are now deprecated, and replaced with Electronic Data Interchange:

- C-2 (Employer's Report of Work-Related Injury/Illness)
- C-7 (Notice That Right to Compensation is Controverted)
- C-8/8.6 (Notice That Payment of Compensation Has Been Stopped or Modified)
- C-669 (Notice to Chair of Carrier's Action on Claim for Benefits)
- VAW-2 (Political Subdivision's Report of Injury to Volunteer Ambulance Worker)
- VF-2 (Political Subdivision's Report of Injury to Volunteer Firefighter)

The following forms replace the prior forms which were used to transmit the same information (see above):

21

- FROI 00 - Original (Mailing to parties is optional)
- FROI 01 - Cancel
- FROI 02 - Change
- FROI 04 - Denial
- FROI AQ - Acquired Claim (Mailing to parties is optional)
- FROI AU - Acquired/Unallocated (Mailing to parties is optional)
- FROI UR - Upon Request (Mailing to parties is optional)
- SROI 02 - Change
- SROI 04 - Denial
- SROI AP - Acquired/Payment
- SROI CA - Change in Benefit Amount
- SROI CB - Change in Benefit Type
- SROI CD - Compensable Death
- SROI EP - Employer Paid
- SROI ER - Employer Reinstatement
- SROI IP - Initial Payment
- SROI PD - Partial Denial
- SROI PY - Payment Report
- SROI RB - Reinstatement of Benefit
- SROI RE - Reduced Earnings
- SROI S1 - Suspension, RTW or Medically Determined/Qualified to RTW
- SROI S2 - Suspension, Medical Non-Compliance
- SROI S4 - Suspension, Claimant Death
- SROI S5 - Suspension, Incarceration
- SROI S7 - Suspension, Benefits Exhausted
- SROI SD - Suspension, Directed By Jurisdiction
- SROI SJ - Suspended Pending Appeal or Judicial Review
- SROI SA - Sub-Annual (Mailing to parties is optional)
- SROI UR - Upon Request (Mailing to parties is optional)

The doctor periodically submits progress reports following every treatment to the Board on Form C-4.2.

§1.24   Practical Advice for Claims Handlers on EDI

For adjusters handling claims, we provide the following practical tips:

1. Download and print out the "event table" cheat sheet (PDF) that lists all the event triggers (for example, reduction in benefits) and identifies the correct electronic form to designate. This "cheat sheet" provides a list of all the prior forms filed (for example, Form C-8/8.6, showing a change or reduction in benefit) and then provides the corresponding EDI equivalents. The "cheat sheet" is available here: http://www.wcb.ny.gov/content/ebiz/eclaims/ReqTables/NYS_R3_EventTable.pdf

2. Download and print out the PDF "cheat sheet" provided by the Board providing all the codes necessary to complete the electronic submissions. The "cheat sheet" is available here: http://www.wcb.ny.gov/content/ebiz/eclaims/ReqTables/NYS_R3_Quick_Code_RefRev.pdf

3. When denying claims (filing FROI-04 or SROI-04) contact counsel to confirm you are entering the appropriate denial codes. A denial reason not raised is waived!

§1.25   Faxing to the Board

In addition to regular US Postal Service mail, claims-related forms and documents may also be faxed to the Board at **1-877-533-0337**. Forms that require verification of the original signature should not be faxed.

PART V: HEARINGS

§1.26   Hearing Basics

Hearings can be scheduled by the Board (without request by either party. The Board will schedule hearings on its own initiative. The goal of every hearing is transmitted to the parties of interest on Form EC-16.1. Initial hearings are held to address the establishment of a case: parties must be prepared to dis-cuss the facts of the accident, notice, and the causal relationship of the al-leged injuries to the employment.

In an admitted case, defense counsel will rely on handling instructions, the Form C-2F (if any), the FROI/SROI screens, the return-to-work information available, and the wage information contained in the FROI. Statements con-tained in the filings (particularly in the Form C-2F) may be considered stipula-tions and binding (on the part of the employer).

Prior to any regularly-scheduled hearing (particularly in an established case) the issues facing the carrier/employer should be well understood. Hearing no-tices are prepared and mailed to all parties by the Board approximately 21 days prior to the date of hearing. Defense counsel should supply the employer with an action plan for upcoming hearings and request any necessary docu-ments/information in preparation for the listing.

§1.27   Requesting Hearings

Any party can request a hearing as per WCL §20, which states:

> [The Board] upon application of either party, shall order a hearing, and within thirty days after a claim for compensation is submitted un-der this section, or such hearing closed, shall make or deny an award, determining such claim for compensation, and file the same in the of-fice of the chair. Immediately after such filing the chair shall send to the parties a copy of the decision. Upon a hearing pursuant to this section either party may present evidence and be represented by counsel.

A carrier requests a hearing by filing a Form RFA-2 ("Request for Further Action by Carrier/Employer"). The most common Request for Further Action filed by employers is a request to stop or reduce benefits in a case where ongoing ben-efits have been ordered by the Court. A carrier/employer cannot simply stop paying benefits because an IME physician says the claimant has reached "MMI" or has a reduced level of disability - there is no "self-help" allowed and the case must be heard by a Law Judge before benefits can be stopped or reduced.

As per 12 N.Y.C.R.R 300.23(b):

> In any case where the board has made an award of compensation for a temporary total or temporary partial disability at an established rate of compensation, and there is a direction for continuation of payments, the employer or carrier shall continue payments at such rate, and such payments shall not be suspended or reduced until: (1) there is filed with the chair in the district office where the case is assigned, a notice of intention to suspend or reduce on a prescribed form accompanied by supporting evidence justifying such suspension or reduction together with proof of mailing of copies thereof upon the claimant, his/her doctor and his/her representative.

Our practical advice for requesting hearings before the Board is to include the documentary evidence in support of the relief requested as an attachment. Another common employer request is to address ongoing benefits in cases where an IME physician has found the claimant to have reached MMI or where there is an issue as to degree of disability. We strongly recommend that a copy of the IME report or medical records to be relied upon be attached to the RFA-2 form.

§1.28   Claimant's Right to Request a 45-Day Hearing

Under the new language in WCL § 25(2)(a), when a claimant or his or her legal representative files the appropriate form, either Request for Assistance by Injured Worker (Form RFA-1W) or Request for Further Action by Legal Counsel (Form RFA-1LC), and checks the appropriate boxes to state that all of the following are true, the Board will expedite the request to schedule a hearing within 45 days of the Board's receipt of the request.

- A claim for workers' compensation has been filed.
- Medical evidence of work-related injury or illness is submitted.
- Claimant is not working in any capacity.
- Claimant is not otherwise barred from receipt of compensation.
- The employer is not paying the claimant as required by law.
- The employer is not controverting the right to compensation (as there is already an expedited process for controverted claims).

- Claimant or his or her legal representative has attempted to resolve the issue with the employer, yet the claimant is still not being paid.

[1]   When a 45-Day Hearing is not Appropriate

The employer is required to make payments required by law. This means that payment must be made within 18 days of disability or 10 days of the employer's knowledge of the disability, whichever is longer (WCL § 25[1][b]). Board rule 12 NYCRR 300.23(a) and (b) sets forth the circumstances under which an employer may suspend or reduce benefits, even cases where the claimant is not working. For example, in cases where there is a medical report from the claimant's doctor indicating no disability, or where a claimant becomes incarcerated for a felony, the employer can suspend or reduce benefits. The Board also issues decisions setting forth awards of compensation, which may indicate no continuing payments because there is no compensable lost time.

A 45-day hearing cannot be requested:

- Initially, until the 18 or 10 days set forth in statute have passed.
- If the Board has issued a decision in the case finding no compensable lost time.
- If the claimant is being paid by the employer directly, and the awards which would be made at the hearing would be to reimburse or credit the employer.
- If the claimant is receiving an indemnity payment, even if not the total rate.

[2]   Revised Request for Further Action (RFA-1LC and RFA-1W) Forms

In 2017 the Board revised versions of Request for Further Action by Legal Counsel (Form RFA-1LC) and Request for Further Action by Injured Worker (Form RFA-1W).

Form RFA-1LC includes a check box to request a 45-day hearing. To qualify for a 45-day hearing, all the conditions listed next to the hearing request check box must be met. Form RFA-1W has a new check box "a" in Section A under Compensation Payments for the claimant to indicate that he or she is not working and to check the following details that apply:

- I have filed a claim for a work-related injury.
- My employer is not paying my wages.
- My claim has not been denied.
- I have not received a decision barring me from compensation.

- I have attempted to resolve the issue with the insurer

Outreach to the employer is a required element. This means that the claimant, or if represented, his or her legal representative, must demonstrate that there was a good faith attempt made to resolve the issue of payment prior to resorting to hearing. Forms RFA-1LC and RFA-1W must set forth that all of the required elements are in place to justify the setting of the 45-day hearing.

§1.26   Conduct of Hearing, and Consequences for Filing Groundless Requests

A workers' compensation law judge (WCLJ) will conduct the hearing and evaluate the request and the evidence. If payments are due, they will be ordered by the WCLJ. The WCLJ will order costs and attorney's fees in the amount of $500 per violation, for raising or continuing an issue without reasonable grounds under WCL § 114-a (3) if the request is baseless, premature, or inappropriate. Additionally, in the event of a finding under WCL § 114-a (3), the claimant's legal representative will not receive a fee, even if an award is made, as the inappropriate use of the 45-day hearing request constitutes a waste of judicial resources that should be utilized for appropriate cases.[33]

WCL § 114-a(3)(i) and (ii) may be imposed where the form is not accurately or completely filled out:

- A claim was not filed, or there is a lack of required medical evidence.
- The requisite time periods in WCL § 25 have not passed. The Board will evaluate the circumstances as they existed at the time the request was sent to the Board. For example, it is inappropriate for a claimant's attorney, as a matter of course, to file Form RFA-1 to request a 45-day hearing when retained by the claimant, without first meeting all the required elements.
- The claim, in whole or part, is controverted.
- There is an existing direction of no further compensable lost time.
- The claimant is not entitled to payments because her or she is not "disabled and not working".
- The claimant's legal representative has not reached out to the employer to make a good-faith effort to resolve the situation.
- The claimant is not out-of-work.

---

[33] Note: These penalties will not be imposed against an unrepresented claimant.

- The claimant seeks to record reimbursement or credit to the employer

If Form RFA-1LC is submitted for a 45-day hearing, and the parties can resolve the issue prior to hearing, the parties should inform the Board. If payments are voluntary (i.e., prior to a formal award having been made by the Board), and the employer agrees to commence payments, no formal stipulation is required. If the parties wish to stipulate, or if a stipulation is appropriate because an award has been previously made, the parties should submit the written Stipulation (Form C-300.5) to the Board and notify the Board that a 45-day hearing is no longer necessary.

§1.27   Trial on Limited Issues – Non-Expedited

In an established cases issues arise that must be resolved by way of trial. Typical trial topics in an established (or admitted) case include: nature and degree of temporary disability, disputes about medical treatment issues, attachment to the workforce, reduced earnings, and employee fraud. Less commonly, trials can be held on issues including establishment of an average weekly wage, concurrent employment, wage expectancy, or any other issues in dispute.

Parties will often bring the disputed issue to the attention of the Law Judge by filing an RFA-2 (by the employer) or RFA-1LC (on behalf of the claimant). Once the issue is raised, the Board will set the matter down for a hearing before a Law Judge. If the issue cannot be resolved, it may be set down for a trial on the issue, by way of a Notice of Decision (Form EC-23).

Trial proceedings are non-continuous. Most medical testimony is produced by way of deposition rather than live testimony. The parties will coordinate the schedule of physician testimony in accordance with the schedule set by the trial judge. Nearly all physician testimony take place by telephone deposition.

All non-medical testimony must be presented before the Law Judge, with rare exception for witnesses who reside out of state. Typically, the testimony of the claimant will be presented last, after medical testimony has been produced.

Each case set down for trial will have a date in which all depositions transcripts must be completed. Extensions of time can be granted by the Court for good cause shown, but the Affidavits in support of a request to extend time must be filed ten (10) days prior to the date the depositions transcripts were to be submitted.

Following the submission of all testimony, the Law Judge will issue a decision from the bench or make a reserved decision. It is the practice of my office to always request an opportunity to submit a memorandum of law and summation of facts to aid the Judge in reaching their final decision.

In my office, simple trials on issues represent approximately 50% of our overall trial practice (with the other 50% being expedited proceedings, generally for denial/controverted claims).

§1.28   Expedited Hearings

WCL §25(3)(d) applies to all cases where "issues have not been resolved within one year after such issues were raised before the Board, or if multiple claims arise from the same accident or occurrence, or if all parties agree to an expedited hearing, or where a notice of controversy has been filed, or if the chair otherwise deems it necessary, the chair may order the case transferred to the special part for expedited proceedings."

The "Special Part for Expedited Proceedings" simply refers to a case being set down for a trial, with a date certain as to the decision. The case is not actually transferred to a new judge or into special courtroom. The goal of transfer to an Expedited Hearing calendar is "for all issues to be decided in one hearing."

The Regulations which govern practice in the Expedited Hearing part are set forth at 12 N.Y.C.R.R. 300.34. A case is moved to the expedited part by way of an Order, issued after a hearing. Within 20 days of transfer to the expedited part, both parties must file a "Pre-hearing Conference Statement" (Form PH-16.2) if one was not previously filed. An initial hearing must be scheduled within 30 days after the Order of transfer to the expedited calendar is issued. There is no "electronic" equivalent of the Pre-hearing Conference Statement."

Adjournments by the defense may be granted for no longer than 30 days. If the adjournment request of the defense is deemed "frivolous" the attorney who makes the request shall be personally liable for a $1,000 penalty.

Only the final decision of the Law Judge in a case assigned to the expedited part can be appealed; all orders concerning the proofs, testimony, or evidence are "interlocutory" and not subject to appeal. Only a final decision, or an interim determination of accident or occupational disease, notice, causal relationship or monetary award can be appealed.

§1.29   Expedited Trial in Controverted Claims

Because ALL controverted (denied) cases (with exceptions for death claims, occupational, and "complex" cases) are automatically assigned to the expedited hearing part, we will explore the rules surrounding these trials. These "hurry up" trials require tight coordination between defense counsel and employer to prepare and present all viable defenses.

We continue to recommend that all denied cases are discussed with counsel before a denial is issued; we also recommend that counsel file the Pre-hearing Conference Statement.

§1.30   The Pre-Hearing Conference

Upon a Notice of Controversy being filed (FROI-04 or SROI-04) the case will be scheduled for a Pre-Hearing Conference but only where the claimant has filed supporting medical. A Form PH-16.2 "Pre-Hearing Conference Statement" must be filed 10 days prior to the Pre-Hearing Conference. Failure to file this form timely may result in defenses being waived!

At the pre-hearing conference, the defense's attorney must be prepared with the following:

- an offer of proof for every affirmative defense raised;
- statutory and case citations for all legal defenses;
- a list of medical witnesses that the employer wishes to cross-examine;
- any additional parties to add to the litigation;
- a plan for any additional discovery necessary.

The Law Judge can order cross-examination of the claimant's treating physician by either deposition or live testimony at a scheduled hearing. Defense counsel should have a plan for requesting whichever mode of cross-examination bests serves the needs of the employer (note that if the medical witness fails to appear at the scheduled hearing, the Judge will authorize a subpoena and give the doctor a "second chance" to appear).

At any pre-hearing conference, the case may be settled under Section 32. Ten (10) days before the pre-hearing conference, claimant's attorney must file forms C-3 and make sure at least one C-4 (medical record) – failure to do so can result in the case being thrown out by the Law Judge. The case can then be re-opened if claimant's attorney files the appropriate forms. Failure by the claimant to proceed (or appear) will result in the case being closed.

If the claimant is represented, a Form PH-16.2 ("Pre-Hearing Conference State-ment") must be filed 10 days before the hearing, or claimant's counsel is not entitled to a fee.

The pre-hearing conference may result in the Judge issuing Orders or directions to the parties. These orders or directions are not appealable (under WCL § 23) until the controverted issues in dispute are resolved.

If everything has been presented and prepared correctly, the Judge will then set the matter down for an Expedited Hearing. Although this sounds "singular" (i.e., one hearing) it includes out-of-court proceedings (usually medical witness depositions). Similarly, there is nothing that prevents the parties from sched-uling necessary depositions or testimony in the absence of specific judicial di-rection to do so.

In cases where medical proofs are going to be required, and the claimant has already produced medical records which will likely be considered prime facie medical evidence, defense counsel may immediately proceed to scheduling necessary medical testimony (by way of subpoenaed deposition) and collecting relevant medical records (using executed C-3.3 "Limited Release" procedures on an expedited basis). These activities may be necessary where the ability of the defense to get organized and present a meaningful defense would be se-verely limited by the scheduling requirements of the expedited hearing pro-cess, which requires a hearing on the lay proofs (with testimony completed) within 30 days of the Pre-Hearing Conference, an IME for the employer com-pleted and served within 27 days of the Pre-hearing Conference, and all medi-cal proofs concluded (including deposition testimony of the claimant's treating physicians and the IME doctor) within 60 days of the Pre-hearing Conference.

Because the specific timelines differ slightly depending on whether or not med-ical proofs will be needed and whether or not the claimant is represented, we will discuss these three separate scenarios, below.

§1.31   The Expedited Hearing Process for Represented Claimants

The Regulations (12 N.Y.C.R.R. 300.38) require that any IME report must be filed and served pursuant to Section 137 no later than 3 days from the date of the initial expedited hearing. In practice, this will be extremely difficult to do if the IME has not already been scheduled by the time of the Pre-hearing Confer-ence, as the minimum time (unless the claimant waives notice) that must elapse before the IME is ten days and scheduling any such IME on short notice is difficult. We recommend that if medical testimony on behalf of the employer is going to be necessary to controvert a claim, an IME be scheduled at the time of denial (concurrent with filing the PH-16.2).

§1.32   Hearing Process Where Medical Testimony Must be Taken

Medical testimony will usually be obtained by deposition. All depositions must be completed, and transcripts submitted to the Board within 85 days of the filing of the FROI-04 electronic denial. Defense can object to any establishing questions (direct testimony) directed to the treating physician, as their reports are deemed to be in evidence as a direct examination.

Represented claimants with medical testimony	Authority
File FROI-04	12 NYCRR 300.38(a)
within 30 days of receipt of FROI-04 and medical report	12 NYCRR 300.38(b)(1)
Pre-hearing Conference held	12 NYCRR 300.38(f) and (g)
no more than 30 days	
Expedited hearing with lay testimony	12 NYCRR 300.38(g)(7) & 12 N.Y.C.R.R. 300.38(h)(2)(i)
No more than 55 days from Pre-hearing Conference	12 NYCRR 300.38(g)(11)
Medical testimony at hearing or by deposition	12 NYCRR 300.38(g)(11)
At the last hearing, unless briefs were ordered (in which case, add 5 days)	
Final Decision	12 NYCRR 300.38(h)(4)

30 days

60 days

33

§1.33   Hearing Process Where Medical Testimony will not be Taken

The following is the hearing process where the defense is purely legal or factual.

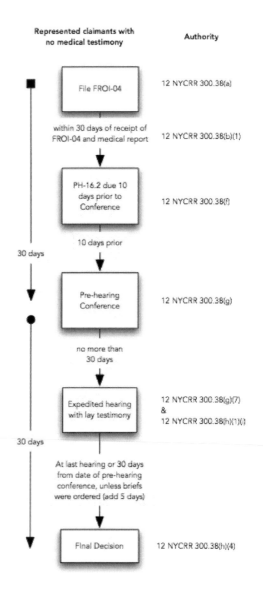

Represented claimants with no medical testimony — Authority

Step	Authority
File FROI-04	12 NYCRR 300.38(a)
within 30 days of receipt of FROI-04 and medical report	12 NYCRR 300.38(b)(1)
PH-16.2 due 10 days prior to Conference	12 NYCRR 300.38(f)
10 days prior	
Pre-hearing Conference	12 NYCRR 300.38(g)
no more than 30 days	
Expedited hearing with lay testimony	12 NYCRR 300.38(g)(7) & 12 NYCRR 300.38(h)(1)(i)
At last hearing or 30 days from date of pre-hearing conference, unless briefs were ordered (add 5 days)	
Final Decision	12 NYCRR 300.38(h)(4)

30 days

30 days

§1.34   Hearing Process for Unrepresented Claimants

In the case of an unrepresented claimant, the rules allow for all testimony to take place at a single hearing, including medical witnesses to appear, within 60 days of the Pre-hearing Conference. In practice, a judge of compensation will usually encourage an unrepresented claimant to obtain counsel, and the matter will not be set down for an expedited hearing until counsel is chosen.

§1.35   Impossibility of Getting an Adjournment

Adjournments of a Pre-hearing Conference, Expedited Hearing, or deposition of a medical witness in a controverted case will only be granted for "an emergency." An "emergency" is defined by the rules as "a serious event" that includes a death in the family, a serious illness, significant prior professional or business commitment, and inclement weather that prevents travel. It does not include any even that could be mitigated "by the timely taking of reasonable action."

Defense counsel that makes a frivolous request for adjournment can be fined $1,000 (personally). Claimant's attorneys who request a frivolous adjournment can be fined $500. Unrepresented claimants are not subject to any penalty.

§1.36   Virtual Hearing Program

Virtual hearings were first tested in the Capital District Office in Menands in November 2017, then rolled out across the state. On October 25, 2018 the "pilot program" was formally made permanent. To participate in a virtual hearing, the party of interest needs only a smart phone, tablet or computer with a microphone and video camera, as well as a high-speed internet connection. All participants can see and hear each other on their respective screens. Additionally, workers' compensation law judges can share claim documents with all involved parties.

Virtual hearings save injured workers the burden of travel, which is particularly helpful for someone with impaired mobility during the harsh winter months, and make it easier for employers and attorneys, to participate in the workers' compensation system.

For more information on the virtual hearing program, see the Board's website.

CHAPTER 2: FIGHTING FRIVOLOUS CLAIMS

PART I: CONTROVERTING CLAIMS

§2.01   Reasons for Controverting Claims

The insurance carrier can contest the claim for a variety of reasons, including that the injury was not related to work, or the employee is not injured to the extent that he or she is claiming. An employer can also request that the insurance carrier contest the claim. However, since the insurance carrier has assumed the liability for the claim, it is not required to comply with the employer's request.

A case may be disputed because:
* The employer alleges that proper notice was not timely given; or
* The claim was not properly filed; or
* A lack of causal connection is alleged between the alleged injury and the accident; or
* The employer-employee relationship is denied[34]; or
* The accident is alleged not to have occurred at work; or
* Any other reason for denying the claim.

§2.02   How a Claim is Controverted

[1]   First Report of Injury – Denial Type 04 Form

File an electronic denial "First Report of Injury - Denial Type 04" (FROI-04) which replaced the Form C-7 "Notice that Right to Compensation is Controverted." The denial filing (FROI-04) provides a description of the legal and factual defenses raised. Once the FROI-04 and a medical record is filed, the case will be set down for an expedited hearing within 30 days.

Because the denial form (FROI-04) must be filed electronically, only the carrier/employer can file this initial pleading, then refer the claim to outside

---

[34] *See* "Chapter 7: Employers and Employees," - this book.

counsel. This introduces delay and a possible dropped deadline into a time-sensitive process.

[2]   Hearings and Pre-Conference Statements

An expedited hearing is scheduled to give a Judge the opportunity to hear both sides of a disputed issue. 10 days before the expedited hearing, a Pre-hearing Conference Statement (Form PH-16.2) must be filed.[35] If the Pre-Hearing Conference Statement is not filed on time, all defenses are **waived**.

The Board may hold a hearing or hearings before a WCL Judge. The Judge may take testimony, order depositions, review medical and other evidence and will decide whether the claimant is entitled to benefits. If the claim is determined to be compensable, the Judge determines the amount and duration of the compensation award.

We counsel our clients that if you are denying a case, **file a Pre-Hearing Conference Statement at the same time** - to avoid the potential for failing to file the Statement (Form PH-16.2) within the 10 days. There is just too much that can go wrong - late notice of the hearing date, no notice at all, etc! If you have enough information to justify a denial, you have enough information to fill out the Pre-hearing Conference Statement - so go ahead and file the PH-16.2 at the same time.

There is no prohibition on *amending* a Pre-Hearing Conference Statement prior to the Pre-hearing Conference. As more information or potential exhibits are obtained through the limited discovery process (such as use of expedited subpoena power) the original conference statement filing can be supplemented.

[3]   Wavier of Defenses for Late Pre-Hearing Conference Statement.

The Appellate court has consistently upheld the waiver of defenses where the employer raised jurisdictional defenses in a timely C-7 but then failed to file a Pre-Hearing Conference Statement on time (ten days prior to the scheduled pre-Hearing Conference). In *Smith v Albany County Sheriff's Dep't*, the Appellate Division ruled that because the carrier submitted an untimely prehearing conference statement the employer waived all defenses to the claim and, upon review of claimant's medical records, established an occupational injury.[36] In a

---

[35] *See* 12 NYCRR 300.38(f)(4). Form PH-16.2 can be downloaded here: http://www.wcb.ny.gov/content/main/forms/ph16_2.pdf. or completed online.

[36] *Smith v. Albany County Sheriff's Dep't*, 82 A.D.3d 1334 (3d Dep't2011).

similar case decided the same day, the Appellate Panel ruled that stripping the carrier of its defenses for failing to file the Pre Hearing Conference Statement on time was "not unreasonable, arbitrary, capricious or contrary to the statute under which it [is] promulgated."[37]

Be wary of the requirement that the Pre-Hearing Conference Statement be filed ten days prior to the expedited hearing - implement a plan to make sure this is done timely or risk a suppression of defenses!

[4]   Filing a Late Pre-Hearing Conference Statement

In a case decided September 29, 2011, the Appellate Division reviewed a situation where the employer denied the case (filed a C-7) but failed to file the PH-16.2 within the time limits.[38] To fix the mistake, counsel immediately filed an "amended notice of controversy" and argued that the originally-scheduled Pre-hearing Conference was therefore "premature" and should have been rescheduled, thereby making the PH-16.2 timely.

The Workers' Compensation Law Judge refused to excuse the late fling, and stripped the employer of its defenses, ultimately establishing the claim. In a decision dated September 29, 2011, the Appellate Division affirmed this outcome.

§2.03   Employer Rights

An employer also has the right to electronically access the Board's case file for a claim filed by the employer's worker by visiting one of the Board's customer service centers. The Board's Electronic Case Folder (ECF) allows parties of interest to view the documents in the claim file electronically. Employers should go to one of the 11 district offices or 30 Customer Service Centers with identification to obtain a password. Based on the confidentiality of workers' compensation records be prepared to offer proof that you are the employer of record in the claim.

An employer has the right to attend any hearings related to a claim filed by one of the employer's workers.

---

[37] *Quagliata v Starbucks Coffee*, 82 A.D.3d 1321(3d Dep't 2011).

[38] *Butler v. General Motors*, 87 A.D.3d 1260 (3d Dep't2011).

A self-insured employer, or an employer who has failed his or her obligation to secure workers' compensation coverage, has the right to participate in the hearing and present relevant evidence about disputed issues at a hearing. Employers may request that a hearing be scheduled on a particular issue by writing to the Board in a timely manner. Corporations must be represented by counsel in proceedings before the Board. Certain defenses will be waived if they are not timely raised or if the employer or carrier does not timely file a "First Report of Injury - Denial 04" (FROI-04).

PART II: FRAUD

§2.04   Defining Fraud

Fraud occurs anytime a person knowingly intends to defraud the workers' compensation system by presenting (or assisting in presenting) an application for benefits, which contains a misrepresentation of a material fact.

§2.05   Penalties

In addition to a Class E Felony conviction, a claimant who is convicted of fraud loses the right to all past and future compensation benefits. Fraudsters must also return any money they got through their fraud.[39] This is contrary to the general rule of law that claimants do not have to pay back money fraudulently obtained.

§2.06   The Role of the Fraud Inspector General

A claimant who applies for workers' compensation benefits is required to provide accurate records and truthful statements to the WCB, the insurance carrier, and the employer. However, the law does not seem to require the claimant to give a truthful account of their condition to their medical care provider.[40]

An employer has the right to report suspected workers' compensation fraud to the Fraud Inspector General.[41] However, fraud will actually be inspected by the office of the Workers' Compensation Fraud Inspector General which is staffed by WCB employees. The Fraud Inspector does not prosecute cases - rather, it refers cases to local authorities for prosecution.

The inspector general may investigate cases involving:

---

[39] WCL § 114.

[40] The prohibition on false representations appears to only apply to false statements made to get a *monetary* benefit – it does not appear to apply to medical awards or benefits, since the prohibition on lying applies only to WCL § 15 (indemnity awards) and not expressly to § 13 (medical benefits) or § 16 (death benefits).

[41] Fraud Referral Hotline: 1-888-363-6001.

- An employer, carrier, or IME causing a medical report to be submitted to the to the WCB as evidence where the opinion of the examiner has been changed;
- Medical opinions that were "encouraged" to be changed;
- Employees lying about material facts to get benefits;
- Attorney-assisted fraud;
- Claimants alleging injuries occurred at work that did not occur at work;
- Lying under oath (perjury);
- Failure to disclose a lack of coverage (no policy in place);
- Failure to inform an employee of the right to benefits;
- Various forms of insurance fraud, including misrepresenting payroll;
- Fraud by health care providers, including billing for services that were not performed.

§2.07   Surveillance as a Tool to Combat Fraud

New York Workers' Compensation Law Section 114-a prohibits the making of false statements to obtain workers' compensation benefits. In practice, this means statements made inside a court room and statements made to doctors in examining rooms. In the real world, two recent cases show exactly how an employer can demonstrate employee fraud.

[1]   Video Evidence

In a recent case, a New York Appellate Court affirmed a disqualification from benefits where video surveillance of the claimant showed him going to and leaving a medical examiner's office with a leg brace and a cane AND A WALKER. While that portion of video[42] showed a severely disabled accident victim, later scenes, in which the claimant is could move his leg freely, without a brace, cane or walker, showed that he actually had no impairment in his daily activities.[43]

The WCB ruled that the claimant had violated WCL § 114(a) and was disqualified from comp benefits. The appellate panel, on review, affirmed that disqualification.

---

[42] A cane and a walker!?! How could he even do that with only two hands!?!

[43] *Retz v. Surpass Chem. Co.*, 39 A.D.3d 1037 (3d Dep't 2007).

[2]   Getting Useful Surveillance Video

Surveillance can be expensive. A single day of surveillance can cost $500-$1,500, depending on the number of investigators used. To conserve litigation resources, we suggest the following "best practices" for obtaining useful surveillance:

· Schedule at least two days of surveillance at a time.

· Always request that any report generated be directed to counsel.

· Request that the surveillance vendor assign a different investigator for each day of surveillance conducted.

· Communicate as much information as possible to the investigator, including a physical description of the claimant, mailing address (use the address the claimant is supplying to medical providers or the address where his checks are being mailed).

· Try to schedule surveillance to take place on days when the claimant has medical appointments. The investigator will have an easier time locating the claimant, and you will be certain to get the claimant "out and about" on the day of the appointment.

· Schedule surveillance on days where the weather is good - you will rarely find a claimant going for a stroll in a rainstorm or during the harsh winter months!

· Take note of the claimant's residence and surroundings before you expend litigation resources on surveillance. If the claimant lives in a gang-infested area, for example, the drug dealers who control the turf will note the presence of your surveillance team or investigator and often "tip off" the local residents as to the surveillance activity.

· Never, ever turn over the surveillance report to the court or adversary. The Board lack authority to compel production of surveillance reports where the report was directed to counsel.

[3]   Statements Outside of Court

Video can be persuasive, but even better than video is the claimant's own words. In another recent case, an employee neglected to reveal a prior, very significant, injury that resulted in neck and back injuries when filling out forms to obtain workers' comp benefits.[44] The claimant repeatedly answered "No" on multiple daily activities questionnaires that asked, "Did you have any injuries, illnesses, or limitations before this workers' comp injury?"

The claimant, who had suffered severe cervical and lumbar injuries just prior to his workers' comp claim, failed to disclose those injuries. The claimant argued that the questions were ambiguous and that he wasn't sure exactly what was being asked. The WCB determined that the claimant knew he was providing false information in connection with his workers' comp claim and disqualified the claimant from further benefits.

[4]   Social Media Information that Shows Fraud

The employer or carrier can utilize publicly available social media evidence as a basis for fraud even when the claimant subsequently makes the social media posts "private." Prior disclosure of social media evidence obtained by the employer is not required and an employer/carrier can introduce "private" social media evidence into the case to cross-examine the claimant.

If investigative material is obtained through covert means, it must be disclosed to the claimant before § 114(a) is raised.   The carrier's obligation to disclose the surveillance materials applies not just before the carrier's questioning of the claimant, but also prior to when the carrier prompts the WCLJ's questioning of the claimant.[45] Generally, the carrier must disclose its surveillance materials at the earliest possible time so that the claimant is aware of the existence of those materials prior to any testimony by the claimant. A failure to notify the claimant of the existence of videotaped surveillance prior to testifying warrants preclusion of the videotaped surveillance, associated investigative reports, and any testimony relating to the reports.[46]

What happens when a claimant posts potentially incriminating videos and materials on social media platforms and then later, during litigation, marks them "private? Are they really "private" (and therefore akin to covert surveillance if introduced by the employer to prove fraud)?

In a recent case, a Board Panel found that investigative materials not covertly obtained are not subject to the same disclosure rules as covert surveillance.

---

[44] *Husak v. New York City Transit Authority*, 40 A.D.3d 1249 (3d Dep't 2007).

[45] *Matter of Morelli v Tops Mkts.*, 107 A.D.3d 1231 (3d Dep't 2013).

[46] Matter of Gary Cummings, 2006 NY Wrk Comp 79911267; Matter of St. Charles R.C. School & Church, 2005 NY Wrk Comp 00048213.

Therefore, if an investigator's report included information publicly available at the time it was obtained, the reports may be admissible with respect to that information. Further, the Board Panel ruled that it does not matter whether the social media post was made private later. The relevant inquiry with respect to the proper disclosure of potential investigative evidence is whether the information at issue was obtained covertly or if it was publicly available at the time at the time it was obtained. The Board noted that any subsequent actions by the claimant to avoid the potential ramification of once public postings are irrelevant. Allowing any other result would encourage the parties to subsequently destroy or remove evidence for their own benefit.

CHAPTER 3: JURISDICTION

PART I: CHAPTER OVERVIEW

§3.01   Workers' Comp Bar – The Exclusivity Provision

Once an employer secures coverage (or self-insures) to provide workers compensation benefits for its employees, the employee cannot sue the employer for damages sustained from an injury or death that result from the employment (exceptions apply). The Workers' Compensation Board becomes the exclusive remedy for the injured worker.[47] This is known as the *exclusive remedy doctrine* or sometimes just the "Workers' Comp Bar" (meaning, the Workers' Compensation Law acts as a "bar" prohibiting direct civil lawsuit against the business owners).

§3.02   Those Subject to the Jurisdiction of the Workers' Compensation Law

Every employer and employee are subject to the jurisdiction of the New York WCB and Law if doing business in New York. There are exceptions – Federal employees, longshoreman, etc., - but for the purposes of this book, we assume you are dealing with a New York claim. Under New York's Workers' Compensation Law, most individuals providing services to a for-profit business will be deemed an employee of that business and therefore must be covered by the employer for workers' compensation insurance. This applies unless those services are specifically excluded as employment under the WCL.

[1]   Resident Alien

Aliens who are in covered employment in New York can be entitled to workers' compensation benefits when injured in the course of that employment.[48]

---

[47] WCL. § 11.

[48] *Keiko Mizugami v. Sharin West Overses, Inc.*, 81 N.Y.2d 363 (1993) *and* WCL §§ 16, 17.

[2]   Illegal Aliens

An illegal alien does not lose the right the right to benefits because of illegal or undocumented status. Further, awarding of benefits does not alter the immigration status of illegal aliens. The Law tries to be as neutral as possible towards illegal aliens, so they do not supply employers with an incentive to hire illegal aliens – and then refuse to provide those workers with benefits when they are injured.[49]

Defending claims filed by illegal aliens is complicated by the lack of reliable identification. This hinders full and proper investigation of claims, as most medical records and accident reports (like CIB indexes) include references to date of birth and social security number information.

[3]   Minors

The employment of a minor – defined as a child under the age of 18 – subjects the employer to the payment of a double compensation award.[50] This double payment must be made by the employer – and not the insurance carrier. It is irrelevant if the minor lied about his age.[51]

§3.03   Intentional Injuries

An employee retains the common-law right to damages where the injury results from an intentional act perpetrated by or at the direction of the employer. The burden falls to the claimant to prove that the employer's acts were intentional and deliberate – not merely reckless.

When a co-employee intentionally injures the claimant, the claimant can sue the co-employee in civil court **and** collect workers' compensation benefits against the employer.[52] Any judgment the claimant receives against the co-employee is subject to the lien or claim for reimbursement (for benefits paid) by the employer or its insurance carrier.

---

[49] *Post v. Berger & Golhke*, 216 N.Y. 544 (1916); *Testa v. Sorrento Restaurant, Inc.*, 10 A.D.2d 133 (3d Dep't 1960).

[50] WCL § 14a.

[51] *Robles v. Mossgood Theatre-Saunders Realty*, 53 A.D.2d 972(3d Dep't 1976).

[52] *Estupian v. Cleanerama Drive-In Cleaners, Inc.*, 38 A.D.2d 353 (2d Dep't 1977).

PART II: TIME LIMITS TO JURISDICTION

§3.04   Notice to the Employer

An employer must provide statutory benefits to employees who have an accident and sustain an injury which arises out of and in the course of employment. It follows that an employer must be notified of the accident and any resulting injury, within a reasonable time, so that it has an opportunity to determine if the claimant is entitled to benefits, and the extent of those benefits, before it can be held responsible for compliance.

Timely notice gives the employer the ability to adequately investigate the circumstances of the accident when information is available, and witnesses can recall the event.[53] Failure to give proper and timely notice may prejudice the rights of the employer to the extent that it may be found to be relieved of its obligation to provide benefits under the law.[54]

[1]   Requirements

The employee must provide notice to the employer within 30 days after the accident causing injury or death to the employee.[55] The notice should be in writing and provide:

- The name and address of the employee;
- The time of the accident causing the injury;
- The place of the accident;
- The nature of the injury sustained by the employee;
- The cause of the injury; and
- The signature of the employee, or a person on behalf of the injured employee.

---

[53] *Ross v. N.Y. Tel. Co.*, 59 A.D.2d 815 (3d Dep't 1977).

[54] WCL § 18; *Serafin v. Pleasant Valley Wine Co.*, 98 .A.D.2d 887 (3d Dep't 1983); *Babington v. Yellow Taxi Corp.*, 219 A.D. 495 (3d Dep't 1927).

[55] WCL § 18.

[2] Manner of Transmission

If the notice is sent to the employer via mail, the notice must be sent via registered mail to the last known place of business.[56]

If the notice is delivered in person, notice must be handed to a partner (if it is a partnership) or someone authorized to receive process (if the employer is a corporation).[57]

Verbal notice – in lieu of written notice – may be sufficient if the employer cannot show prejudice.

[3]   Constructive Notice

Constructive notice can be found where:

- The events, facts and circumstances surrounding the accident provide notice to the employer; and
- The employer was not prejudiced by the lack of formal notice.
- The employer's report (Form C-2) is not sufficient to be relied upon as a claim for compensation.[58]

[4]   When Failure to Provide Timely Notice will be Excused

Failure to provide timely notice will be excused when:

- Notice for some reason could not be given – such as when the claimant is hospitalized and in a coma; or
- The employer had knowledge of the accident – like cases where the employer provides first aid at the time of the accident – or takes the employee to the emergency room; or
- The employer has not been prejudiced.

§3.04 Proving Employer Prejudice in regards to notice

As we have seen (above) an employee must provide notice to the employer to obtain benefits within 30-days – but the claimant can report it later – and get benefits – if the employer is not prejudiced by this late reporting.

---

[56] *Id.*

[57] *Id.*

[58] *Bielat v. Alco Products, Inc.*, 28 A.D.2d 747 (3d Dep't 1967).

Whether or not late reporting prejudices the employer is a fact question for the Board. The burden of proof rests with the claimant to demonstrate[59] that the employer was provided with oral notice and that the employer's defense was not prejudiced. Late notice may also be excused by the WCB without consideration of prejudice if the claimant was not aware of the seriousness of the injury, or the causal relationship of the injury to the employment.[60]

In a case decided December 15, 2011, the Appellate Division reviewed the denial of a claim based on the failure of the claimant to provide timely notice to the employer. In *Dudas v. Town of Lancaster,* the claimant allegedly injured his ankle from slipping on ice while working at Town Hall on February 28, 2007.[61] The employee continued to work and did not seek medical treatment until 10 days later. The claimant reported the injury as work-related on June 27, 2007. The employer filed denial pleadings raising "notice" as a defense. The employer also obtained the original emergency room intake records, in which the claimant was recorded as stating he was injured when he "fell off a porch" - a story at odds with his "slip on ice at Town Hall" claim.

Here, the Board disallowed the claim and the Appellate Division upheld that denial, as the claimant's failure to report the injury within the period required by law (30 days) prejudiced the employer's ability to investigate the underlying accident.

§3.05   Notice to the Board – Section 28

A claim for compensation must be filed with the WCB within two (2) years of the occurrence of the accident causing injury or death.[62] Form C-3 is used for this purpose (*see* Chapter 1). A claim for disability caused by occupational disease must be filed within two years after the disablement and also after the

---

[59] By "substantial evidence."

[60] Claim of McEnaneney, 426 N.Y.S.2d 440 (3d Dep't 1981); *Peters v. Putnam Hosp. Center,* 146 A.D.2d 834 (3d Dep't 1989); Blain v. Emsig Mfg. Corp., 249 A.D.2d 602 (3d Dep't 1998).

^THE FIRST CASE I CAN'T FIND ON LEXIS

[61] *Dudas v. Town of Lancaster,* 90 A.D.3d 1251 (3d Dep't 2011).

[62] WCL § 28.

claimant knew or should have known that the disease causing the disability is or was due to the nature of the employment.[63] The WCB can decide (within its discretion) that the date of disability is the date of last employment – rather than the date medical treatment was provided (if earlier).

§3.06   When the Statute of Limitations Defense MUST be Raised

The employer must raise all defenses under § 18 ("notice") and § 28 (two-years to file claim) at the very first hearing. The failure of the employer to raise the statute of limitations defense – that the claim is time-barred – at the first hearing will result in that defense being waived. The Law requires that the defense be raised at the first hearing 'at which all parties in interest are present.'[64]

§3.07   Occupational Disease

The statute of limitations is different for occupational disease than for accidental injury. The claim for occupational disease disability must be filed within two years after disablement and after the claimant "knew or should have known that the disease is or was due to the nature of the employment."[65] Generally speaking, this means two years from when the claimant is specifically told his condition may be work-related.

§3.08   Infants & Mental Incompetents

The Statute of Limitations does not run against infants or mental incompetents if no committee or guardian has been appointed.[66] A mental incompetent is defined as "one who is unable to protect his or her legal rights because of an overall inability to function in society."[67]

---

[63] *Hastings v. Fairport Cent. Sch. Dist.*, 274 A.D.2d 660 (3d Dep't 2000); *Graniero v. Northern Westchester Hosp.*, 265 A.D.2d 638 (3d Dep't 1999).

[64] WCL § 28.

[65] *Id.*

[66] WCL § 115.

[67] This is the same definition for insanity as found in the Civil Practice Law and Rules, N.Y.C.P.L.R. § 208.

§3.09   Continuing Jurisdiction

The Board continues to have jurisdiction over claims, even after an award has been made.

[1]   Frequently Asked Question on the Statute of Limitations

Q: Does payment of benefits toll the statute of limitations for providing notice?

A: Yes. Medical expenses, wages, and funeral expenses provided before a claim is filed or notice is given enlarge the time for the claimant to file notice or a claim. This is so a claimant is not lulled into not filing because medical expenses and wages are being provided.

CHAPTER 4: EMPLOYERS AND EM-PLOYEES

PART I: DETERMINING EMPLOYMENT

§4.01   Employer-Employee Relationship

To be entitled to benefit, the WCB must find an employer-employee relationship exists. An employer (defined below) must provide coverage for all of its employees.[68]

[1]   Employer Defined

Any employer is defined as "anyone who has employees." [69] An employer can be a natural person, an association or partnership, a corporation, or a municipal organization.

Virtually all employers in New York State must provide workers' compensation coverage for their employees.[70] Employers must post notice of coverage in their place(s) of business.[71] Employers must cover the following workers for workers' compensation insurance:

- Workers in for-profit employments, including part-time employees, borrowed employees, leased employees, family members and volunteers.[72]
- Employees of counties and municipalities engaged in "hazardous" work.[73]
- Public school teachers and aides (excluding those employed by New York City.[74]

---

[68] WCL § 10.

[69] Even just one.

[70] WC §§ 2, 3.

[71] WCL § 51.

[72] WCL § 3 Groups 1-14-a.

[73] WCL § 3 Groups 15, 15-a and 17.

[74] WCL § 3.

- Employees of the State of New York.
- Domestic workers employed forty or more hours per week by the same employer.[75]
- Farm workers.[76]
- Any other worker determined by the Board to be an employee.
- All corporate officers if the corporation has more than two officers and/or two stockholders.[77]
- Officers of one-or-two-person corporations if there are other individuals in employment. These officers may choose to exclude themselves from coverage.[78]
- Most workers compensated by a nonprofit organization.
- Volunteer Firefighters and Volunteer Ambulance Workers are provided benefits for death or injuries suffered in the line of duty under the Volunteer Firefighters' Benefit Law and Volunteer Ambulance Workers' Benefit Law.

[2]   Employee Defined

Most individuals providing services to a for-profit business will be deemed an employee of that business and therefore must be covered by the employer for workers' compensation insurance. This applies unless those services are specifically excluded (*see* the second half of this chapter for a discussion of excluded employments).

The term *employee* includes day laborers, leased employees, borrowed employees, part-time employees, unpaid volunteers (including family members) and most subcontractors.

§4.02   Factors to Consider in Finding Employment

---

[75] This includes full-time sitters, companions, and live-in maids

[76] Farm workers are entitled to benefits if their employer paid $1,200 or more for farm labor in the preceding calendar year.

[77] WCL § 54.

[78] *Id.*

A common question before the WCB is whether an injured claimant is an employee or an independent contractor. The Board defines an "employee" differently than does the Federal government (for example, tax filing status is immaterial in a determination of employment.)

The Board considers the following factors in determining whether an injured claimant is an employee or was an independent contractor (and therefore not eligible for benefits):

[1]   Who has the right to control the claimant?

- A person or organization controlling the manner in which the work is to be performed indicates that the task is being performed by an employee.

- If the person doing the labor controls the time and manner in which the work is to be done this may indicate that the task is being done by an independent contractor.

Rule of thumb: If an individual is truly independent, the individual generally works under his/her own operating permit, contract or authority.

[2]   Whether the character of the work performed by the claimant was the same as the employer?

- Work done consistent with the primary work performed by the hiring business indicates that the labor was done by an employee. *Example*: Someone paving a driveway for a driveway contractor is generally considered the employee of that paver.

- Work done by a person that is different than the primary work of the hiring business may indicate the task is being performed by an independent contractor. *Example*: A plumber hired on a one-time basis to fix a broken pipe for a retail store owner is generally considered an independent contractor.

[3]   What Was The Method of Payment?

- Employees tend to be paid wages on an hourly, daily. weekly, or monthly basis.

- Employment is indicated if the hiring business withholds taxes and/or provides other employee benefits (Unemployment Insurance, health insurance, pensions, FICA, etc.) Whether the labor is paid using a W2 or 1099 Form for tax purposes does not matter in determining an employer/employee relationship for workers' compensation purposes.

57

- A business paying cash to an individual for services usually indicates that the individual is an employee.

- Payment made for performance of the task as a whole may indicate the task is being done by an independent contractor.

[4]   *Who Furnished the Equipment and Materials for the job?*

- A business providing the equipment and/or materials used by people in performing the work tends to indicate an employer-employee relationship.

[5]   *Who has the right to Right to Hire/Fire at the worksite?*

- A business retaining the authority to hire and fire the individuals performing the work indicates an employee is performing the work.

- An independent contractor retains a degree of control over the time when the work is to be accomplished and is not subject to be discharged by the hiring entity because of the method he chooses to use in performing the work. An independent contractor's services may be terminated if the services rendered do not meet contractual requirements.

All factors may be considered, and no one factor alone determines whether a person will be considered an employee under the WCL.

PART II: SPECIFIC EMPLOYMENT SITUATIONS

§4.03   Owner Controlled Insurance Policies ("Ocips")

Discussed in chapter 24, this book.

§4.04   Wrap-Up Policies

On large construction projects, the general contractor may obtain a workers' compensation insurance policy to cover all workers on the job site - this policy is called a "wrap-up" policy. A wrap-up policy has an expiration date that coincides with the planned completion date of the project.

All the subcontractors should be listed as policyholders on the wrap-up policy. The general contractor and most of the sub-contractors should each also have their own separate workers' compensation insurance policy. See chapter 24.

§4.05   Unions

Generally, all for-profit unions in New York State need coverage – no exceptions.

§4.06   Taxi Cab Operators

A taxi driver, operator or lessee is an employee, so they must be covered for workers' compensation purposes. For the lessee to be considered an independent contractor, the owner-operator may not control, direct, supervise, or have the power to hire or fire such lessee.

§4.07   Student Interns

Student interns are individuals that are providing services to gain work experience. Workers' Compensation Law Judges have ruled that the training received by student interns constitutes compensation – in lieu of wages – and that workers' compensation coverage must be obtained for even unpaid interns.[79]

---

[79] Exception: Student interns (paid or unpaid) doing "non-manual" work for a religious, charitable or educational institution (covered under § 501(c)(3) of the IRS tax code) are exempt from mandatory coverage.

§4.08   Spouses

Except for the spouses of farmers, spouses providing paid or unpaid services to a for-profit business are counted as employees for workers' compensation coverage purposes under the Workers' Compensation Law (regular owner/officer exclusions apply).

§4.09   Sole Proprietorships

Workers' compensation coverage is not required for a sole proprietor who does not have employees. If a sole proprietor has no employees but obtains a workers' compensation policy, the sole proprietor is automatically included in that policy, unless the sole proprietor elects himself out of that coverage.

§4.10   Real Estate Brokers

Licensed real estate brokers or real estate sales associates are independent contractors if the licensed real estate broker or sales associate meets all of the following requirements:

1) Has income based upon sales and not on the number of hours worked (*i.e.*, not salaried);
2) Has a written contract that outlines the services that they are to perform - this contract may be terminated by either party at any time upon notice given to the other party;
3) Works any hours they choose;
4) Can engage in outside employment;
5) Incurs their own expenses including automobile, travel and entertainment (office facilities and supplies may be provided by real estate firm); and
6) Shall not be treated as an employee for state and federal tax purposes.[80]

§4.11   Partnerships

Workers' compensation coverage IS NOT required for partners of a partnership under the laws of New York State if there are no employees.

---

[80] For the written contract requirements, refer to WCL § 2.

§4.12   Out-of-State Employees Working in New York State

As of September 9, 2007, all out-of-state employers with employees working in New York State are required to carry a full, statutory New York State workers' compensation insurance policy.[81]

§4.13   Other States' Government Employees

New York's Workers' Compensation Law does not cover the government employees of any other states.

§4.14   LLCs & LLPs

Members of a Limited Liability Company (LLC) or a Limited Liability Partnership (LLP) are treated the same as partners of a business that is a partnership under the laws of New York State.[82] Workers' compensation coverage is not required for members of a LLC or LLP that does not have employees.

§4.15   Leased Employees: Professional Employer Organization

Leased employees are the employees of the company that is paying to lease them, and that company must have a workers' compensation policy in its name.[83] The employer generally recruits and hires its employees and contracts with the leasing firm to handle the payroll, taxes and benefit packages for its employees.

Clients of PEOs may be covered by either of the following methods:
- Each business using leased employees may procure its own workers' compensation insurance policy to cover its leased employees (as well as any non-leased employees), or

---

[81] To be considered a full, statutory New York State workers' compensation insurance policy, "New York" must be listed under Item "3A" on the Information Page of the policy.

[82] WCL § 54.

[83] Leasing firms (PEOs) must be licensed by the New York State Department of Labor. Article 31 Section 922 of the Labor Law defines the relationship between the PEO and the client employer.

61

- The leasing firm can procure a separate workers' compensation insurance policy to cover the leased employees of each of its client firms.[84]

§4.16   Independent Contractors and Subcontractors

A business cannot require employees working for that business to obtain their own workers' compensation insurance policy or contribute towards a workers' compensation insurance policy.

---

[84] The policy should identify the insured as: XYZ Leasing Company Inc. L/C/F ABC Business Entity, Inc.

PART III: THOSE NOT COVERED BY THE WCL

§4.17   Those Not Covered by the Workers' Compensation Law

Generally, *see* § 3 of the Workers' Compensation Law.
1) Independent contractors.
2) Individuals who volunteer their services for nonprofit organizations and receive no compensation.[85]
3) Clergy and members of religious orders.
4) Members of supervised amateur athletic activities operated on a non-profit basis (i.e., Little League coaches, etc.).
5) People engaged in a teaching capacity in or for a nonprofit religious, charitable or educational institution (Section 501(c)(3) under the IRS tax code).
6) People engaged in a non-manual capacity in or for a nonprofit religious, charitable or educational institution (Section 501(c)(3) under the IRS tax code).
7) Persons receiving charitable aid from a religious or charitable institution who perform work in return for such aid and who are not under any express contract of hire and sheltered workshop workers.[86]
8) People who are covered for specific types of employment under another workers' compensation system (such as maritime trades, interstate rail-road employees, federal government employees and others covered under federal workers' compensation laws).
9) Farmers' spouses and minor children (under 18 years old).
10) Employees of foreign governments and Native American Nations.
11) New York City police officers, firefighters, and sanitation workers who are covered under provisions of the New York State General Municipal Law. Uniformed police officers and firefighters in other municipalities may also be excluded.
12) People, including minors, doing yard work or casual chores in and about a one-family, owner-occupied residence or the premises of a nonprofit, noncommercial organization.[87]

---

[85] WCL § 3.

[86] New York Mental Hygiene Law § 33.09.

[87] "Casual" means occasional. Coverage is required if the minor handles power-driven machinery, like a power lawnmower.

13) Certain real estate salespersons who sign a contract with a broker stating that they are independent contractors[88];
14) Certain media sales representatives who sign a contract stating that they are independent contractors[89];
15) Certain insurance agents or brokers who sign a contract stating that they are independent contractors[90]; and
16) Sole proprietors, partners, and certain one/two-person corporate officers with no other individuals providing services integral to the business[91] (although coverage may be obtained voluntarily).

§4.18   Independent Contractors

To be considered an independent contractor, and thus not an employee, the Board has stated that an individual must meet and maintain **all ten** of the following conditions:

1) Obtain a Federal Employer Identification Number from the Federal Internal Revenue Service (IRS) or have filed business or self-employment income tax returns with the IRS based on work or service performed the previous calendar year;
2) Maintain a separate business establishment from the hiring business;
3) Perform work that is different than the primary work of the hiring business and perform work for other businesses;
4) Operate under a specific contract and is responsible for satisfactory performance of work and is subject to profit or loss in performing the specific work under such contract and be able to succeed or fail if the business's expenses exceed income.
5) Obtain a liability insurance policy (and if appropriate, workers' compensation and disability benefits insurance policies) under its own legal business name and federal employer identification number;
6) Have recurring business liabilities and obligations;

---

[88] WCL § 2 (4); and *see* Real Estate Brokers - this chapter.

[89] WCL § 2 (4); and *see* Media Sales Representatives - this chapter.

[90] WCL § 2 (4); and *see* Insurance Agents - this chapter.

[91] WCL § 2 (4); *and* Sole Proprietorships, Partnerships, and Corporate Officer Coverage Requirements *and* Who Is an Employee Under the Workers' Compensation Law - this chapter - for exceptions.

7) If it has business cards or advertises, the materials must publicize itself, not another entity;
8) Provide all equipment and materials necessary to fulfill the contract;
9) Control the time and manner in which the work is to be done; and
10) The individual works under his/her own operating permit, contract or authority.

Although the Board has issued this ten-part test, note that the case law contains less restrictive definitions - and this list is helpful, but **is not** precedent.

§4.20   Trucking and the Independent Contractor Defense

To be considered an independent contractor, drivers must also be transporting goods under

- their own bill of lading and
- their own Department of Transportation Number

A business CANNOT require employees working for that business to obtain their own workers' compensation insurance policy or contribute towards a workers' compensation insurance policy.[92]

§4.21   Other Employment Situations

[1]   Volunteers

Unpaid and uncompensated volunteers doing charitable work for a nonprofit organization are not considered employees and do not have to be covered by a workers' compensation policy.[93]

[2]   Family Members

Family members providing paid or unpaid services to a for-profit business are counted as employees for workers' compensation coverage purposes (regular owner/officer exclusions apply). Coverage is not required for the spouses and minor children of farmers.

---

[92] WCL§§ 31, 32, 32-a.

[93] "Compensation" includes stipends, room and board, and any "perks" that have monetary value.

[3]   Domestic Workers

Domestic workers employed forty or more hours per week by the same employer (including full-time sitters or companions, and live-in maids) are required to be covered by a New York State workers' compensation insurance policy.

Domestic workers include gardeners, chauffeurs, nurses, nannies, home health aides, au pairs, baby-sitters, maids, cooks, housekeepers, laundry workers, butlers, and companions.

[4]   Corporate Officers

An executive officer of a corporation who owns all the shares of stock, holds all the offices of the corporation, and has employees is automatically included in the corporation's workers' compensation insurance policy. The officer may choose to exclude him/herself by filing an exclusion form with his/her insurance carrier at the time the policy is written or renewed.[94]

[5]   Media Sales Representatives

A media sales representative is an independent contractor if the representative:

1) Is a contractor engaged in the sale or renewal of magazine advertising space;

2) Has income based upon sales/services and not on the number of hours worked;

3) Is incorporated and shall be solely liable for payment of workers' compensation premiums;

4) Has entered into a written contract (not entered under duress) that outlines the services that the Media Sales Representative will perform. This contract must include the following statements: The media sales representative:

· Shall not be treated as an employee for State and Federal tax purposes;

· Can work any hours they choose subject to restrictions in the New York State Business Law;

· Can work at any site other than on the premises of the person for whom the services are performed;

---

[94] Form C-105.51

- Incurs his/her own expenses other than those outlined in the written contract; and
- Can terminate the contract with two weeks notice given to the person for whom the services are performed.[95]

[6]   Nonprofit Organizations

Individuals that volunteer their services for not-for-profits are not eligible for workers' compensation benefits, so the not-for-profit entity using volunteers is not required to obtain a workers' compensation insurance policy.

Not-for-profits that are paying individuals for their services are required to obtain a workers' compensation insurance except for:

- Paid clergy and members of religious orders are exempt from mandatory coverage (but can be covered voluntarily). To be exempt the clergy and members of religious orders must be performing only religious duties.
- Members of supervised amateur athletic activities operated on a nonprofit basis, provided that such members are not otherwise engaged or employed by any person, firm, or corporation participating in such athletic activity (like Little League Coaches).
- Paid individuals teaching for a religious, charitable or educational institution (Section 501(c)(3) under the IRS tax code) are also exempt from mandatory coverage (but can also be covered voluntarily). To be exempt, the teachers must only be performing teaching duties.
- Paid individuals working in a non-manual capacity for a religious, charitable or educational institution (Section 501(c)(3) under the IRS tax code) are also exempt from mandatory coverage.[96]
- Persons receiving charitable aid from a religious or charitable institution (Section 501(c)(3) under the IRS tax code) who perform work in return for such aid (such as a sheltered workshop for handicaps).

[7]   Nonprofit Executive Officer Exclusions

A not-for-profit entity that is not compensating individuals (including executive officers) for their services is not required to obtain a workers' compensation

---

[95] For the written contract requirements, refer to WCL § 2 (4).

[96] Manual labor includes filing; carrying materials such as pamphlets, binders, or books; cleaning; playing musical instruments; moving furniture; shoveling snow; and mowing lawns.

insurance policy. All compensated executive officers of a not-for-profit corporation or unincorporated association that is not classified as religious, charitable or educational (Section 501(c)(3) under the IRS tax code) must be covered by a workers' compensation insurance policy.

[8]   Black Car Operators

Limousines and other black car operators, as defined in Article 6-F of the executive law ("The Black Car Law"), is an "employee" of the New York Black Car Operators' Injury Compensation Fund, Inc. (NYBCOICF).

[9]   Native American Enterprises

Workers' compensation insurance coverage is not required for Native American enterprises owned by the Native American tribe itself, such as casinos.

[10]   Religious Organizations

Workers' compensation insurance coverage is not required for a religious organization that only pays clergy and/or teachers and/or individuals providing non-manual labor.

CHAPTER 5: DEFENSES

PART I: CHAPTER OVERVIEW

§5.01   Background

Workers' Compensation benefits are analogous to no fault benefits because the employee will be entitled to benefits regardless of whether the employee was negligent in causing the injury or death. By the same token, an employer's negligence is not considered. Comparative negligence, contributory negligence, or the *act of God* doctrines are not applicable in determining entitlement to workers' compensation benefits in New York.[97]

There are some exclusions from compensation. Keep these possible defenses handy when analyzing claims.

§5.02   Non-Employee (Independent Contractor Defense)

Only an employee is entitled to workers' compensation benefits.

Whether a claimant is an employee or an independent contractor is a factual issue for the WCB. After the facts of the relationship have been presented, the board will decide if there is an employee-employer relationship exists. Appeal can be made to the Appellate Division Third Department.[98]

In a 2010 case, the claimant was a cleaner who worked in a number of buildings owned by the employer.[99] The claimant was paid a fixed amount per week by check. According to the claimant, he worked for the alleged employer exclusively. Most telling, the claimant was told "where to work as well as what to do." According to testimony, "(we) instructed and supervised the claimant,

---

[97] *Pierce v. Young*, 252 N.Y. 520 (1929).

[98] For more on this defense, as well as application of the relevant law to specific occupations, *see* Chapter 4, this book.

[99] *Lew v. Younger*, 69 A.D.3d 1161 (3d Dep't 2010).

(and) would ordinarily contact him if he was required to do specific cleaning work."

The Board found that the claimant was an employee and not an independent contractor. The Appellate Court agreed, stating "relevant considerations include the right to control the work, the method of payment, the right to discharge and the relative nature of the work; however, no single factor is dispositive."[100]

§5.03   Intentional Injury

Not a defense *per se*, but a circumstance where the Workers' Compensation law will not apply, is when there is an intentional injury. If the claimant was injured by an employer or co-employee intentionally, the injured worker can seek damages in civil court.[101]

To seek damages for intentional injury, the employee must show that there was specific intent to harm the claimant – not mere gross negligence or reckless conduct by the employer.

§5.04   Intoxication

An employee is not entitled to benefits if his injuries are caused **solely** by his intoxication. This defense is largely illusory because of the word "solely." If the claimant can show any other contributing other factor, the injuries will be found compensable. For example, if the claimant can show the intoxication along with another factor, such as fatigue, caused the injury, the fact that the claimant was drunk at the time of the accident will not be a bar to compensation – the claimant will likely be successful arguing that the fatigue contributed to the accident and resultant injury, and the matter will likely be found compensable. In fact, there is a statutory presumption that the intoxication was not the sole factor in any injury.[102]

"Intoxication" refers to alcohol- and drug-related behavior.

---

[100] *Id.,* (citing *Matter of Park v. Lee,* 53 A.D.3d 936 (3d Dep't 2008).)

[101] WCL § 10(1).

[102] WCL § 21(4).

§5.05   Suicide

Intentional self-injury is not compensable. However, a line of cases has developed since 1991 finding some suicides compensable. For example, a suicide may be found compensable where:

- There was a work-related injury which caused insanity, derangement, or mental deterioration;[103]
- There was a depressive condition causally related to the employment (presume causal connection between work and mental illness);[104]
- Work-related stress contributed to a depressive illness (which may have been pre-existent in nature and in which suicidal tendencies were a feature).[105]

[1] Recent Case on Suicide: Veeder

Forensic Investigator Gary Veeder specialized in trace fiber evidence for the New York State Police Forensic Investigation Center.[106] His findings were relied upon by prosecutors and juries in sending people to jail. Unfortunately, a state investigation found that in nearly 1/3 of all the cases Veeder worked on there were "serious problems" with the evidence Veeder provided.

A very public scandal erupted ("Troopergate" and "Dirty Tricks Scandal") when it was learned that Veeder "routinely failed to conduct a required test when examining fiber evidence, then falsely indicated in case records that he had performed the test," according to the audit of his practices. It appears that Veeder had no knowledge of the tests he was supposed to be conducting and could not even properly operate a microscope.

A lot of people may have gone to jail because of Veeder's fake evidence. Veeder first retired and then 15 days later committed suicide by hanging himself in his garage. His widow claimed that his death was caused by work-related stress and filed for workers' compensation benefits.

---

[103] *Cf. Musa v. Nassau County Police Dep't*, 276 A.D.2d 851 (3d Dep't 2000).

^I COULD ONLY FIND THIS CASE FROM 2000 NOT 1991

[104] *Friedman v. NBC, Inc.*, 178 A.D.2d 774 (3d Dep't 1991).

[105] *Miller v. IBEW Local 631*, 237 A.D.2d 641 (3d Dep't 1997).

[106] *Veeder v. N.Y. State Police Dep't*, 86 A.D.3d 762 (3d Dep't 2011).

71

The widow's claim was denied, on the basis that the stress was the result of personnel actions, which are excluded from workers' compensation eligibility.

The case was appealed and the decision to deny benefits was reversed. The case was sent back to the Workers' Compensation Board for reconsideration. The reversal was based upon the fact that at the time of Veeder's suicide, no personnel actions had been implemented. The Appellate court stated that "the unrefuted psychiatric evidence contained in the record, as well as the suicide letters, make clear that decedent's suicide was predominantly the product of the depression and stress he experienced from the employer's inquiry into the inconsistencies in his fiber analysis tests." The state was investigating the situation; they had uncovered problems in Veeder's work, but they were on a narrowly defined "fact finding" mission. No action had been taken against Veeder: he was not suspended or demoted or disciplined in any manner. Thus, the stress was purely the result of the investigation, not of any personnel action.

In other words, had the employer simply announced to Veeder that the investigation was the initial phase of a disciplinary process, he would probably not have been eligible for workers' compensation benefits. The facts that count: he was under enormous work-related stress (of his own making) and he killed himself as a direct result of the work-related situation.

Based on the decision in the appeal Veeder's widow is eligible for burial and indemnity benefits.

§5.06   Athletic (Recreational) Activities

Injuries from voluntary athletic activities are not compensable. The general rule is that activities which improved the health or morale of the employee, without any specific benefit to the employer, are not compensable, unless the employer does something (affirmatively) to seek benefit or participate in the activity. The actions of an employer can transform a purely voluntary recreational activity into an activity where compensation for injuries can be awarded. For example:

- If the employer mandates that the employees participate in some recreational activity, then the immunity from compensation is destroyed.[107]
- If the claimant is paid to participate in the activity.

---

[107] *Kobre v. Camp Mogen Avraham*, 255 A.D.2d 636 (3d Dep't 1998).

- If the employer sponsors the activity, by purchasing equipment (such as uniforms) or otherwise.[108]

What constitutes *sponsoring* an activity is the subject of debate. The law judges will look at this issue on a case-by-case basis.

§5.07   Picnics

Injuries occurring during company picnics will be looked at with the same analysis as injuries occurring during recreational activities. Basically, encouraging employees to attend a company picnic to promote morale is not a basis for finding compensability.[109]

§5.08   Purely "Personal Acts"

Injuries from purely personal acts are not compensable. This is the "personal risk doctrine." Simply stated, activities which are purely personal, or demonstrate a purely personal pursuit, do not fall within the scope of employment. In cases where the employer raises this defense, the WCB will consider how work-related the activity was that led to the injury.

A good example is the retail employee who is attacked at work. If the attacker was a random store customer, or someone who walked into the store to rob it, then the incident will likely be found to be compensable. However, if the employee is attacked by an estranged lover, for purely personal reasons, and the attack just happened to take place at work, then the injuries resulted from a purely personal circumstance and should not be found to be compensable.

Injuries that arise out of and in the course of employment are compensable, unless they are the result of some intervening cause.

§5.09   Injuries Occurring Outside Regular Duties

In *Murphy v. Mt. Sinai Hospital*, a nurse practitioner sustained multiple injuries in a traffic accident while attending a continuing education conference.[110]

---

[108] *Diem v. Diem & Buerger Ins. Co.*, 146 A.D.2d 840 (3d Dep't 1989).

[109] *Briand v. N.Y. State Dep't of Envtl. Conservation*, 186 A.D.2d 308 (3d Dep't 1992).

[110] *Murphy v. Mt. Sinai Hospital*, 37 A.D.3d 919 (3d Dep't 2007).

Attendance at the conference was a mandatory requirement of his position. The claimant had been encouraged to go to the conference by his supervisor. The claimant testified that his supervisor had handed him the brochure advertising the conference.

The employer denied that the injuries were a direct result of the employment - and that attendance at the conference did not directly benefit the employer.

The WCB found that "an act outside of an employee's regular duties which is undertaken in good faith to advance the employer's interests is generally within the course of employment." Therefore, any injuries arising from the act (in this case, a motor vehicle accident) were compensable.

In so ruling, the WCB looked at the factual circumstances surrounding the educational conference. The WCB was impressed by the following: (1) The employer paid remuneration for two "conference days"; (2) the employer encouraged the employee to attend the conference; and (3) attendance was a mandatory requirement for the position.

§5.10   Lunchtime Injuries

Lunch is generally considered to be a personal act (*see* above), so lunch-time injuries are generally not compensable. This is especially true where the employee eats his lunch off-site.

§5.11   Voluntary Withdrawal from the Labor Market

A claimant who has voluntarily withdrawn from the labor market is not entitled to receive temporary disability benefits. The burden of proof of this defense falls upon the employer. For example, if an employer can show that the claimant retired from the workforce, the claim for compensation can be defeated. However, the WCB can find that the claimant's retirement was not entirely voluntary if the retirement was caused by the injury; in that case the employer will have to pay compensation.

PART II: BREAKING DOWN THE "ATTACHMENT" DEFENSE

§5.12   Applying "Attachment to the Workforce" as a Defense

A claimant who is receiving temporary disability benefits has an ongoing obligation to show "attachment to the workforce" - that he is actively seeking a job within his restrictions - in order to continue to be eligible for weekly benefits. In April 2017, the Legislature statutorily removed "attachment" as a defense to paying ongoing permanent partial disability benefits. Therefore, a claimant who receives an award for permanent partial disability does not have to show any effort to secure work to remain eligible for ongoing payments.

§5.13   The "Many Places" Argument on Attachment

The employer/carrier can use the legal requirement that the claimant demonstrate "the many places she has looked for work within her restrictions" as a basis for challenging ongoing benefits.

The Workers' Compensation Board has issued <u>Form C-258</u> for claimants to use to keep track of "the many places they have looked for work within their restrictions."

§5.14   Demonstrating Attachment to the Labor Market

To demonstrate **attachment to the labor market** the claimant in a workers' compensation case must show:

1) the **many places** they have looked for work within their restrictions AND
2) provide documented evidence of active participation in at least one NYSDOL re-employment service. "Active Participation" is defined in the case law as
   a) calling for an appointment at OneStop or VESID;
   b) attending an orientation session;
   c) meeting with a One-Stop counselor to develop a resume;
   d) registering a resume in the One-Stop system;
   e) following up to determine whether there were any job matches; and
   f) following up on all job referrals and matches.

The case law instructs that merely signing up for VESID[111] is insufficient; the injured worker must also follow through with all of the additional steps in order to receive Workers' Compensation benefits.[112]

§5.15   Reasons to Pursue the "Attachment" Defense

Many claimants, deemed either temporarily- or permanently-partially disabled, have not conducted any sort of meaningful work search. For many claimants, it is not until the employer/carrier raises attachment as a defense to further benefits that a work search is even considered.

In other words - this is a defense that is waived until affirmatively raised.

In the long-run, it is relatively easy for a claimant to assemble proofs and get an ongoing disability benefit reinstated - they merely have to follow the steps (above) to demonstrate attachment. Upon doing the required steps, they can file an RFA-1LC and ask a Workers' Compensation Judge to reinstate benefits. Generally, most Judges of Compensation will accept even a modest work search as meeting the requirements for showing attachment and will reinstate benefits.

Even though a successful "attachment" argument may result in only a short-lived termination of benefits (for the motivated claimant), it is a useful tool in gaining traction in a slowly-progressing case. At the time benefits are discontinued for lack of attachment, an offer to resolve the claim amicably can be made.

The problem with this defense is that when you get a hearing on attachment, the claimant will show up in Court with a (typically) handwritten list of places where she sought work. The list will be purposefully vague. A common practice is for the claimant to write down a list of stores near their home that they allegedly went to in order to look for work (usually "Home Depot," "Walmart", "Walgreens" etc). The Board has created a voluntary form (Form C-258.1 "Claimant's Record of Independent Job Search Efforts") for claimants to use to keep track of the places they have sought work.

---

[111] VESID (Vocational and Educational Services for Persons with Disabilities).

[112] *American Axle*, 2010 WL 438153 (N.Y. Work. Comp. Bd.)

§5.16   Practical Tips on Challenging Attachment

1. Job search questionnaires should regularly be sent to partially tempo-
    rary or partially permanently disabled workers. We recommend that
    every thirty days you send a Form C-258.1 and request it be returned.

2. If the claimant fails to return a completed form, or the form is vague or
    incomplete, issue an RFA-2 to have the matter set down for a hearing
    on attachment.

3. Using the list of potential employers supplied by the claimant, ask your
    defense counsel to subpoena the records of every single employer
    where the claimant alleges they applied for work. This sets up two de-
    fenses - an "attachment" defense and a potential fraud defense (Section
    114a).

4. If the claimant has identified an employer - stating they applied for a job
    electronically - and the employer responds to the subpoena *duces te-
    cum* by stating they never received an employment application from the
    claimant, the employer/carrier is well armed to argue that the claimant
    has not pursued employment "at many places" within her restrictions,
    and that benefits should be terminated.

5. If the claimant completes a work search questionnaire saying that they
    sought work and submitted applications to entities that ultimately deny
    contact with them, may constitute fraud under WCL Section 114a. Spe-
    cifically, an argument should be made that the claimant "knowingly
    made a false statement or representation as to a material fact" to obtain
    a cash benefit.

6. In high-exposure, disputed cases consider using a labor market survey
    to demonstrate suitable alternative employment.

CHAPTER 6: ARISING OUT OF AND IN THE COURSE OF EMPLOYMENT

PART I: CHAPTER OVERVIEW

§6.01 Presumptions and Purely Personal Injuries

A New York Workers' Compensation claimant is availed five (5) presumptions, though we will only discuss the first presumption in this chapter.[113]

The first presumption is that **an accident which occurs in the course of employment is presumed to arise out of the employment.** This is a temporal/substantive link: if the injury occurs at work and during the work day, it is presumed the injury arose out of and in the course of employment.

If the activity the claimant was undertaking at the time of the accident was purely personal it would not be within the scope of the employment and the presumption would be rebutted. An injury must be work-related to be compensable.

Injuries from purely personal acts are not compensable. This is the "personal risk doctrine." Activities which demonstrate a purely personal pursuit, do not fall within the scope of employment. An assault occurring at work is accordingly presumed to have also arisen out of the employment, a presumption that can be rebutted with substantial evidence that the assault was motivated by purely personal animosity.[114]

In looking at cases where the employer raises this defense, the WCB will consider how work-related the activity was that led to the injury.

---

[113] Here is the complete list of presumptions - 1: An accident which occurs in the course of the employment is presumed to arise out of the employment; 2: "Notice" is presumed to have been received by the employer; 3: Benefits are denied for intentional injury; 4: Benefits are denied for injuries solely caused by intoxication; and 5: Claimant's medical reports are accepted *prima facie* by the WCB. New York Work. Comp. Law § 21.

[114] *See* WCL § 21; *Rosen v. First Manhattan Bank*, 84 N.Y.2d 856, 857 (1994); *Turner v. F.J.C. Secs. Servs.*, 306 A.D.2d 649 (3d Dep't 2003).

A good example is the retail employee who is attacked at work. If the attacker was a random store customer, or someone who walked into the store to rob it, then the incident will likely be found to be compensable. However, if the employee is attacked by an estranged lover, for purely personal reasons, and the attack just happened to take place at work, then the injuries resulted from a purely personal circumstance and will likely not be found to be compensable.

Two recent cases applied this rule.

In *Wadsworth v. K-Mart Corp.*, the Workers' Compensation Board found emotional injuries sustained by a claimant whose car was stolen while she was at work were compensable.[115] Bizarrely, a week after the car was stolen, the claimant saw the car idling in the parking lot at work. When the claimant approached the vehicle, she became involved in a scuffle with the driver. At the same time, a co-worker emerged from the place of work, jumped in the car, and the stolen car took off. The Board ruled against the employer, citing the fact that a co-worker was apparently involved in the theft of the car, and found the matter compensable.

The employer appealed, arguing that the incident did not arise out of the course of the employment and was purely a personal matter.

The Appellate Court agreed with the employer and overturned the award. The Appellate Court ruled that while there was a question of fact for the Board to decide, and an award of benefits is proper if "there is any nexus, however slender, between the motivation for the assault and the employment,"[116] the decision must be based on "such relevant evidence as a reasonable mind might accept as adequate to support a conclusion."[117]

The Appellate Court reasoned that "the statutory presumption was rebutted by substantial evidence presented that the motivation for the assault was purely personal animosity between claimant and the individual she discovered driving her stolen vehicle. . . Claimant's assailant was not a coworker or

---

[115] *Wadsworth v. K-Mart Corp.*, 72 A.D.3d 1244 (3d Dep't 2010).

[116] *Baker v. Hudson Valley Nursing Home*, 233 A.D.2d 608 (3d Dep't 1996), *lv. denied* 89 N.Y.2d 813 (1997); *accord* 2 A.D.3d 963 (3d Dep't 2003).

[117] *Consolidated Edison Co. v. NLRB*, 305 U.S. 197, 229, (1938); *accord*, 246 A.D.2d 933 (3d Dep't 1998), *lv. denied* 91 N.Y.2d 1002 (1998).

otherwise connected to her employment and there is no work-related explanation given for the altercation." The decision of the WCB was overturned as
arbitrary.

In a second case, decided May 6, 2010, the Appellate Division reviewed an
award of compensation benefits filed by Deborah Wilson.[118] In the *Wilson* case,
the Claimant, a general mechanic, filed a claim for workers' compensation benefits after a coworker struck her in the face with what was variously described
as an air regulator or valve. The claimant and her assailant had a long history
of difficulties. While claimant described repeated harassment due to race and
gender, she also testified that the assailant had "defamed" her abilities and
work as a mechanic by stating that she was a "bad mechanic," and influencing
other coworkers to believe this was true. Even the affidavit that the claimant
filed with the Equal Employment Opportunity Commission in support of her
discrimination complaint, upon which the employer and its carrier relied upon,
suggested that at least some of the assailant's offensive comments and conduct stemmed from a promotion and pay raise that the claimant received in
2005.

In *Wilson*, the Appellate Court found a "nexus between the employment and
the injury" and so found the assault injury compensable.

§6.02   Going-and-Coming Rules

Employees are not deemed to be in the course of their employment when they
are traveling to-and-from work. This rule of thumb is referred to as the "going-
and-coming rule" or the "portal-to-portal" rule. Basically, there is no door-to-
door coverage: the risk of travel to and from work is not distinctly related to
any specific employment, and so is generally considered not *arising out of and
in the course of* any particular employment.

§6.03 Exceptions to Going-and-Coming Rules

[1]   *Outside workers*

Outside workers – like traveling salesmen – who do not work at a fixed location
and are required to travel between work locations.[119]

---

[118] *Wilson v. General Mills*, 73 A.D.3d 1246 (3d Dep't2010).

[119] *Bennett v. Marine Works*, 273 N.Y. 429 (1937).

[2]   Special errands

Special errands – being sent by the employer to do something specific (and work-related).[120]

[3]   Paid travel expenses

Paid travel expenses – where an employee is paid to use their own car for work-related travel, an injury occurring during that travel may be found to be compensable.

[4]   Some home office situations

Some home office situations – the WCB recognizes that it is not unusual for management and professional workers to have home office with links to the employer's office, making injuries in those locations compensable.[121]

[5]   Entering or leaving the employer's premises

Entering or leaving the employer's premises – in particular, injuries sustained while the employee is entering the worksite have been held compensable where the entrance to the worksite posed a special hazard.[122]

In a recent case[123] the WCB denied a claim for dependency benefits to the widow and two children of a worker who died in a car accident while traveling in a carpool arranged by his employer to a job site.

The claimant was an employee of "Labor Ready" which provides temporary workers. Labor Ready did not provide the employee with a ride to his work location or pay for his travel time or travel expenses. Instead, the employer encouraged employees to carpool to remote locations.

---

[120] *Neacosia v. N.Y. Power Auth.*, 85 N.Y.2d 471 (1995).

[121] Note: The factors to be considered are: (1) the regularity of work done at home; (2) the home office is permanent; and (3) the employer is benefited from the arrangement. *See Hille v. Gerald Records*, 23 N.Y.S.2d 135 (1968);*Bobinis v. State Ins. Fund*, 235 A.D.2d 955 (3d Dep't 1997); *Fine v. S.M.C. Microsystems Corp.*, 75 N.Y.2d 912 (1990).

[122] *Bigley v. J & R Music Elec.*, 269 A.D.2d 667 (3d Dep't 2000).

[123] *Davis v. Labor Ready*, 69 A.D.3d 1214 (3d Dep't 2010).

In that case, the claimant was killed in a car accident on the 26-mile return trip. A Workers' Compensation Law Judge awarded benefits to the decedent's widow and two minor children.

The employer argued that the claimant was not in the course of his employment at the time of the accident. Labor Ready argued that the claimant was not paid an hourly wage while he traveled to the work site. It was undisputed that Labor Ready did not provide the transportation, and that the claimant was paying his co-employee $2 in gas money for the ride to the work site. The driver, a Labor Ready employee, was not paid for driving the co-workers to-and-from the worksite.

The Appellate Division upheld the denial of benefits, stating "we cannot conclude that Labor Ready had 'exclusive control of the conveyance' that was used to provide transportation.

PART II: EXPLORING COMPENSABILITY

§6.03   The Outer Bounds of What is "Work-Related"

An April 2010 case provides a real-world illustration of the challenges to determining compensability. While attending a training conference and after an employer-sponsored dinner, Emily Maher and a group of co-workers took a shuttle into downtown Saratoga and visited three bars on Caroline Street. According to one witness Maher consumed five beers but did not appear drunk. Around midnight, Maher and two of her coworkers took a taxi back to the Gideon Putnam Hotel, where they had overnight accommodations, and eventually worked their way to a second-floor suite occupied by one of the coworkers.[124]

After arriving in the suite, claimant and her two coworkers stepped out onto the roof of the hotel, which was accessible only via the bathroom window in the suite. Approximately 20 minutes later, claimant placed her hands on the railing surrounding the roof, heard a loud crack and fell to the ground below. She brought a claim for workers' compensation benefits against her employer.

Was it compensable?

Both the Workers' Compensation Board and the Appellate Division agreed that the injuries did not "arise out of and in the course of employment." Whether a particular activity is compensable is a factual issue for the Board to resolve,[125] "with the test being whether the activity is both reasonable and sufficiently work related under the circumstances."[126]

Although the employer did not raise a defense of intoxication, our review of the case does not indicate that such a defense would be successful. An employee is not entitled to benefits if his injuries are caused solely by his intoxication. This defense is largely illusory, though, because of the word "solely." If the claimant can show another contributing factor – **any** contributing other factor – the injuries will be found compensable.

---

[124] *Maher v. NYS Div. of Budget*, 72 A.D.3d 1380 (3d Dep't 2010).

[125] *Pedro v. Vill. of Endicott*, 307 A.D.2d 598 (3d Dep't 2003), *lv. dismissed* 1 N.Y.3d 546 (2003), *lv. denied* 2 N.Y.3d 706 (2004).

[126] *Marotta v. Town & Country Elec., Inc.*, 51 A.D.3d 1126 (3d Dep't 2008); *Pedro v. Village of Endicott, supra; Grady v. Dun & Bradstreet*, 265 A.D.2d 643 (3d Dep't 1999).

For example, if the claimant can show the intoxication along with another factor, such as fatigue caused the injury, the fact that the claimant was drunk at the time of the accident will not be a bar to compensation – the claimant will likely be successful arguing that the fatigue contributed to the accident and resultant injury and the matter will likely be found compensable. In fact, there is a statutory presumption that the intoxication was not the sole factor in any injury.

In this case, there was eyewitness testimony that Maher drank "five beers over four hours" - not enough to establish her intoxication. However, diligent investigation should have obtained the blood-alcohol results from the Emergency Room visit so that the defense could have been explored.

CHAPTER 7: INDEMNITY BENEFITS

PART I: BASICS OF WAGES & WAGE REPLACEMENT

§7.01 Entitlement to Benefits

A workers' compensation claimant is entitled to medical care and wage replacement. If the worker is killed by the accident, his dependents may be eligible for death benefits.

When an employee sustains an injury, medical benefits must be provided immediately.[127] There is no waiting period before medical benefits must be provided. Wage replacement (as discussed below) has a waiting period before benefits must be provided.[128]

§7.02 Valuing Injuries

The happening of an injury is not enough (by itself) to warrant the payment of an award. Awards are issued for residual permanent impairment. If the claimant is due an award, the amount of money the claimant receives will depend on the nature and degree of the loss. The Workers' Compensation Law breaks down the amount payable into two broad categories: "scheduled losses" and "unscheduled losses."

§7.03 Wage Compensation: Cash Benefits

Cash benefits are not paid for the first seven days of the disability unless it extends beyond fourteen days. In that case, the worker may receive cash benefits from the first work day off the job.

Rules: Compensation (money allowance – the wage replacement) is not paid to the injured employee for the first seven days of disability.[129] If the disability continues for 15 days or more, the compensation will be paid going back to the

---

[127] *See* Chapter One, *this book,* and WCL § 13.

[128] WCL § 12.

[129] *Id.*

first day of time lost. The fourteen lost days do not have to be consecutive. If the disability is for fourteen days or less, then there is no wage replacement for the first seven calendar days, only the eight through fourteen days lost.

Claimants who are totally or partially disabled and unable to work for more than seven days receive cash benefits. The amount that a worker receives is based on his/her average weekly wage for the previous year.

§7.04   Supplemental Benefits

Supplemental benefits were made available to claimants thought to be most affected by rising costs.[130] The combination of weekly benefits, death benefits and supplemental benefits cannot exceed $215 per week. This is the rate that was in effect on January 1, 1979.

Two categories of claimants/beneficiaries are eligible for supplemental benefits by making application to the Board:
1.   Claimants classified permanently and totally disabled as the result an injury or disability incurred on the job prior to January 1, 1979;
1.   Widows or widowers receiving death benefits as the result of the death of their spouse occurring prior to January 1, 1979.

§7.05   How to Stop Paying Temporary Disability Benefits

We can stop paying temporary disability benefits in New York when:
·   The claimant has reached "maximum medical improvement" and is discharged from further care.
·   The claimant has voluntarily withdrawn from the labor market.
·   The claimant has refused a light duty offer that complies with the treating doctor's work restrictions.

---

[130] These benefits must be applied for; Form SC-4.

PART II: TEMPORARY TOTAL DISABILITY BENEFITS

§7.06   Calculating Benefits

The following formula is used to calculate benefits:
2/3rds of the pre-accident average weekly wage x % of disability = weekly benefit

This formula is subject to minimums (currently $150 per week for a totally disabled claimant) and maximums (currently $870.61 per week), which are set by the Commissioner of Labor.

Therefore, a claimant who was earning $400 per week and is totally (100%) disabled would receive $266.67 per week. A partially disabled claimant (50%) would receive $133.34 per week. The weekly benefit cannot exceed the following maximums, however, which are based on the date of accident:

§7.07   Schedule of Benefits

Date of Accident	Weekly Maximum (Total/Partial)
July 1, 1985 - June 30, 1990	$300 / $150
July 1, 1990 - June 30, 1991	$340 / $280
July 1, 1991 - June 30, 1992	$350 / $350
July 1, 1992 - June 30, 2007	$400 / $400
July 1, 2007 – June 30, 2008	$500 / $500
July 1, 2008 – June 30, 2009	$550 / $550
July 1, 2009 – June 30, 2010	$600 / $600
July 1, 2010 - June 30, 2011	$739.83
July 1, 2011 - June 30, 2012	$772.96
July 1, 2012 - June 30, 2013	$792.07
July 1, 2013 - June 30, 2014	$803.21
July 1, 2014 - June 30, 2015	$808.65

July 1, 2015 - June 30, 2016	$844.29
July 1, 2016 - June 30, 2017	$864.32
July 1, 2017 - June 30, 2018	$870.61
July 1, 2018 to June 30, 2019	$904.74

The benefit rate a claimant receives (determined by his/her date of injury) does not change if new maximum benefit rates are adopted into law.

Temporary disability payments of 66.6% of the injured worker's wages for the year in which the injury occurred or his occupational disease manifested, subject to the annual maximum and minimum, are payable until he can return to work.

For accidents occurring after July 1, 2010 the rate is two-thirds the State Average Weekly Wage (SAWW) decided by the Commissioner of Labor. From July 1, 2018 to June 30, 2019 the rate is $904.74.

PART III: TEMPORARY PARTIAL DISABILITY BENEFITS

§7.08   Degrees of Partial Disability

The degrees of partial disability are "mild" (25%), "moderate" (50%), and "marked" (75%). The degree of disability is equivalent to the loss of earning capacity.

§7.09   Calculating Compensation

Compensation is calculated as follows:

$$AWW * \frac{\text{degree of disability}}{150} = \text{rate of compensation}$$

This is the same formula as for total temporary disability compensation. The difference is that the degree of disability is the loss of earning capacity - which can be demonstrated by lost wages. However, most of the time the claimant will not be working, and the IME physician will state that the claimant has a "mild" or no temporary disability and the attending doctor will opine that the claimant is totally disabled. The claimant generally does not return to work, and the impasse is often resolved by the Court issuing a "tentative" disability rate.

PART IV: PERMANENCY BENEFITS

§7.10   Types of Permanent Disabilities

There are three types of permanent disability in New York: (1) Scheduled Loss of use; (2) Permanent "partial" disability; and (3) Permanent "total" disability. These three types of disability are compensated at different rates.

[1]   Scheduled Loss of Use

"Scheduled loss of use" relates to injuries to specific, enumerated body parts which are listed on a "scheduled loss of use chart" (found in this book). This is a fixed amount of compensation for injuries to fingers, toes, hands, feet, arms, ankles, knees, etc. In other words, the Workers Compensation Law states that if you lose your thumb in accident, you get a fixed benefit – a number of weeks of compensation times your weekly rate – which is determined by the injury. The Law affixes a specific maximum exposure (expressed as a maximum number of weeks of benefits) for each enumerated body part.

Prior payments of compensation and wages (all wages, not just those paid at the compensation rate) are deducted from the award.

> *Example: If an injured worker made $200 per week and lost her thumb, according to the Scheduled Loss of Use chart, she would be entitled to 100% loss of the thumb – 75 weeks of compensation. This would be paid at a rate equivalent to 2/3 (66.6%) of her average weekly wage – or approximately $133.34 per week (2/3 of $200 per week). So, in this example, the loss of the thumb would give rise to an award of $10,000 for permanent disability. The other benefit the injured worker would receive is medical treatment for life regarding the lost thumb.*

Scheduled Loss of Use - Checklist
- Has the claimant reached MMI?
- Has the claimant's physician issued a C-4.3 Report (Doctor's Report of MMI/Permanent Impairment[131])?
- Has the IME physician given an estimate of scheduled loss of use?

If the answer to two or more of these questions is "yes" then consider the potential for a scheduled loss of use award or settlement.

---

[131] http://www.wcb.ny.gov/content/main/forms/c4_3.pdf

[2]   Classification – Permanent Partial Disability

The second type of permanent disability award is called a "classified award" or sometimes it is called a "classification." This term "classification" doesn't really mean anything – it just means the claimant sustained injury to a body part which is not specifically listed as a "scheduled loss of use." For example, injuries to the head, neck, and low back are considered "classifiable" injuries – and they are compensated in terms of a fixed number of weeks – up to 600 weeks.

> **Example**: If an injured worker earned $200 per week and sustained an injury to her low back, such an injury (if permanent) could give rise to a classification award. Any amounts already paid to me – the claimant – during the claim for my lost wages – for example, if I lost a few weeks from work – would be subtracted from the overall award.

[3]   Permanent Total Disability

Permanent total disability is just that: total disability that is not temporary and which prevents the claimant from engaging in the work giving rise to his earnings that he enjoyed before the disabling accident. The benefit rate is 2/3 of the Average Weekly Wage (subject to the maximum rate caps depending on the year of injury). This benefit is payable weekly. There is no cap on weeks – this benefit may be payable for the remainder of the claimant's life.

§7.11   Awards for Permanent Disability

Some specific injuries, such as loss of an extremity, vision loss, hearing loss, or facial disfigurement have "scheduled" or **set** payment amounts. Other losses, called "unscheduled" or "classifications" compensate the injured worker for injuries which are not on the schedule (such as a spinal injury, disc herniation, a cardiac injury, abdominal injury, etc.) but which cause continuing partial or total disability in the claimant. These unscheduled losses are classified into permanent partial disability and permanent total disability.

§7.12   Stipulating to a Disability

In many simple cases, where the body part injured is scheduled (hands, fingers, feet, toes, etc.) the parties can reach amicable settlement. Under a stipulated scheduled loss of use, the claimant's right to future medical remains open. The stipulation will be prepared on Form C-300.5 and submitted to the Board for approval.

The parties should clearly state whether the payment of the scheduled weeks will be "accelerated" so that the claimant can receive all future weeks in one immediate payment.

§7.13   What a Treating Doctor must do

Often, there is not a simple agreement between the parties as to the extent and nature of the claimant's residual permanent disability. In such a case, we will often have a trial. During the pendency of the trial both parties can present their own witnesses.

A treating physician must provide the Board with medical evidence that the Workers' Compensation Law Judge will consider when making their legal determination about disability. The health provider can make a recommendation about whether the claimant can return to their regular employment. If the medical provider states that the claimant cannot return to his previous employment, the medical provider should state what medical limitations exist.

The 2012 Guidelines envision that the treating physician's evaluation of medical impairment should include the relevant basis for the impairment classification, including the relevant history, physical findings, and diagnostic test results and be provided on Form C-4.3.

§7.14   The Scheduled Loss of Use Guidelines Change in 2018

As part of the April 2017 legislation, the Board was directed to issue new guidelines for medical professionals to rely on when evaluating permanent impairments to "scheduled" body parts. In September, 2017 the Board issued "draft" proposed guidelines. At the time this book goes to print, the draft guidelines were being debated.

PART V: LIGHT DUTY WORK

§7.15   Why Seek a Return to Work in a Light Duty Capacity?

Employees who do not return to work (transitional or otherwise) within 6 months of the date of loss have a less than 50% chance of returning to gainful employment. Injured workers who remain out of work for more than one year, but less than two years have a 25% chance of returning to employment. Workers who have lost two or more years to injury have less than a 1% chance of returning to any type of employment.[132]

The Workers' Compensation Board envisions a process in which an employer "creates" a light duty job tailored to each injured worker. In reality, most employers have a limited amount of potential light duty employment. In those cases, the goal of the claims professional is to get a clear statement of the claimant's work ability from the treating physician and then to issue an appropriate offer letter to the claimant.

§7.16   Make a Valid Light Duty Offer

If a light duty offer is made, and the claimant does not return to the workplace to accept the work, the employer can stop paying benefits by arguing that the claimant has voluntarily withdrawn from the labor market.

Some claimants don't want to come back to work. They are quite happy to sit home, collect their benefits, drink beer and watch "Judge Judy" all day. They regularly employ two excuses to avoid light duty work:

"I never got the offer to return in any capacity;" and

"I tried the job, it was too hard."

The Courts have consistently upheld these excuses. In cases where the employer could not document that a valid light duty offer of work was made, the Courts have found in favor of the claimant. The light duty offer should be made in writing.

---

[132] New York State Workers' Compensation Board "Return to Work Program Handbook" page 2.

Claimants who argue that the offered job was "too much" consistently prevail where the offer letter fails to address exactly what job the claimant was being offered.[133] Similarly, if the offered work is "more active" that the work release provided by the treating physician, the Board has been upheld in ruling that refusal to do the "more active" work does not constitute a voluntary removal on the part of the claimant.[134]

§7.17   Light Duty Return to Work Action Plan

If the employer can offer light duty work, the goal is to identify whether the potential light duty employment can be performed by the worker. The first step is getting a light duty release. The carrier/employer can communicate with the claimant's treating health care providers. Then, communicate with the treating doctor to get a statement of work ability. If the work restrictions can be accommodated, issue an offer to the claimant. If the claimant refuses to return to the employment, file the appropriate RFA-2 (if you are under an order to continue benefits) or stop paying partial benefits!

[1]   Determine if Light Duty Work can be Offered

If the employer is willing to provide light duty work, a written job description detailing the skill requirements necessary, job duties, physical demands, and environmental conditions should be obtained.

[2]   Model Release from Claimant to Communicate with Physician

Here is a model release to be adapted to your needs[135]:

AUTHORITY TO RELEASE MEDICAL INFORMATION

DATE: (Dated)

TO: TREATING DOCTOR

RE: (Employee Name) (Employee Address) (Date of Birth)

---

[133] Hatter v. New Venture Gear, 305 A.D.2d 757 (3d Dep't 2003).

[134] Turner v. Erie Cty. Med. Ctr., 250 A.D.2d 1020 (3d Dep't 1998).

[135] *See* Appendix "C,", Page 15, New York State Workers' Compensation Board "Return to Work Program Handbook."

I, (Employee Name), authorize (name of treating doctor) to release medical information to my employer, (name and address of employer), regarding my on the job injury that occurred on (date of injury). This information is confidential and may not be used for any purpose other than facilitating the claimant's return to work.

This information may facilitate my return to medically appropriate productive work.

Print Employee Name _____

Employee Signature _____ Date

[3]   Communicate with the Treating Physician

The employer/carrier may communicate with the claimant's treating physician about workplace demands (following receipt of employee consent). This communication should be in writing and should be copied to the claimant and her attorney (if she has one). We recommend that you describe the work duties, physical demands, and environmental conditions for the proposed light duty work in written format. Here is a model letter to the treating doctor to be adapted to your needs:

[4] Model Letter to Treating Physician

SAMPLE LETTER TO TREATING DOCTOR.

DATE: (Date of letter)

TO: TREATING DOCTOR

RE: (Employee's name and date of injury)

Dear Dr._____:

Our Company has implemented a return to work program designed to return any injured employee to medically appropriate work as soon as possible. Enclosed is a detailed job description for the regular job of the employee named above, which may be modified, if possible, to meet medical restrictions that may be assigned.

If our employee is unable to return to his or her regular job, we will attempt to find an appropriate alternate work assignment. We will ensure that any assignment meets all medical requirements as directed toward your specific treatment strategies.

We will consider re-arranging work schedules around medical appointments if necessary. To that end, we request that you complete the enclosed Transitional Assignments Form with as much detail as possible.

If you need additional information about a possible work assignment or about our return to work program, please call (Return to Work Program Contact name and number). Our insurance carrier is (name and address of insurance carrier).

Thank you for your participation in our efforts to return our employees to a safe and productive workplace.

> Sincerely,
>
> (Signature of company representative or owner)
>
> (Title),
>
> (Name of Company)

cc: Claimant, claimant's attorney

Encl. (2 enclosures):

> (1) Claimant's Signed authorization; and
>
> (2) Job descriptions and task analysis

[5]   The "Light Duty Offer" Letter

The "perfect" light duty offer letter contains the following elements:
- Sent to the claimant's correct address.
- Sent "certified" mail or with proof of delivery.
- Includes the following information:
- Job title.
- Location (address).
- Duration of assignment.
- Wages.

- Department (or Name of Supervisor).
- Start date.

We strongly recommend that the offer letter include a "start date" and an "expiration date" for the return-to-work offer.

[6] Model Light Duty Offer Letter

Here is a model "offer letter" that can be modified to suit your needs:

BONA FIDE OFFER OF EMPLOYMENT (Sent Certified Mail – Return Receipt)

DATE: (Date)

TO: (Employee name) (Employee address line 1) (Employee address line 2) (City, State, Zip)

RE: Bona Fide Offer of Employment

Dear (Employee Name):

After reviewing information provided by your doctor, we are pleased to offer you the following temporary work assignment. Please see the attached Individual Return to Work Plan for details. We believe this assignment is within your capabilities as described by your doctor on the attached Transitional Work Assignment Form. You will only be assigned tasks consistent with your physical abilities, skills, and knowledge.

If any training is required to do this assignment, it will be provided.

Job Title:

Location:

Duration of Assignment:

Wages:

Department:

This job offer will remain available for five (5) business days from your receipt of this letter. If we do not hear from you within five (5) business days,

99

we will assume that you have refused this offer. Please note that refusal of an employment offer may impact your Temporary Income Benefit payments.

We look forward to your return. If you have any questions, please do not hesitate to contact me.

Sincerely,

(Signature)

(Printed Name and Title)

(Contact Information)

§7.18   When the Claimant Fails to Come Back to Work

OK, so the treating physician has released the claimant to light duty work, with specific lifting and activity restrictions. The employer can accommodate the restrictions and has sent a "perfect" letter to the claimant offering a light duty position and telling the claimant when the position will start.

The start day comes and goes, and the claimant fails to report to work.

What to do next?

[1]   No Order Directing Employer/Carrier to Pay Benefits

Per 12 NYCRR § 300.23, in any case where the carrier or employer has made payment without waiting for an award by the board, the carrier or employer should file a C-8/8.6 form with the chair accompanied by supporting evidence that the suspension or reduction of payment is appropriate such as the notice to return to work justifying the suspension or reduction of payments.

[2]   Order Directing Employer/Carrier to Pay Benefits

If there is a direction for continuation of payments, the employer or carrier must continue payments at such rate [beyond the period covered by the award], and such payments shall not be suspended or reduced until:

- an RFA-2 is filed, accompanied by supporting evidence justifying the proposed suspension or reduction together with proof of mailing of copies thereof upon the claimant, his/her doctor and his/her representative, and,

- after a hearing finding that such suspension or reduction is justified. At said hearing, meeting, or conference, if either party fails to appear or fails to submit any evidence as to the above issue, the Workers' Compensation Law judge may continue, suspend, or reduce the award.

CHAPTER 8: MEDICAL BENEFITS AND THE MEDICAL TREATMENT GUIDELINES

PART I: OVERVIEW OF MEDICAL TREATMENT

§8.01 Medical Benefits

The injured or ill worker who is eligible for workers' compensation will receive necessary medical care directly related to the original injury or illness and the recovery from his/her disability. The treating health care provider must be authorized by the Workers' Compensation Board, except in an emergency. In an emergency, the employer can provide the medical care – choosing doctors, facilities, etc. However, when able to do so, the employee can change the physician to one of his own choosing.[136]

Unlike wage-replacement benefits, medical benefits must be provided from the date of the loss – there is no waiting period for medical benefits.[137]

The claimant must be provided care "as long as the nature of the injury or the process of treatment may require." This means that treatment must be provided so long as it is directed at returning the claimant to gainful employment. Not all medical treatment relates to disabilities that 'arises out of and in the course of employment' – and those disabilities that do not arise from the employment (such as those from the natural aging process) are not compensable. Medical evidence must be presented to the WCB of the employer believes that the claimant's medical care is not properly directed at treating an industrial disability.[138]

---

[136] WCL § 13-a.

[137] WCL § 4.13.

[138] *Kapogiannis v. Vassar Coll.* 141 A.D.2d 947 (3d Dep't 1988); *Murtagh v. St. Theresa's Nursing Home, Inc.*, 84 A.D.2d 587 (3d Dep't 1981); *Stiso v. Hallen Constr. Co.*, 135 A.D.2d 974 (3d Dep't 1987); *Evans v. Great E. Lumbar Co.*, 141 A.D.2d 937 (3d Dep't 1988).

§8.02   Medical Treatment Guidelines

On December 1, 2010, the Medical Treatment Guidelines became the manda-tory standard of care for injured workers, regardless of the date of injury or accident.[139] These Guidelines have been supplemented and amended, effec-tive September 15, 2014, and now include treatment pathways for carpal tun-nel syndrome and non-acute pain. Medical care providers are required to treat all existing and new workers' compensation injuries in accordance with the Medical Treatment Guidelines (MTG) which are incorporated by reference into the regulations.

The MTG body-part specific guidelines are:

- Non-Acute Pain Medical Treatment Guideline, First Edition, September 15, 2014.[140]

- New York Mid and Low Back Injury Medical Treatment Guidelines, Third Edition, September 15, 2014.[141]

- New York Neck Injury Medical Treatment Guidelines, Third Edition, September 15, 2014.[142]

- New York Knee Injury Medical Treatment Guidelines, Third Edition, September 15, 2014.[143]

- New York Shoulder Injury Medical Treatment Guidelines, Third Edition, September 15, 2014.[144]

---

[139] 12 NYCRR 324.2.

[140] http://www.wcb.ny.gov/content/main/hcpp/MedicalTreatmentGuidelines/Non-AcutePainMTG2014.pdf

[141] http://www.wcb.ny.gov/content/main/hcpp/MedicalTreatmentGuide-lines/MidandLowBackInjuryMTG2014.pdf

[142] http://www.wcb.ny.gov/content/main/hcpp/MedicalTreatmentGuidelines/NeckIn-juryMTG2014.pdf

[143] http://www.wcb.ny.gov/content/main/hcpp/MedicalTreatmentGuidelines/Knee-InjuryMTG2014.pdf

[144] http://www.wcb.ny.gov/content/main/hcpp/MedicalTreatmentGuidelines/Shoul-derInjuryMTG2014.pdf

- New York Carpal Tunnel Medical Treatment Guidelines, Second Edition, September 15, 2014.[145]

Medical care for workers' compensation injuries to the neck, low back, mid back, shoulder, knee and for carpal tunnel syndrome must be provided in a manner "consistent with the MTG." This is the standard for doctors and health care providers to follow. "Consistent with the MTG" means that care is provided within the criteria and based upon a correct application of the MTG. What is within the criteria and a correct application is left open for the WCB's WC Judges to interpret.

8.03   General Principles of the Treatment Guidelines

The Medical Treatment Guidelines include statements of "General Principles" in each MTG's first section. These are the key principles necessary to apply and interpret the MTGs.

There are 23 general principles divided into 6 categories. Of these, the two most important are:

1. **Medical Care.** The purpose of medical care is to restore functional ability required to meet daily and work-related activities, to obtain a positive patient response primarily defined as functional gains which can be objectively measured, and to provide effective treatment which includes evaluations and re-evaluations of treatment and which discontinues ineffective treatments.

1. **Treatment approaches.** Treatment should emphasize active interventions over passive modalities (i.e., therapeutic exercise instead of manipulation), should include passive intervention to facilitate progress in an active rehabilitation program, and should resort to surgical interventions only when there is correlation of clinical findings, clinical course, imaging and other diagnostic tests.

§8.04   When Authorizations are Required

All medical care consistent with the MTG is pre-authorized and the health care provider is not required to obtain prior authorization.[146] There are eleven (11) exceptions to this rule which are defined in the regulations and one (1)

---

[145] http://www.wcb.ny.gov/content/main/hcpp/MedicalTreatmentGuidelines/Carpal-TunnelMTG2014.pdf

[146] N.Y.R.R.C. 324.2(d)(1).

additional exception defined in the regulations. So, in total there are twelve official exceptions - 12 specific procedures that a doctor must get pre-authorization to do.

Now, if you pay close attention, you will realize that there are really 19 exceptions. Check out the WCB's published list of procedures that require the health care provider to obtain pre-authorization.

- Mid- and Low Back: lumbar fusion, vertebroplasty, kyphoplasty, and spinal cord stimulator;

- Neck and Low Back: artificial disc replacement and spinal cord stimulator;

- Knee: Chondroplasty, osteochondral autograft, autologous chondrocyte implantation, meniscal allograft transplantation and knee arthroscopy (total or partial knee replacement); and

- Duplicative surgery/treatment.

If you list all these procedures separately, you see that there are actually 19 different procedures or treatment scenarios listed here - 6 for the low back, 4 for the mid back, 2 for the neck, 6 for the knee, and all *duplicative treatment*.

Providers who want to perform one of these procedures must request pre-authorization from the carrier before performing the procedure. In addition, the MTG specifically forbids any "medical treatment that is experimental and not approved by the FDA." If the MTG do not address a condition, treatment or diagnostic test for one of the covered body parts, then a variance request can be made to determine whether a carrier will be obligated to pay for the treatment or medical care.

§8.05   Duplicate Treatment

Duplicate surgery or treatment is not automatically authorized. Referred to by practitioners as the "13th Exception", this exception requires a medical provider to seek prior approval for repeat or revision care - for example, removal of hardware in a failed fusion attempt.

§8.06   Out-of-State Claimants and the MTG

In a Board Panel Decision dated May 24, 2017, the Board found that the Medical Treatment Guidelines apply to the out of state treatment of a claimant residing outside of New York State. The decision in *In Re Hospice* is important because it reverses the Board's previous statements that out-of-state treatment was immune from the application of the restrictive Medical Treatment Guidelines ("MTG"). This meant that New York claimants merely had to "cross the river" into New Jersey or any other state and obtain medical treatment and medications which far exceeded the treatment or medications allowed under the Medical Treatment Guidelines, needlessly increasing the costs in their cases. Now employers and carriers have a Board Panel decision supporting the argument that law judges should apply the MTG's to out of state cases.

[1]   In Re Hospice Facts

The claimant had a New York workers' compensation claim with a 1995 date of loss. He moved to Nevada where he received treatment for low back pain with Dr. Fisher. The doctor prescribed and dispensed LidoPro ointment ($1,883) and Terocin patches ($2,576). "LidoPro" is nothing more than a mixture of lidocaine and capsaicin. "Terocin" is also lidocaine with menthol.

The carrier objected to the prescriptions (by filing C-8.1Bs). All bills were found in favor of the provider. The carrier appealed, conceding that the Medical Treatment Guidelines do not apply out of state but arguing that the doctor had not established medical necessity for the treatments.

[2]   In Re Hospice Legal Decision

The Board directly addressed the fact that in dozens of prior decisions it has held that the Medical Treatment Guidelines do not apply when the claimant resides out of state and receives medical care out of state. In the new decision, the Board panel states that "the plain language of the regulations governing the Guidelines, 12 NYCRR 324, do not limit their applicability to treatment rendered to New York residents or treatment rendered in New York."

The Board applied Mid and Low Back Medical Treatment Guideline D.7.j.i & D.7.j.ii which state that

- Optimal Duration for lidocaine is one to two weeks and that long-term use is not recommended, and

- Topical lidocaine is only allowed where the physician has documented neuropathic pain and for no longer than four weeks unless there are functional gains (documented improvement).

Although the facts of the case do not include a lengthy medical history, it is quite obvious from the date of loss (1995) and the dates of treatment (2016) that at least 21 years elapsed (clearly longer than the one to four week trial periods for the topical medications prescribed). The Board also noted that the two prescriptions (ointment and patch) were just two different delivery mechanisms for the same medication.

The Board panel reversed the Law Judge and ruled in favor of the carrier, finding that the medications exceeded the Guidelines. The Board found that the Medical Treatment Guidelines apply to out of state residents.

> *Practical Advice:* Even though the carrier did not raise the argument that the Medical Treatment Guidelines should not apply to out of state claimants the Board Panel used that basis to reverse the Law Judge. This is important - for two reasons. First, it shows how entrenched the Board's prior direction in this topic - that the Medical Treatment Guidelines do apply to out of state claimants has become in the New York Workers' Compensation arena. It is notable that the carrier did not even bother to raise the inapplicability of the MTG's to out of state treatment in their appeal. Second, by addressing the applicability of the MTGs to out of state treatment on their own accord signals that the Board is taking a new direction on out of state treatment which exceeds the Guidelines. This decision is great for employers and carriers in New York!

[3]   Important Takeaways from In Re Hospice

Medical Treatment Guidelines apply to out of state residents obtaining medical treatment outside of New York State.

Employers and carriers can challenge out of state treatment by filing C-8.1B's stating that "medical treatment exceeds the Guidelines" with a reference to the Guideline. Risk professionals may want to append a copy of the Board panel decision in In Re Hospice to their C-8.1 filings to remind the board employees reviewing the medical fee disputes that the Board's position on out of state treatment has changed.

An out of state medical provider does not have to use New York forms, for example a MG-2 (variance) or C-4AUTH (request for authorization) but still must request permission from the carrier when their proposed treatment course will exceed the Medical Treatment Guidelines.

§8.07   Managed Care

Insurance carriers, which includes self-insured employers, may contract with a legally and properly organized diagnostic network to perform diagnostic tests, x-ray examinations, magnetic resonance imaging or other radiological tests or examinations or tests. The Workers' Compensation Law allows insurance carriers and self-insured employers to contract with New York State Health Department certified Preferred Provider Organizations (PPOs) to provide services, to diagnose, treat and rehabilitate an injured or ill worker requiring medical treatment. PPOs are required to make available at least two providers in every medical specialty and two hospitals. An injured worker is required to seek initial treatment with a provider affiliated with the PPO however, after initial treatment, he/she may select any authorized provider outside the PPO 30 days after the initial treatment.

The Workers' Compensation Law also allows, by negotiated labor agreement, a non-Workers' Compensation Board adjudication claim process called the Alternate Dispute Resolution (ADR) system for employers and employees in the unionized construction industry. Injured workers covered by the ADR program are required to obtain medical treatment from medical providers participating in the ADR program.

§8.08   M&T Reimbursement

The Workers' Compensation Law requires the employer/carrier to reimburse the claimant for out-of-pocket expenses related to certain categories of expenditures. Specifically, the Law allows for *certain medication, durable medical goods,* and *mileage.*

Just fare or car mileage to and from doctor's appointments (including hospital parking fees) and prescription drug or apparatus costs. These expenses should be recorded on Form C-257.[147]

Expenses NOT eligible for reimbursement include:

- Round trip mileage to hearings.
- Round trip mileage to pharmacy.
- Round trip mileage for out of state medical treatment not previously approved.
- Round trip mileage to Workforce One, VESID or any similar vocational rehabilitation program.
- Anything that does NOT have a receipt for proof of payment.
- Doctor appointments which do NOT have corresponding medical reports to show proof of attendance.

---

[147] http://www.wcb.ny.gov/content/main/forms/c257.pdf

- Housekeepers, prepared meals, other domestic help not previously approved or ordered.

PART II: AUTHORIZATION & APPROVAL PROCESS

§8.09   The Optional Prior Approval Process

The Optional Prior Approval process allows a medical treatment provider the opportunity to confirm that medical treatment is consistent with the MTG.[148] While participation in this process is voluntary, as of the date of this writing, all carriers have been "opted in" to this system. To opt out a carrier or third-party administrator must issue a written notice of the desire to get out and must give the Chair 60 days notice.

The carrier must provide a qualified employee as a point of contact for the medical providers. The required information for the point of contact is to be placed on the WCB's website. Medical providers must submit a written form (Form MG-1 for the first request and Form MG-1.1 for all subsequent requests) and are encouraged to call the qualified employees directly to discuss authorizations.

Medical providers must use Form MG-1 and it must be sent using "same day transmission" (either fax or email) to the carrier. The carrier has eight (8) days to respond.

The carrier can respond one of three (3) ways:
1. Grant the request;
1. Grant the request Without Prejudice; or
2. Deny the Request.

If the request is denied because the requested medical treatment departs from the MTG, further explanation is not required - the carrier should note which specific MTG section supports the denial. The denial must include the name of the medical professional (which could be a LPN, PA-C, MD, or RN) who reviewed the request along with the MTG section that supports the denial. However, this medical professional (who reviewed the request on behalf of the carrier) does not have to sign the Form MG-1.

If the request is denied, the medical care provider has 14 days to request a review of the denial. The matter then goes to the Medical Arbitrator who will

---

[148] N.Y.C.R.R. 324.4.

issue a decision within 8 days. The decision of the medical Arbitrator is not appealable under WCL Section 23.[149]

This process is only to be used for knee, neck, shoulder, and mid- and low back cases. The claim does not have to be established for this process to be used.

§8.10   The Variance Process

When a medical care provider wants to provide specific medical treatment that does not fit the MTG they can request prior authorization for the treatment by requesting a variance. This procedure is similar to a "Request for Authorization" under WCL § 13-a(5). The regulation that permits variances is found at 12 N.Y.C.R.R. 324.3.

[1]   Variance Basics

A variance is a license to do something that varies from the MTG. A treating medical provider must request this approval from the carrier. A variance request must be made even if the claim is controverted or the time to controvert the case has not yet expired.

A variance request must be made before treatment is provided that differs from the Guidelines. Requests made after treatment has already been provided that differ from the MTG will not be considered.

Important timelines for variance requests:
- 5 (five) business days to respond if obtaining an IME;
- 15 (fifteen) days for a final response if not obtaining an IME;
- 30 (thirty) days for a final response along with a copy of the IME;
- 8 (eight) business days to discuss denial informally;
- 21 (twenty-one) business days for claimant to request review.

[2]   When a Variance will be Sought

A variance will be sought in four circumstances:
- **EXTRA-MTG:** The treating doctor believes that the claimant would benefit from medical care that is not within the MTG;

---

[149] Please note: if the carrier fails to respond to the *Optional Prior Approval Request* a *Notice of Resolution* will be issued   approving the procedure and the carrier loses the ability to challenge the necessity or appropriateness of the treatment later.

- **NOT RECOMMENDED BY THE MTG:** The treating doctor believes that the claimant would benefit from medical care that is within the Guidelines but not recommended;

- **NOT YET RIPE:** The treating doctor believes that the claimant would benefit from medical care that is within the Guidelines but not specified at that point in the claimant's treatment; or

- **FREQUENCY:** The treating doctor believes that the claimant would benefit from medical care that is within the Guidelines but exceeds the maximum number or frequency limit for that particular treatment.

[3]   Making a Variance Request

Variance requests must be made on Form MG-2, "Attending Doctor's Request for Approval of Variance and Carrier's Response.'"[150] The treating physician must complete all sections of the Form MG-2, which includes information about the claimant, employer, carrier, the Medical Treatment provider, the body part, the section of the MTG that applies, the specific treatment requested, a statement as to why the treatment is medically necessary, reference to records in the WCB's file, and a certification that the claimant understands and agrees to undergo the proposed medical care.

It is possible for attending doctors to request treatment which is not addressed specifically in the MTG. In those cases, the attending doctor is not seeking a variance from the Guidelines as much as they are asking for permission to do something not contemplated by the MTG. In those cases, the attending doctor must show the same proofs as a doctor seeking simple variance.[151]

If more than one Treating Medical Provider needs a variance for more than one procedure or test at the same time, Form MG-2.1 should be used. The MG-2 form must be transmitted the same day to the WCB, the carrier, the claimant, and claimant's attorney. Form MG-2 must be sent by either email or fax - mail is acceptable only if the provider does not have fax or email capabilities.[152] This is likely to cause problems as the attending doctor is unlikely to have an email address for the claimant or the claimant's attorney. All carriers are required to designate a "qualified employee "to receive these requests.

---

[150] Form MG-2 is available here: http://www.wcb.ny.gov/content/main/forms/MG2.pdf

[151] 12 N.Y.C.R.R. 324.5.

[152] 12 N.Y.C.R.R. 324.3(a)(3).

113

[4]   Burdens of Proof for Making a Variance

The medical provider requesting the variance has the burden of proof to show that the treatment requested is appropriate and medically necessary for the claimant.[153]

The attending doctor requesting the variance must provide:

- the basis for the opinion that the specified treatment or test is appropriate and is medically necessary;
- a statement that the claimant agrees to the proposed medical care;
- an explanation why alternatives contained within the Guidelines are not appropriate or sufficient; and
- any signs or symptoms which failed to improve with treatment provided in accordance with the Guidelines; or
- the objective improvements made by a particular treatment and the expected improvements with more of the same treatment.[154]

The attending doctor may also submit copies of relevant articles from peer-reviewed medical journals which lend support for the variance request but ONLY for treatments not otherwise addressed by the MTG. If the claimant is seeking a treatment (like discography) which has been specifically eliminated by the MTG, then NO AMOUNT of contrary articles in support of the procedure will be persuasive. The attending doctor must refer to medical reports that get attached to the MG-2 form or already within the WCB's file (E-case).

[5]   When an Insurance Carrier Receives a Variance Request

Upon receipt of a variance request the carrier must decide if it will obtain an IME or review of the records report. If the carrier is going to obtain an IME or records review, the WCB must be notified within 5 business days of receipt. (Receipt of variance is calculated as 'same day' if email or fax transmission is used; if sent by mail then receipt is 5 business days after treating doctor certified it was mailed). The carrier notifies the WCB that they are obtaining an IME or records review by completing Section "D' of the MG-2 form.

If the carrier decides not to get an IME or records review, then the carrier must transmit its response within 15 calendars after receipt of the variance request. If the carrier has selected to get an IME or records review, the response is due within 30 days from receipt of variance request. Obviously, this

---

[153] 12 N.Y.C.R.R. § 324.3(a)(2).
[154] See N.Y.C.R.R. 324.3(a)(3).

creates an enormous burden for carriers: it will be a challenge to get an IME scheduled and completed and a report generated and reviewed within 30 days from receipt of a variance request. One response to this time challenge may be to get examining physicians to set one day aside per month for these emergent variance review IMEs.

The possible responses to a variance request are:

* **Approval;**
* **Denial.** Remember to issue a denial even if you have already filed a C-7 to controvert the case - controverting the case is not enough - the WCB can rule on variance requests where no denial was issued.
* **"Grant without prejudice."** This is only available if the claim has been controverted or the time to controvert the claim has not yet expired.
* **Do nothing.** if this happens (you do not respond within the time limitations) the Chair will issue an Order of the Chair. This decision will likely result in an approval of the variance. An Order of the Chair issued under these circumstances (untimely or no response) is not subject to an appeal under WCL Section 23.

[6]   Rejecting Variance Requests Based on Defective Filing

The MG-2 variance request form is a multi-page document with plenty of small type. Certain information is essential to the Board's internal procedures and if that information is missing or incomplete, the Board cannot process the form. For the Board to take action on an MG-2 form, the Board requires that the following fields be completed.

Check the MG-2 - if any the following sections are incomplete or missing - issue a denial and alert the Board as to your reasons!

Required in Section A:

* Patient's name, and
* Insurance carrier's name & address.

Please note that the Insurance carrier's or TPA's name and address must match the information the Board has on file.

Required in Section B:

* Individual provider's WCB authorization number for all providers authorized by the New York State Workers' Compensation Board

Required in Section C:

- Date variance request submitted and method of transmission,

- Guideline reference for the body part followed by the 2 to 4 character corresponding reference in the Medical Treatment Guidelines or followed by the four letters N-O-N-E if there is no listed procedure,

- Written description of the treatment requested,

- Description for statement of medical necessity. *If there is a supporting medical report in the Board's case file, the requesting physician should enter the date of service or if there is no supporting medical report in the case file, attach a medical report and enter "See attached medical report" on the form;*

- A check box selected for how the carrier was contacted; and

- The provider's signature or stamp. *Please note that initials next to the signature or stamp are not acceptable.*

Note that **physical therapists are not "medical providers"** under the MTG and cannot issue an MG-2 to request authorization for additional physical therapy visits beyond the Guidelines - only a doctor can issue the MG-2 to request additional PT. Issue a summary denial to any variance request issued by a physical therapist.

[7]   Variance Denials

The carrier must explain any denial of requested variance in Section "E" of Form MG-2. Any reason for denial that is not raised is deemed waived. The possible grounds for denial are:

- The medical care requested has already been rendered (if the request was submitted after treatment already rendered, an IME or records review is not necessary)[155];

- The Treating Medical Provider did not meet the burden of proof (appropriateness and medical necessity);

- The treatment request is not medically necessary or appropriate for the claimant - this would be coming from your IME or records review; or

- The claimant failed to appear for the scheduled IME examination. In this situation, the WCB may extend the time for IME by thirty days.[156]

---

[155] 12 N.Y.C.R.R. 324.3(i)(b)

[156] 12 N.Y.C.R.R. 324.3.

If the denial is based on the grounds that the treatment sought is not medically necessary or appropriate, the carrier must:

- Have the case reviewed by its own medical professional, independent medical examiner, or records reviewer;

- Attach the written report of its own medical professional, independent medical evaluator, or records reviewer;

- Submit citations to peer-reviewed medical journals in support of the denial (if such articles formed the basis of the denial).

[8]   After a Denial

One path to resolution is informal discussions between the medical care provider seeking the variance and the carrier. The parties have eight (8) business days to attempt an informal resolution - and if the dispute can be resolved, the insurance carrier confirms the agreement by completing Section "G" ('Carrier's Granting of Attending Doctor's Variance Request after Initial Denial').

If 'informal' resolution fails, the treating doctor notifies the claimant and claimant's counsel. The claimant can then seek review of the denial by the Board. If the claimant decides to request review, a request for review must be filed within 21 business days of the receipt of denial (once again, 'receipt' is deemed the date of transmission of the denial was sent via fax or email and 5 business days of the denial was sent via mail). If the claimant is represented, the request for review must be on the Form MG-2 (Section F). If the claimant is not represented, the request for review must be in writing (but does not have to be on Form MG-2).

When informal resolution fails, and the claimant requests a review, there are two pathways the review can take:

- Submission to a medical arbitrator if both parties agree in writing to the submission; or

- By a Workers' Compensation Law Judge through the expedited hearing process ("Rocket Docket").

The choice of either medical arbitration or 'rocket docket' is up to the claimant - the claimant elects the method for resolving the dispute on Section "F" of Form MG-2. If the claimant is not represented, then they have 14 days after the WCB responds to select either an expedited hearing or medical arbitration. If the claimant makes no choice the case is set for an expedited hearing.

The carrier may also elect either expedited hearing or medical arbitration - but in the case of arbitration the claimant must agree to it. Ultimately, the choice will reside with the claimant: unless the claimant agrees to medical arbitration, the matter goes to expedited hearing.

[9]   Medical Arbitrator Process

By agreeing to have the denial of waiver decided by a medical arbitrator, the parties give up the right to an expedited hearing and accept a final decision that CANNOT be appealed under WCL Section 23 (so don't file an RB-89 if you are unhappy with the outcome!). The review is conducted without participation of the parties - the arbitrator reviews the request for review, variance request, and denial (and all papers including medical reports, IMEs or record reviews, and articles from peer-reviewed journals). The Medical Arbitrator then issues a notice of resolution setting forth the ruling and the basis for the ruling.

[10]   Expedited Hearing Process

The expedited hearing will be held within 30 days after the period of informal resolution has ended if the matter could not be resolved informally. One or both parties must request the expedited hearing (or not waive the right to expedited hearing). Medical testimony will be taken. If the claimant is unrepresented then medical testimony is always taken at the hearing. If the claimant is represented, then medical testimony may be by submission of deposition transcripts at the hearing (the transcripts must be submitted to the WCB at or before the expedited hearing). Adjournments are possible, but only for up to 30 days and only for cases in involving complex medical issues of causation or diagnosis.

CHAPTER 9: DEATH BENEFITS

PART I: CHAPTER OVERVIEW

§9.01   When a Worker Dies from a Compensable Injury

If the worker dies from a compensable injury, the surviving spouse and/or minor children or other dependents as defined by law, are entitled to weekly cash benefits. The amount is equal to two-thirds of the deceased worker's average weekly wage for the year before the accident. The weekly compensation may not exceed the weekly maximum, despite the number of dependents.

If there are no surviving children, spouse, grandchildren, grandparents, brothers or sisters, parents or grandparents entitled to compensation, the surviving parents or the estate of the deceased worker may be entitled to payment of a sum of $50,000. Funeral expenses may also be paid, up to $6,000 in Metropolitan New York counties; up to $5,000 in all others.

§9.02   Trial Presumption in Death Cases

New York workers who die on the job are entitled to a presumption that the death was work-related where the death is unwitnessed or unexplained.[157] This section of the statute is meant to encourage employer vigilance regarding employees in dangerous circumstances and encourage proper supervision.

§9.03   Employer Must be Afforded Opportunity to Rebut Claims

The employer bears the burden of refuting the allegations that the onset of the claimant's symptoms occurred while he was at work and that therefore the claimant was entitled to the statutory presumption that stroke or cardiac claims arose out of the employment.[158] Appellate courts have ruled that the WCB erred by requiring the claimant to establish his case before the employer refuted it: in essence, the panel found that the employer "must . . . .be afforded the opportunity to rebut the presumption (of compensability)."

---

[157] WCL § 21.

[158] WCL § 27.

§9.04   Same-Sex Members of Civil Unions Not Eligible for Dependency Benefits

Death benefits are payable to the spouse and minor children and other bene-ficiaries allowed by law on behalf of a worker killed at his employment. What about members of a civil union? In a recent decision[159], the WCB denied death benefits to the surviving "member" of a civil union which had taken place in Vermont. A divided Appellate Panel agreed and ruled that the surviving mem-ber of the civil union was not entitled to benefits.

The decision of the WCB strictly construed that workers' compensation law - the *surviving spouse* language. According to the facts of the case, John Langdon and his partner, Neal Spicehandler participated in a civil union ceremony in Vermont in 2000. According to the Vermont special statute authorizing the cer-emony, the participants in the union ceremony are not legal "spouses." For that reason, the New York court refused to grant death benefits to Spicehandler.

This is a significant departure from New Jersey law, which specifically includes members of a domestic partnership recognized under New Jersey law (since 2007) - and provides the same benefits to parties in a civil union as to married spouses.

---

[159] *Langan v. State Farm Fire & Cas.*, 48 A.D.3d 76 (3d Dep't 2007).

PART II: DEATHS FOUND NOT RELATED TO WORK

§9.05   Employee's Death Found Not Work-Related

In *Frederick v. Lindenhurst*, decided October 8, 2009, the Appellate Court reviewed a case where a custodian employee was found dead in the school's boiler room. An autopsy was performed and according to the autopsy report, the death was attributed to arteriosclerotic heart disease. This disease is frequently referred to as "hardening of the arteries" and comes from a buildup of fatty plaque on the walls of the main arteries. This disease is not peculiar to any employment.

Both the autopsy report and the death certificate found that the decedent's cause of death was arteriosclerotic heart disease. The employer disputed that the death was related, and the WCB agreed. The decedent's dependent's appealed.

The Appellate Panel found that "substantial evidence" will rebut the presumption that unwitnessed deaths are related to the employment. In this case, the cause of death was known: arteriosclerotic heart disease. The Appellate Division stated that absent any medical evidence that would call that conclusion into question or otherwise suggest that the decedent's work and his death were causally linked, the opinion of the WCB must stand.

The Appellate Panel repeated the case law that instructs that the employer does not have to rebut or meet every allegation presented by the dependents in order to overcome the assumption: in other words, if the claimant alleges that the 'heat' of the boiler-room, plus the claimant's work effort, 'combined' to cause his cardiac condition to erupt, the employer does not have to meet each theory separately in order to overcome the presumption of compensability, just offer a medically-sound evidence of contrary causation.

121

CHAPTER 10: OFF THE JOB INJURIES; DISABILITY BENEFITS

PART I: GENERAL OVERVIEW

§10.01   New York Disability Benefits Law

New York Disability Benefits Law (DBL) is a state disability insurance program designed to provide employees with some level of income replacement in case of disability caused off-the-job. The DBL is found under Article 9 of the New York State Workers' Compensation Law.

[1]   Eligibility

To be required to have DBL coverage for its employees, a company must employ at least one person besides the proprietor within the state of New York. Full-time employees are eligible for coverage after four consecutive weeks of work, and part-time employees are eligible after their twenty-fifth day of employment.

Out of state employees can be covered under some DBL policies, but the employer must have some New York employees to attain DBL coverage.

[2]   Benefits

The DBL offers a benefit of 50% of weekly wages up to a maximum of $170 per week of benefit ($340 per week of covered salary). The normal waiting period for DBL benefits to start is seven days, and benefits can extend to a maximum duration of 26 weeks.

It is possible for carriers to offer benefits that extend beyond the statutory DBL coverage known as "enhanced" or "enriched" DBL. This extended coverage usually takes the form of a higher maximum benefit but can also include shorter waiting periods or a longer maximum duration. Carriers take these factors into account when underwriting DBL coverage, and so enriched DBL is often more costly than statutory DBL coverage.

[3]   Penalties

Excerpt from 12 NYCRR § 220:

Any employer who fails to make provision for payment of disability benefits as required by section two hundred eleven of this article within ten days following the date on which such employer becomes a covered employer as defined in section two hundred two shall be guilty of a misdemeanor and upon conviction be punishable by a fine of not less than one hundred nor more than five hundred dollars or imprisonment for not more than one year or both, except that where any person has previously been convicted of a failure to make provisions for payment of disability benefits within the preceding five years, upon conviction for a second violation such person shall be fined not less than two hundred fifty nor more than one thousand two hundred fifty dollars in addition to any other penalties including fines otherwise provided by law, and upon conviction for a third or subsequent violation such person may be fined up to two thousand five hundred dollars in addition to any other penalties including fines otherwise provided by law. Where the employer is a corporation, the president, secretary, treasurer, or officers exercising corresponding functions, shall each be liable under this section.

CHAPTER 11: TRAUMATIC INJURIES

PART I: CHAPTER OVERVIEW

§11.01   Types of Injuries

Injuries can be mental or physical.[160] As long as the injury arises out of the course of the employment it may be compensable. Damages to personal property are not compensable, except for prosthetic devices.

[1]   Compensable Injuries

To be compensable under the Workers' Compensation law, an accidental injury must have arisen both out of and in the course of employment.[161] Accidents arising "in the course of employment" are presumed to arise out of the employment, and this presumption must be rebutted by "substantial evidence to the contrary" for the employer to succeed in denying a claim.[162]

[2]   Death

To be compensable, the death must "arise out of and in the course of employment." Death benefits are payable to a decedent's spouse, children, or dependents in the case of work-related death.[163] Benefits are payable at the total disability rate in effect for the year of death.

When a claimant receiving workers' compensation benefits dies – and the death is not related to the employment-injury – the benefits end.

[3]   Mental Injuries

Psychiatric injuries caused by trauma arising out of the course of the employment are compensable in the same way traumatic physical claims are. However, "stress" resulting from a lawful personnel action, like firing or reprimand, are not compensable.[164]

---

[160] WCL § 2(7).

[161] See WCL § 10.

[162] See WCL § 21.

[163] WCL § 16.

[164] WCL § 2(7).

If a claimant alleges a mental stress injury, the WCB will consider three thresh-old questions:

- Was the injury *solely* mental?
- Was the injury solely the consequent of a lawful personnel decision?
- Was the personnel decision made in good faith?[165]

[4]   Assaults

Assaults occurring in the course of employment that cause injuries are com-pensable. The assault must be related to the employment – it must have arisen out of some duty performed for the benefit of the employer – to be compen-sable.[166] A purely personal assault –for example an attack on an estranged lover – will not be compensable.

[5]   Chemical Exposures

Exposure to noxious fumes or other exposures may be held to constitute an accident, and therefore could be compensable.[167]

[6]   Purely Personal Injuries

Typically, purely personal injuries are not compensable. For example, injuries arising from diabetic collapse or fainting in the workplace are sometimes re-ferred to as "idiopathic" injuries. More commonly, the employee who alleges that their leg "just gave out" causing them to fall to the ground. In one memo-rable case, a claimant stated that her ankle twisted, and testified that she did not trip or fall - her ankle simply twisted while she was walking. In these types of injuries, the employer must decide whether to accept the claim or deny it as "did not arise out of or in the course of the employment."

[7]   Idiopathic Injuries

The term "idiopathic" means "spontaneous injuries or injuries whose causes are unknown" but we use this term to refer to an injury that likely arose from something "personal" to the employee - not a common or shared workplace risk. Generally speaking, idiopathic conditions or injuries arising from purely idiopathic events are not compensable.

---

[165] Basically, unless the personnel action was retaliatory it will be considered to have been undertaken in good faith.

[166] WCL § 21.

[167] *Johannesen v. N.Y.C. Dep't of Hous. Pres. and Dev.*, 84 N.Y.2d 129 (1994).

§11.02   Defending Traumatic, Specific Claims

During and after treatment, it is imperative that defense counsel be provided with all medical records, which include:

- Operative Notes; and
- discharge summaries; and
- Results from any objective tests.

PART II: WHEN AN IDIOPATHIC OR PURELY PERSONAL RISK CAN BE COMPENSABLE

§11.03   Case Law

The application of this rule is very fact specific.

In cases of epileptic seizures occurring in the workplace, where the claimant is injured not by the seizure but by coming in contact with the employer's premises during the thrashing episode, the Board has previously ruled that the claim was not compensable, because "in any epileptic fit anywhere the ground or floor would end the fall." In other words, there is nothing uniquely impeding about the employer's workplace floor that distinguishes it from any other which would have been encountered by the epileptic during a fit.

However, in a recent case where a claimant passed out and fell to the ground because of a personal health condition, and the claimant's head struck a bathroom wall - not the floor, the Board ruled that the it was the wall that interfered with the fall - not the floor - and therefore the claim was compensable. [168] The claimant fell while exiting a bathroom at work. She testified that "she did not trip over anything." A co-worker testified that about an hour before the fall, the co-worker had called the nursing office about the claimant, telling them that she was throwing up and feeling sick. It was determined that the underlying health condition (a vasovagal reaction due to pregnancy) had nothing to do with the employment. The trial judge found that the claimant had blacked out and fell at work due to a condition not connected to her work activity.

However, the Board ruled that while falling due to her purely personal condition, she stuck her head on the wall of the bathroom she was exiting. The Board ruled that even though the fall was precipitated by a reason purely personal to the employee, the fall was "impeded by the work environment" and the resulting injuries were therefore compensable. This decision was based on a longstanding line of cases (going back to 1932) in which the Board finds that objects such as a table or the employer's building itself "impede" the fall and therefore render a claim for injury compensable.

---

[168] Matter of Manhattan Psychiatric Center, 113 NYWCLR 86, N.Y.W.C.B. Full Board 2013, Decided March 28, 2013.

CHAPTER 12: OCCUPATIONAL CLAIMS

PART I: CHAPTER OVERVIEW

§12.01 Compensable Occupational Claims

Occupational diseases/conditions can be compensable if they result from the nature of the employment and were caused by the employment.[169] To establish a claim for workers' compensation benefits allegedly resulting from occupational disease the claimant must provide a recognizable link between the disease and a distinctive feature of the employment.[170] The pre-employment "health state" of the employee is not considered when assessing the compensability of an allegedly occupational condition – whether the employee is predisposed to some condition is not important.

The following diseases and conditions have been found compensable:

- Orthopedic injuries resulting from repetitive movement;
- Silicosis;
- Pulmonary diseases - including pulmonary fibrosis, pulmonary asbestosis, emphysema, bronchitis, and asthma.
- Hearing Loss;
- Dermatitis;
- Hernia produced by repetitive straining;
- Nervous system injuries;
- Infectious diseases, such as hepatitis or tuberculosis when the exposure was to patients (ex: in a hospital setting) or infected materials.
- Blood poisoning, such as lead poisoning.

§12.02 Non-Compensable Occupational Claims

Occupational claims related to the location or environmental conditions are **not** compensable under workers' compensation law because if all the

---

[169] WCL § 2(15), WCL § 39.

[170] *Id.*

employees were exposed to the same condition (ex: poor ventilation) then it is not possible to say that a resultant pulmonary condition was related to the peculiar nature of the work rather than to the nature of the location. However, exposure to specific agents, like carcinogenic compounds, which then caused a related condition – will be found compensable.[171]

Determining which factors are "merely environmental" and which are truly "peculiar" to the work is done on a case-by-case basis. Shared risks (like heat and cold) - common to all employments - as well as risks that are not common to the particular work - will not be found to be "occupational" in nature and therefore not compensable.

Generally, claims related to incidental exposures - for example, during a building renovation in which construction dust is in the workplace for a short time - are more likely to be characterized as a "specific " accident rather than an occupational.

Similarly, health conditions contracted from contact with co-employees are not compensable.[172]

§12.03   Benefits Payable

Benefits payable for occupational disease are the same as those payable for traumatic specific injury claims.[173] For example, where the occupational disease leads (like scoliosis) to a panic disorder (or other psychiatric manifestation of the condition) then the resulting mental condition is considered part of the underlying occupational condition.

---

[171] *In re Leventer*, 257 A.D.2d 903 (3d Dep't 1999).

[172] *Paider v. Park Movers*, 19 N.Y.2d 373 (1967).

[173] WCL § 39.

PART II: DEFENSE AGAINST OCCUPATIONAL CLAIMS

§12.04   Denying Occupational Claims

Occupational claims are generally denied. The filing of the FROI-04 denial pleading will result in the matter being listed for a Pre-Hearing Conference (if the claimant has filed medical).

§12.05   The Statute of Limitations for an Occupational Claim

The two-year statute of limitations applies to occupational claims.[174] The statute begins to run "from the date of disablement and within two years from the date the claimant knew or should have known that the disease is due to the nature of the employment." This is important because fixing the claimant's knowledge of the alleged occupational condition is important for defending against these claims. Specifically, we are looking for any documentation showing that the claimant was advised of the alleged condition and the relationship of the condition to the work.

§12.06   Investigating Occupational Claims

Investigation is the key to defending against occupational claims. A strong medical opinion (IME) on causal relationship is needed. To provide counsel and the IME doctor with the most useful information possible, defense should be provided with the following:

- Results of any environmental (ex: air quality testing) studies performed at the location;
- Any ergonomic studies;
- A complete job description for the claimant, with description of work duties;
- Any OSH filings for the location, including MSDS (material safety data sheets) or SDS (safety data sheets) for all materials in location;
- Information regarding any abatement or remediation projects at location;
- Any internal surveillance depicting conditions within location;
- Employee health records;

---

[174] WCL § 28

131

- Employee human resources/personnel file;
- Information about any union membership of claimant (because medical records/health information may be domiciled at union);
- Information regarding prior employers (usually a resume submitted to the current employer);
- Prior medical information;
- Information about other similar claims for the same employer/insured location;
- Contact information for witnesses who can testify about the claimant's actual work activities;
- Surveillance of the claimant;
- Prior claims history of the claimant (usually an ISO claims index bureau search report).

[1]   *Practical Advice on Defending Occupational Exposure Claims*

- The defense should obtain information relating to any prior workers' compensation or other claims filed by the claimant. Even if the body parts alleged in the instant occupational claims are not implicated, prior medicals may contain information about prior disease/illness manifestation.
- The defense should visit the insured location to assess the risk.

§12.07   Defense Experts

The defense medical expert is usually an IME physician. However, consideration should be given toward obtaining reports/testimony from ergonomic experts, environmental testing experts/laboratories, etc., and presenting that information to the defense medical expert to help inform the opinion regarding causality.

§12.08   The Role of the Defense

You should expect the defense to subpoena or obtain by way of medical release authorization prior medical records. The purpose of such an investigation will be to obtain information that the condition is pre-existing/arose during a prior period of employment. Employers can use prior medical documentation to argue that the claimant's condition manifested during a prior period of employment or that the claimant "know or should have known" about the injuries and their relationship to the employment for purposes of raising a Statute of Limitations defense.[175]

At trial, defense counsel must be prepared to vigorously cross-examine the claimant and her expert witnesses.

---

[175] WCL § 28

PART III: APPORTIONING LIABILITY BETWEEN EM-PLOYERS

§12.09   Apportioning Liability Between Successive Employers

New York allows for the apportionment of liability for payment of any award among several employers.[176] The last employer pays the entire award to the claimant. Then, that last employer can seek apportionment against the claimant's prior employers (who exposed the claimant to the same condition leading to the occupational disease).

§12.10   Investigating Apportionment

Enabling this apportionment, the claimant must provide the last employer with the names and addresses of all his prior employers; the failure to provide those prior employer's contact information may result in the claimant being stripped of all compensation until he complies with the request.[177]

§12.11   Medical Witnesses

When both of the claimant's injuries are due to work-related accidents, apportionment can be found if it is supported by medical evidence.[178] When the prior condition is the result of a compensable work-related injury, apportionment is simply a factual issue for the Board to determine based by the medical evidence in the record.[179]

The Board can find one doctor more credible than another on the issue of "how much apportionment" is due to each successive accident where one doctor examined the claimant multiple times. Further, where a doctor changes his opinion on apportionment without reviewing additional medical information

---

[176] WCL § 44. Successive insurance companies have the same liability as successive employers; the one "last on the risk" pays the award and then seeks apportionment from the prior carriers.

[177] WCL § 46.

[178] *McCloskey v. Marriott Corp.*, 290 A.D.2d 671 (3d Dep't 2002).

[179] *Id.* and *Huss v. Tops Mkts.*, 13 A.D.3d 768 (3d Dep't 2004).

(example: additional interim records) that medical opinion can be discounted by the fact finder.[180]

---

[180] Fashion Marketing Inc. and Travelers Indemnity Co., 113 NYWCLR 166 (September 12, 2013).

CHAPTER 13: TRIALS AND HEAR-INGS

PART I: SUBPOENAS

§13.01   Subpoena Power

A subpoena is simply a legal command, instructing someone to show up and give testimony at a certain place on a certain date and time. A "judicial subpoena" is returnable in a court.

The New York Workers' Compensation Law allow litigants to use subpoenas to obtain information necessary to the defense of a claim.[181] Used frequently by the defense, the subpoena power is an invaluable tool to obtain necessary information to fully defend a claim.

We regularly use subpoenas to investigate prior claims, uncover information (including medical reports) from prior settlements, and to obtain medical records. We also use subpoenas to obtain information regarding the claimant's employment history and the validity of statements made by the claimant regarding work searches (in the context of attachment to the workforce investigations).

§13.02   Subpoena Duces Tecum

A subpoena *duces tecum* requires the production of books papers or other things and is commonly used to request medical records or employment records. A subpoena *duces tecum* can be served separately or jointly with a subpoena for testimony.[182]

A subpoena *duces tecum* requires the personal appearance of the custodian of the records to be present. The custodian of the records is then expected to give testimony to authenticate the documents being produced. However, the requirement of personal appearance by the records custodian has almost entirely been replaced by acceptance of certified copies. In most cases when a

---

[181] WCL § 119.

[182] New York CPLR § 2305(b).

subpoena *duces tecum* is issued, we are satisfied by receiving copies of the documents requested along with the certification by the custodian that they are accurate and complete, or "kept in the usual course of business."

§13.03   Issuing Subpoenas

A subpoena can only be issued in connection with an ongoing litigated matter. There must be some type of legal action – such as our workers compensation cases – pending. Subpoenas should be signed by the attorney at law under the authority of the particular court or administrative agency.

New York Worker's Compensation Law § 119 has a specific enabling provision allowing the Workers' Compensation Board the authority to issue subpoenas. The procedure for issuing and responding to the subpoena is been the same as that followed in the civil courts.

[1]   Information in a Subpoena

Every subpoena will state the name of the court or administrative body under whose authority the subpoena is being issued. The subpoena also provides the names of the parties to the action or proceeding and usually a case reference number (in New York, it will contain a Workers Compensation Board number).

The subpoena always indicates to whom it is directed – which may be an employer, hospital, etc. In the case of a subpoena seeking records (a subpoena *duces tecum*) the subpoena must describe with particularity what documents are being sought. This is especially important in subpoenas seeking medical records.

The subpoena also provides a date, time, and place for which the appearance of a witness or the production of documents must be provided. The subpoena will also typically include language indicating that the recipient risks "contempt of court" for failing to comply with the subpoena. Finally, every subpoena should bear the signature of the attorney who issued it and a statement regarding the court or administrative body under whose authority the subpoena was issued.

[2]   Out-of-State Subpoenas

Out-of-state subpoenas - issued from the court or agency of another state and seeking records - are not valid in New York (unless it is a federal subpoena bearing the name of the US District Court, which may be valid – ask counsel). There is no obligation to respond to out-of-state subpoenas. However, if the out-of-state subpoena is accompanied by a properly executed authorization for medical records, you may want to honor just as you would any other request for records (in other words, treat it as any request for records that does not contain a subpoena).

[3]   Serving Subpoenas

In New York, a subpoena must be served in the same manner as a summons.[183] This means that it must be served by personal delivery. Under the rules, a subpoena must be delivered to a person of suitable age or to a designated agent. The subpoena can be served by affixing the subpoena to the door of the business or residence or by mail (but only if the recipient cannot be personally served).[184]

Service by fax is not allowed. Further, service by first class mail is not generally valid except under certain circumstances. Generally, if a subpoena is received in the mail, you should contact counsel to determine its validity.

Subpoenas may be served statewide in workers compensation proceedings in New York.

§13.04 Witness Fees

In New York, the person subpoenaed is entitled to receive traveling expenses and one days witness fee (in advance). The dollar amounts are specified in the law. At present, New York allows a witness fee of $15 plus $.23 per mile for travel.[185]

§13.05 Advance Notice

In New York, some subpoenas have specific notice requirements. A subpoena for a deposition must be served with 20 days notice.[186] Subpoenas for hospital records must give at least three days notice.[187] Outside of these situations,

---

[183] CPLR § 2303.

[184] CPLR § 2303(a), CPLR §§ 307-312-a.

[185] CPLR § 8001.

[186] CPLR § 2106.

[187] CPLR § 2306.

there are no stated minimum or maximum time periods – but the courts have consistently held that "reasonable notice" must be presented for a party to be compelled to produce documents. What is "reasonable notice" is up for interpretation.

§13.06   HIPAA Rules and Subpoenas

A litigant in a workers' compensation proceeding has no federally-protected privacy interest in his medical records relating to that condition or claim. In fact, the Health Insurance Portability and Accountability Act (HIPAA) has three specific "exemptions" for workers compensation related matters:

1. If the disclosure is "as authorized and to the extent necessary to comply with laws relating to workers compensation or similar programs established by law that provide benefits for work-related injuries or illness without regard to fault."[188]
2. If the disclosure is required by state or other law, in which case the disclosure is limited to whatever the law requires.[189]
3. If the disclosure is for obtaining payment for any healthcare provided to injured or ill employee.[190]

Regardless of these exemptions in the HIPAA rules, parties receiving a subpoena generally do not understand the HIPAA requirements nor do they understand the subtleties of the exemptions drafted for workers compensation proceedings. Therefore, subpoenas issued to healthcare providers in the case of an injured worker should also contain an executed medical release authorization (HIPAA-compliant) to ensure that the entity actually responds to the subpoena. It has been my experience that despite the fact that there are three clear "exemptions" in the case of workers compensation claims – and despite the fact that our subpoenas clearly identify that it is being issued in connection with a workers' compensation claim – medical care providers are extremely unlikely to respond to a subpoena without a HIPAA release attached.[191]

---

[188] 45 C.F.R. § 164.512(l).

[189] 45 C.F.R. § 164.512(a).

[190] 45 C.F.R. § 164.502(a)(1)(ii)

[191] Please also note that in 2003 the New York law was changed to indicate any subpoena for medical records must be accompanied by the patient signed HIPAA authorization. CPLR § 3122.

§13.07   Motions to Quash

In cases where a subpoena appears to have been improperly issued, or request information which may be privileged (attorney-client privilege), the recipient cannot simply ignore the subpoena but must make a formal request to withdraw or modify the subpoena. In New York, the recipient should contact the issuer.[192]

§13.08   Subpoena Checklist

When you receive a subpoena asking for medical records or the proceeds of your workers' compensation file, consider the following:

- Was the subpoena appropriately served according to all the rules?
- Does the caption of the subpoena provide you with information regarding the nature of the legal proceeding? The caption of the subpoena tells you whether the subpoena was issued by an administrative agency, a court, or government official.
- The subpoena must contain the identity of the person or entity to whom the subpoena is directed.
- Does the subpoena call for personal testimony or records?
- If the subpoena is requesting medical records, does it include a HIPAA authorization?

---

[192] CPLR § 2304.

PART II: MEDICAL WITNESSES

§13.09   Medical Evidence

Physicians may be required to testify as to the causal relationship of the claimed disability to the employment injury. Physicians may also be called to testify as to the nature and extent of disability and the necessity of specific treatment.[193]

The testimony of physicians may be required even though the WCL allows for medical reports and records to be introduced by claimants and accepted as prima facie evidence of facts as to the matter contained therein.[194] Despite this presumption, issues of credibility, reasonableness, and weight of medical opinion are for the Board to decide – and so medical proofs in the form of physician testimony are permitted.[195] Medical opinions which are mere speculation or surmise and not sufficient for the Board to rely upon.[196]

§13.10   Proving Depression: An Example of Battling Doctors

Proving depression is related to the employment is difficult for New York claimants. The claimant bears the burden of establishing, by competent medical evidence, a causal relationship between his or her employment and the psychiatric disability. In a recent case claimant Janina Guz alleged her employment at Jewelers' Machinist, Inc., caused her to develop a psychiatric disability: major depression.[197]

Guz last worked in 2002. Her claim for major depression was initiated in 2007. In the meantime, she had received psychiatric treatment with her own psychiatrist, Dr. Alina Marek, in five occasions beginning after she filed her claim for benefits (she first sought treatment in January 2008). Dr. Marek diagnosed

---

[193] WCL § 13-1.

[194] *See* review of the "5 presumptions," of WCL § 21, discussed elsewhere.

[195] *Blaine v. Big Four Industries, Inc.*, 17 A.D.2d 881 (3d Dept' 1962); *Amato v. Sklar Lumbar & Millwork Co.*, 430 N.Y.S.2d 425 (App. Div. 3d Dep't 1980).

[196] *Ayala v. DRE Maint. Corp.*, 656 N.Y.S.2d 71 (3d Dep't 1997), *aff'd*, 90 N.Y.2d 914 (1997).

[197] *Guz v. Jewelers Machinist, Inc.*, 71 A.D.3d 1272 (3d Dep't 2010).

Guz as suffering from major depressive disorder and causally related same to her 2002 employment (Guz allegedly suffered bilateral carpal tunnel syndrome in 2002).

The employer had Guz examined by Dr. Areyek Klahr, who performed two independent medical examinations. Dr. Klahr concurred that the claimant had the condition but found it would not interfere with her ability to work. Dr. Klahr also testified that the claimant's responses were inconsistent and that her complaints did not correlate to his objective findings. On the stand, Dr. Klahr testified that the claimant did not suffer a work-related disability.

While testifying on behalf of the claimant, Dr. Malek admitted that she had no information about the claimant's work or her 2002 carpal tunnel injury. Dr. Malek testified that she was unaware of the claimant's prior claims history (which included multiple MVAs, etc.) although she agreed that knowing the claimant's prior medical and claims history would be useful in assessing Guz's condition. Further, Dr. Malek stated that she had no information about the claimant's activities of daily living or her personal life history and admitted that her opinion was based on the claimant's subjective account of the cause of her depression.

The Workers' Compensation Board found against the claimant. The decision was upheld by the Appellate Division.

PART III: HEARINGS

§13.11   Pre-Hearing Conferences

The purpose of pre-hearing conferences is to allow the parties to address the issues, identify relevant issues and allow the parties to exchange information and assess their case so that outstanding issues can be resolved prior to trial. In cases where a notice of controversy has been filed (Form C-7) these pre-hearing conferences must take place no more than 60 days after the C-7 has been filed. The parties are provided with 21 days notice of the scheduled pre-hearing conference.[198]

At the pre-hearing conference, your attorney must be prepared with the following[199]:

- Confirmation that all appropriate forms, information, medical reports, etc., have been submitted to the Board;
- Confirmation that the submitted forms and information is accurate;
- The addition of any necessary parties, where appropriate;
- Limitations of the factual and legal issues, if appropriate;
- A list of proposed witnesses;
- Depositions of prose's witnesses (if any);
- Calendaring information so the case can be scheduled for a hearing;
- Written stipulations.

At any pre-hearing conference, the case may be settled under Section 32. 10 days before the pre-hearing conference, all parties must file Form PH-16.2 ("Pre-Hearing Conference Statement") – failure to do so can result in the case being thrown out by the Judge or conciliator or defenses barred. The case can then be re-opened if claimant's attorney files the appropriate forms. Failure by the claimant to proceed (or appear) will result in the case being closed.[200]

---

[198] 12 NYCRR 300.33.

[199] *Id.*

[200] *Id.*

The pre-hearing conference may result in the Judge issuing Orders or directions to the parties. These orders or directions are not appealable (under § 23) until the controverted issues in dispute are resolved.

§13.12   Hearings

Hearings refer to trial-like activities in which testimony is taken and evidence presented. The claimant and all witnesses testify under oath.[201]

Notices of hearings are sent by the Board to the carrier for the employer, or directly to the employer if self-insured.[202] An employer having knowledge of a hearing is not obligated to attend unless a hearing notice is sent to the employer, specifically requesting attendance, or unless a representative of insurance carrier requests attendance.

Every case filed with the WCB (all claims) receive a decision or award – but an award or decision does not necessarily require a hearing before a Workers' Compensation Law Judge. Hearings are required in cases where there is a dispute – the controverted cases. This is a small percentage of all claims – roughly 10%. Most claims are paid by the employer and resolved without contest. (The WCB also handles disputes regarding Disability Benefits Law claims).

§13.13   Adjournments

If the claimant (or his representative) fails to appear at the first hearing of a case, the matter will generally be adjourned to permit the claimant another opportunity to appear. The WCB, in its discretion, may continue to carry the matter until resolution is reached (which may include having the supervising law judge doing an investigation as to the reason for the continued nonappearance of the claimant).

On the employer side, nonappearance (or failure to provide evidence at a scheduled hearing) may give rise to an adjournment, but failure to present evidence or nonappearance at a rescheduled hearing will result in the evidence

---

[201] 12 NYCRR 300.9.

[202] *See* 12 NYCRR 300.7 "Hearings" *and* 12 NYCRR 300.8 "Notice of Hearings" for the specifics.

being excluded unless there are extraordinary circumstances which warrant the delay/adjournment.[203]

§13.14   The Duties of the Workers' Compensation Law Judge

In disputed cases, the Workers' Compensation Law Judge considers the employer's defenses and makes a determination regarding accident, notice, and causal relationship. In practice, most cases do not involve disputes about whether the accident took place, except for occupational claims, in which there may be serious issues of notice and causal connection. The Law Judge must be made aware of any pre-existing conditions the claimant had, prior claims and awards, and any subsequent injuries or claims.

---

[203] 12 NYCRR 300.10.

PART IV: DECISIONS AND REVIEW

§13.15   Decisions

Decisions by Workers' Compensation Law Judges may be made orally and read into the record (stenographically).[204] The Workers' Compensation Law is expected to make a brief summary of the reasoned decision upon the contested points. The parties to any claim before the board may stipulate to uncontested facts or proposed findings.

In every claim where the disability exceeds seven days, a Judge makes a finding as to whether or not an accident arising out of and in the course of employment or an occupational disease has been established.

§13.16   Board Panel Review

An appeal from a Workers' Compensation Judge's decision is not made to the appellate court. The first opportunity for review is to a WCB panel.

Either side may seek administrative review of the decision within 30 days of the filing of the Judge's decision. There is no specific form for this – but it must be done in writing. A panel of three Board Members will review the case.

The employer's attorney does not have to make a record (by taking exceptions, etc.) below to preserve issues for appeal. The WCB panel does a fresh look at all of the evidence from the hearing below in reaching their decision. It is the written findings of fact and law of the panel that becomes the record for appeal to the Supreme Court.

This three-judge panel may affirm, modify or rescind the Judge's decision, or restore the case to the calendar for further development of the record. If the panel is not unanimous, any interested party may make application in writing for mandatory review of the full Board. The full Board must review and either affirm, modify, or rescind such a decision. In addition, following a unanimous decision of the Board panel, a party may file an application for discretionary full Board review. The application for discretionary full Board review will either be denied by the Board or, when warranted, the Board panel decision may be

---

[204] 12 NYCRR 300.5.

rescinded by resolution of the full Board. When the original Board panel decision is rescinded a new panel decision will be issued.

Appeals of Board Panel decisions may be taken to the Appellate Division, Third Department, Supreme Court of the State of New York, within 30 days.[205] The decision of the Appellate Division may be appealed to the Court of Appeals.

> **Note:** When seeking administrative review, the carrier does not pay for any contested weekly benefits while the claim is being reviewed by a Board Panel.[206] The carrier must pay any portion of the award that is not the subject of dispute. For example, if the carrier concedes that the employee has a mild disability and the WCLJ found the disability was total, the carrier must pay the employee at the mild rate while it seeks administrative review of the finding of total disability. When the carrier does not concede any liability, then the entire WCLJ award is stayed pending administrative review by the Board panel.

Following administrative review, the carrier must make any payment of compensation and physician's bills directed by the Board Panel, even if an application for discretionary full Board review and/or an appeal is made to the Appellate Division.[207]

The upshot of this is that the appeal process delays payment to the claimant. Be warned of using this process for purposes of delay: the statute provides that if appeal is made on frivolous grounds for the purposes of delaying the claim's adjudication, a penalty of $250 (payable to the claimant) may be awarded.[208]

§13.17   WCB Review in Practice

The Appellate Division issued a new opinion regarding the Workers' Compensation Board's discretionary power in reviewing cases.[209]

---

[205] WCL § 23.

[206] *Id.*

[207] *Lehsten v. NACM-Upstate N.Y.*, 93 N.Y.2d 368 (1999).

[208] WCL § 23.

[209] D'Errico v. N.Y.C. Dep't of Corr., 65 A.D.3d 795 (3d Dep't 2009).

In *D'Errico*, a city corrections officer alleged that his employment experiences caused him to suffer permanent "major depressive disorder with psychotic features, post-traumatic stress disorder, and panic disorder." The WCB ultimately denied his claims - finding that the claimant was no exposed to a greater amount of work stress than any other normally-situated correctional officer. The claimant applied for a full Board review and his request was denied.

The Appellate panel found that the WCB had properly exercised its discretion and ruled that the claimant was not due a second review of his case by the WCB. Two of the three Judges on the appeals panel agreed that the claimant was out of luck - that the Board did not have to review its decision. The third judge issued a dissenting opinion - laying the foundation for the claimant to seek appeal to New York State's highest court, the Court of Appeals. The dissenting opinion argued that the WCB had failed to fully consider the issues in the first hearing the WCB granted the claimant. Specifically, the third judge questioned "whom" the average correctional worker was that comprised the normally-situated correctional officer baseline used by the WCB to determine that the claimant was not exposed to 'extraordinary' occupational stressors. The Appellate Court upheld the denial of full Board review - finding that the claimant could not (1) show that newly discovered evidence existed; (2) that he had a material change in condition; or (3) or that the Board improperly failed to consider issues raised in the application for review in making its initial determination. The Appellate Court also noted that in "rare instances" the WCB was found to have abused its discretion in not granting a review of a prior board decision - but those rare instances were confined to cases where the Board failed to consider new evidence or disregarded a material change in the claimant's condition.

PART V: CLOSING CASES

§13.18 Closing Cases Under Section 32 (Dismissal of Claims)

WCL § 32, in general states that the parties may enter into an agreement settling upon and determining the compensation and other benefits due to the
claimant or their dependents. The agreement shall not bind the parties to it,
unless approved by the Board. Such agreements, when so approved, notwith-
standing any other provisions, shall be final and conclusive upon the claimant,
the claimant's dependents, the employer and the insurance carrier.

The WCB has at least ten days to review a Section 32 before it can render a
decision. The agreement shall be approved by the board in a decision duly filed
and served unless the proposed agreement is unfair, unconscionable, or improper as a matter of law (illegal), or the proposed agreement is the result of
an intentional misrepresentation of material fact, or one of the parties objects
to the proposed settlement.

Note: a "section 32" settlement is different than a 'lump-sum' settlement under Section 15 – a Section 32 can't be re-opened.[210] There can be multiple Section 32 settlements in one case: for example, one Section 32 for the medical
benefits, and then a later one for the compensation benefits.

§13.19 Section 32 & Medicare Secondary Payer

The WCB has issued the following statement:

> The Board has been asked about the use of indemnification or hold
> harmless provisions in Section 32 agreements to protect a carrier or em-
> ployer from liability of Medicare payments related to an established
> workers' compensation claim. The Board will not approve agreements
> containing such indemnification for payments made by Medicare for
> services provided prior to the Section 32 agreement.

Workers' Compensation Law §32 (part b1) directs the WCB to disapprove unfair agreements. We expect the WCB to decline to approve §32s where there
have been conditional payments made by Medicare and the carrier seeks

---

[210] A §15 settlement can be later re-opened if the claimant can show a change in the
medical condition which was not anticipated at the time of the original settlement.

indemnification. (We also think such a disapproval would be appealable under Section 23).

Of course, a §32 can be silent on the conditional payment issues, but we continue to recommend that the payments be addressed at time of settlement.[211]

---

[211] *See* Medicare Secondary Payer Act, Chapter 20, this book

CHAPTER 14: INDEPENDENT MEDI-CAL EXAMINATIONS

PART I: IMEs in General

§14.01 Background

Independent Medical Evaluations ("IMEs") are relied upon to dispute ongoing care, to challenge the necessity of specific treatment under the Medical Treatment Guidelines, and to contest the nature and degree of permanent disability.

The WCB will consider the report of an independent medical examiner who is New York State licensed and board-certified to perform a physical examination, review medical records, and issue reports regarding the claimant's injury or illness. The IME doctor can be a surgeon, podiatrist, or any other person who the WCB has authorized to evaluate the claimant. The WCB can appoint an examiner who has never treated the claimant for the injury for which benefits are claimed.

Notice of the exam must be provided at least seven (7) business days in advance (by mail) on Form IME-5.[212] In practice, this is usually taken care of by the IME vendor. The claimant can have anyone they want to come with them to the exam (including an attorney) and can videotape the process. Travel to and from the exam is a reimbursable expense.

§14.02 Claimants Residing in Another State

For claimants that reside in another state, but seek benefits under the New York law, the WCB will appoint a practitioner it finds qualified to perform an IME. The qualifications of any doctor performing an out-of-state exam are subject to challenge by the employer.

The doctor assigned must be within a reasonable distance of the claimant; the claimant cannot be forced to endure a hardship to attend an IME. The claimant may challenge the examination if the travel involved is onerous. The challenge must be made to the WCB, and the burden is on the claimant to demonstrate that the request is "onerous."

---

[212] http://www.wcb.ny.gov/content/main/forms/ime5.pdf

§14.03   IMEs in Permanency Cases

The Workers' Compensation Law presumes that the medical records and re-ports from both treating physicians and IME doctors will be "adequate, com-plete, and objective." In reality, medical reports often contain subjective im-pressions, such as a treating doctor's feeling that a claimant cannot return to work based on non-medical factors such as age, education, occupation, etc.

Evaluating doctors are expected to produce reports which measure, to a rea-sonable degree of accuracy and uniformity, the nature and extent of the im-pairment experienced by the individual claimant. IME physicians should base their determinations of permanent residual disability on the 2012 Guidelines for Determining Permanent Impairment and Loss of Wage Earning Capacity, effective January 2012[213] and the 2018 Scheduled Loss of Use Guidelines (for scheduled body parts). The LWEC guidelines require that the IME physician opine as to the claimant's medical condition, degree of impairment, and func-tional abilities.

The Guidelines provide detailed criteria for determining the severity of a med-ical impairment, with a greater weight given to objective findings. To prepare a report on permanent impairment, the physician should do the following:

* Review the Guidelines
* Review the medical records
* Perform a thorough history and physical examination and recount the rel-evant medical history, examination findings and appropriate test results
* State the work related medical diagnosis(es) based upon the relevant medical history, examination and test results
* Identify the affected body part or system (include Chapter and Table No. for non-schedule disabilities)
* Follow the recommendations to establish a level of impairment
* For a non-schedule disability, evaluate the impact of the impairment(s) on claimant's functional and exertional abilities

---

[213] New York State Guidelines for Determining Permanent Impairment and Loss of Wage Earning Capacity, January 2012 ("2012 Guidelines") at 9.

The Board publishes Loss of Wage Earning Capacity Guidelines which are available here: http://www.wcb.ny.gov/content/main/hcpp/ImpairmentGuidelines/2012ImpairmentGuide.pdf

The Board publishes Scheduled Loss of Use Guidelines which are available here: http://www.wcb.ny.gov/2018-Impairment-Guidelines.pdf

PART II: APPLICABLE LAWS

§14.04   Statute and Regulations

The rules surrounding IMEs are found in two places: the statute (§ 137 of the Workers' Compensation Law) and the regulations (12 NYCRR § 300.2).

§14.05   Serving the Report

A copy of each report of independent medical examination must be submitted to all parties at the same time.[214] This eliminates the possibility of destroying or hiding an unfavorable IME report.

The report must only be copied to "the board, the insurance carrier, the claimant's attending physician or other attending practitioner, the claimant's representative and the claimant."[215] The applicable statute (§ 137) does not define who the "attending physician is" but the New York Code, Rules & Regulation (NYCRR) does: "Attending physician or other attending practitioner means those providers or practitioners who have primary responsibility for treating the claimant for the injury or illness for which such claimant is being examined."[216]

This has been interpreted by the Board to mean that "physicians or provider who has examined the claimant for the sole purpose of a consultation or diagnostic examination or test is not an attending physician or provider within the meaning of the Workers' Compensation Law." This means that radiological test facilities and purely diagnostic testing providers are not to be copied. This is a common-sense approach.

Case law examining this issue is scant. There are reported decisions which hold that only doctors who treat claimants for injuries at the time of the IMEs are to be considered attending physicians and copied. (cf. Estanluards v. Amer. Mus. Of Nat. Hist., App. Div., Decided July 31, 2008). Based on the text of the statute and regulation's definition of "attending physician," it is not necessary

---

[214] WCL § 137(1).

[215] See WCL § 137.
[216] 12 NYCRR 300.2.

to copy every facility and doctor who treated the claimant at any time during the course of care.

Only the physician "primarily responsible" and currently treating the claimant should be copied. However, when obtaining and IME and serving the resulting report, the employer/carrier must copy all providers who saw the claimant for the preceding six months, excluding purely diagnostic testing facilities/physicians.

§14.06   Stopping Benefits Based on the IME Report

You cannot stop payments if under an Order (CCP) based solely on the results of your IME. If the IME finds the claimant able to work (light duty or full duty) an RFA-2 must be filed and a Judge must rule.

WCL § 137 (2) states as follows:

> In any open case where an award has been directed by the board for temporary or permanent disability at an established rate of compensation and there is a direction by the board for continuation of payments, or any closed case where an award for compensation has been made for permanent total or permanent partial disability, a report of an independent medical examination shall not be the basis for suspending or reducing payments unless and until the rules and regulations of the board regarding suspending or reducing payments have been met and there is a determination by the board finding that such suspension or reduction is justified.

§14.07   Conditions of the IME Exam

WCL § 137(8) states as follows:

> Independent medical examinations shall be performed during regular business hours except with the consent and for the convenience of the claimant. Claimants subject to such examination shall be notified at the time of the exam in writing of the available travel reimbursement under law.

§14.08   Notice to the claimant of the IME.

The claimant must be provided mailed notice of the scheduled independent medical examination at least seven business days prior to such examination. In practice, this is usually taken care of by the IME vendor.

§14.09   Failure to Appear at Exam

The carrier or employer is "entitled to have the claimant examined by a physi-cian authorized by the chair...at a medical facility convenient to the claimant and in the presence of the claimant's physician, and refusal by the claimant to submit to such independent medical examination at such time or times as may reasonably be necessary in the opinion of the [Board, bars] the claimant from recovering compensation for any period during which he or she has refused to submit to such examination."[217]

When a claimant frustrates the employer's right to engage an independent medical consultant, a suspension of payments for the challenged injuries is warranted.[218] In contrast, there is no basis to bar payments where the claim-ant's failure to attend an IME is not due to a refusal to submit to such exami-nation, or where the claimant's refusal is reasonable.[219]

If the claimant simply fails to appear for an exam, benefits cannot be termi-nated.[220] Instead, the exam should be rescheduled. if the claimant fails to at-tend a rescheduled exam, an RFA-2 ("Request for Further Action on behalf of the Carrier/Employer") should be filed to get the matter listed for a hearing. At the hearing, counsel should request that benefits be suspended until the claim-ant attends to an exam.

§14.10   Denial of Benefits Pending Exam

If a claimant refuses to submit to a physical examination ordered by the WCB, she loses her compensation benefits during the period of refusal.[221]

---

[217] WCL § 13-a(4)(b) *see also* 12 NYCRR 300.2(d)(8).

[218] *Jasmine v Rainbow Grill*, 115 A.D.2d 862 (3d Dep't 1985).

[219] *Ferguson v Fruehauf Corp.*, 156 A.D.2d 880 (3d Dep't 1989).

[220] WCL § 137(10) states as follows: "The ability of a claimant to appear for an exam or hearing shall not be dispositive in the determination of disability, extent of disability or eligibility for benefits."

[221] WCL § 13-a(4)(b) *and* § 19.

PART III: AVOIDING PRECLUSION OF THE DEFENSE IME REPORT

§14.11   Best Practices for Avoiding Preclusion of the Defense IME Report.

New York Workers' Compensation Law §137 and 12 NYCRR §300.2 governs IMEs. Section 137 provides eleven specific requirements. Of the eleven requirements, the following are two basic requirements that can and are easily overlooked:

1. A copy of each report of independent medical examination shall be submitted by the practitioner on the same day and in the same manner to the board, the insurance carrier, the claimant's attending physician or other attending practitioner, the claimant's representative and the claimant.

2. The claimant shall receive notice by mail of the scheduled independent medical examination at least seven business days prior to such examination. Such notice shall advise the claimant if the practitioner intends to record or video tape the examination, and shall advise the claimant of their right to video tape or otherwise record the examination. Claimants shall be advised of their right to be accompanied during the exam by an individual or individuals of their choosing.

Based on the above, it is important that each and every one of the above parties (the Board, the carrier, the claimant's attending physician or other attending practitioner, the claimant's representative and the claimant) is served with a copy of the IME report. Keep in mind, the failure to send the report to even one of the parties could result in the IME report being precluded.

In addition, it is important to verify that the notice of examination was sent to the claimant's correct mailing address. If appropriate notice is not provided (i.e., seven days prior to the scheduled IME), then you can expect the report to be precluded. A simple step to avoid this mistake is to confirm the claimant's correct address prior to scheduling the IME and serve the IME-5 immediately after it is scheduled.

There is not much that can be more frustrating than obtaining a favorable IME report only to discover that a basic requirement in serving the report was overlooked and likely have that report precluded. So it is important to keep the aforementioned two basic requirements in mind in relation to IMEs.

§14.12   Defending the IME Physician at Trial.

It is the role of the defense attorney to present the IME physician's testimony in a contested workers' compensation case. There are three phases to this: first, qualifying the doctor as competent to testify. Next, presenting the direct testimony of the IME doctor - usually through the use of pre-planned direct questions designed to elicit favorable testimony. Finally, the claimant's attorney has an opportunity to cross-examine the IME doctor and defense counsel must be prepared with legal objections to ensure fair questioning.

§14.13   Direct Examination - Qualify the doctor.

If possible, skip voir dire by asking the judge to accept your proffered physician as an expert. If the expert testifies regularly enough, the Judge and adversary may simply accede. If the court or opposing counsel will not accept the expert without voir dire, the following script can be employed:

Q. Please state your name for the record.

Q. What is your profession or occupation?

Q. Where are your offices located?

Q. In what states are you licensed to practice medicine?

Q. Please describe your educational background.

Q. Are you Board certified?

Q. What does it mean to be Board certified?

Q. Does Board certification require record reviews of your patients, confirming that the treatment course pursued in individual cases was appropriate?

Q. Is an exam required to be Board certified in your area of expertise?

Q. Doe you have admitting privileges? If so, where?

Q. Do you maintain a private practice where you treat private patients?

Q. When did you last perform surgery?

Q. Have you performed the type of surgery (identify treatment) that was undertaken in this case?

Following this basic voir dire, the Court should be asked to accept the physician as an expert. Note that the questions elicited on voir dire reflect the qualification questions considered by the court in Sanchez, above.

§14.14   Direct Examination - Direct questioning.

The purpose of the direct examination of the defense IME physician is to describe the work the expert actually did on the case, the time spent with the petitioner, how the interactions were recorded, how the objective medical testing was conducted, and to explain the final conclusions to the Law Judge. To the extent possible, the IME physician should constrain their responses to the objective medical findings. The testificant is expected to be able to explain the various tests and findings referenced in the report and to state for the record whether the test or finding is "objective" or "subjective."

§14.15   Defending the cross-examination.

Defense must be wary of purely hypothetical questions, with no basis in fact that may serve to confuse or mislead the law judge. Defense should confine the expert, to the extent possible, to the findings made in the narrative report.

CHAPTER 15: UNDERSTANDING LOSS OF WAGE EARNING CAPACITY (LWEC)

PART I: CHAPTER OVERVIEW

§15.01 Calculating Exposure

The Judge must establish a loss of wage earning capacity based on the facts in the case, considering medical evidence and vocational factors. **The Judge is not expected to presume that the wage-earning capacity of the non-working claimant is zero.**

Calculating exposure in New York for permanent partial disability (non-scheduled losses) is supposed to be simple:

> Rate x Number of Capped Weeks = Exposure (plus the cost of medical)

The number of weeks ranges from a minimum of 225 weeks (for Loss of Wage Earning Capacity of 15% or less) to a maximum of 525 (applicable to Loss of Wage Earning Capacity of 95% or more.)

The tricky part is figuring out the Rate and the Number of Capped Weeks in the formula. The Rate and Number of Capped Weeks is dependent on a concept called "Loss of Wage Earning Capacity" ("LWEC"). The Workers' Compensation Law Judge (WCLJ) finds the level of disability or loss of wage earning capacity (LWEC) based on the proofs submitted by the parties.

§15.02 The Concept from 50,000 Feet

Once the claimant has reached maximum medical improvement (MMI), determining a worker's loss of wage earning capacity (LWEC) is a three-part analysis:

1. Evaluation and ranking of medical impairment. This is done by a doctor. The Board has issued the Disability Duration Guidelines and a special Form (Form C-4.3) to be used by the Doctor in evaluating the impairment.

1. Medical evaluation and determination of functional ability/loss (functional assessment). This is also (strangely) done by a doctor.

2.   Consideration of vocational factors. This includes prior work history, education, skills, and aptitudes.

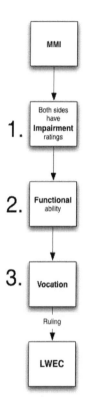

After factoring these three inputs (impairment, function, and vocational factors) the Judge of Compensation is expected to come up with a number, expressed as a percentage.

This number we shall call "Loss of Wage Earning Capacity" and it will be used to plug into a formula and arrive at two things: first, a dollar figure, and second, a number of weeks.

Here it is again:

> **Rate** x **Number of Capped Weeks** = **Exposure** (plus the cost of medical)

Both the **Rate** and the **Number of Capped Weeks** are derived from **LWEC**, which itself is derived from the impairment, function, vocational factors.

This formulation is meant to imply that there is a straightforward application of relatively "objective factors" which will be used to determine disability. In truth, arriving at LWEC is not straightforward at all. There is no "weighting" of the various factors, and no clear "formula" to apply in considering the various inputs.

§15.03   The Process

[1]   MMI

- The big questions are: does our IME doctor say the claimant has reached MMI?
- Has the claimant's physician filed a Form C-4.3 stating that the claimant is at MMI?

[2]   Impairment

- Does our doctor provide a ranking and severity finding for the permanent impairment?
- Has the claimant's physician filed a Form C-4.3?
- Has the physician answered question "E-2" on Form C-4.3 ("Could this patient perform his/her at-injury work activities without restrictions?") by examining physician on understanding of claimant's actual at-injury work duties.

[3]   Function

- Has a Functional Capacity Evaluation been obtained?
- Is the Form C-4.3 section on functional impairment complete?
- Is there surveillance available?
- Do the claimant's doctors objective findings of functional limitations (Part F2 of Form C-4.3) comport with the observations made on surveillance?
- If the claimant has returned to work, counsel must be prepared with a complete understanding of the job duties and work requirements of the current position. To the extent that these current duties exceed the functional capabilities/exertional abilities identified on the C-4.3 form, counsel must be prepared to make a complete record.
- Counsel should examine the treater on question "F-6" regarding the physician's investigation into the claimant's work status.

[4]   Vocational Factors

· Is the claimant's personnel file, to include a job application available? This reveals the skills the claimant had pre-injury.

· Is a job description available to demonstrate the pre-injury work requirements that this claimant could fulfill?

· Should the testimony of the employer and the claimant be obtained on this issue?

· Is a Labor Market Survey available?

§15.04   The 2012 Guidelines

The Guidelines are intended to provide a standard framework and methodology for physicians to evaluate and report a worker's
1. medical condition (work-related medical diagnosis(es)),
1. degree of impairment, and
2. functional ability/loss.

The Guidelines also contain detailed documentation requirements for the physician's evaluation of non-schedule PPD.

Chapters 2 through 8 of the guidelines are taken, unchanged, from the 1996 guidelines and are devoted to Schedule Loss of Use awards. Chapters 9 through 17 deal with Non-Schedule Permanent Disabilities (the focus of this Chapter).

[1]   Obtaining a Copy of the 2012 Guidelines

The 2012 Disability Duration Guidelines are available as a free download from the Board's website.[222]

[2]   Reliance on Objective Tests

Objective tests generally carry more weight than subjective symptoms. The performance of objective tests should be determined by the patient's clinical condition. Inclusion of objective tests as criteria in the 2012 Guidelines does not imply the tests should be performed.

§15.05   Best Practices: Cross-Examination of Claimant's Doctors

The cross-examination should cover the doctor's opinions on impairment and functional ability. Counsel must be prepared to cross examine the claimant's

---

[222] http://www.wcb.ny.gov/content/main/hcpp/ImpairmentGuidelines/2012ImpairmentGuide.pdf

physician about the alleged diagnosis, injury severity ranking, and objective findings on examination, as well as any diagnostic testing/imaging results.

If surveillance video is available, the activities of daily living/demonstrated abilities may form the basis of a cross-examination if the physician's report finds functional limitations which are inconsistent with the video evidence.

Counsel should have a thorough understanding of the claimant's work activities in the at-injury job. Generally, claimant's physicians will only have a vague idea of the claimant's at-injury work, often provided solely by the claimant. Claimants often report to their treater that there is no light or accommodated duty work available.

PART II: THE LAW

§15.06   The 2007 Reform Bill

The 2007 Reform Bill amended the WCL to impose caps on non-schedule per-manent partial disability (PPD) awards based on Loss of Wage Earning Capacity (LWEC). This is the part of the Law that employers like - the capping of the maximum number of weeks for a permanent partial disability. The Board has promulgated Disability Duration Guidelines (2012) to provide guidance regard-ing how medical and vocational factors are considered in determining how much earning capacity an injured worker has lost because of a non-scheduled permanent injury.

Section (3)(w) states:

> Other cases. In all other cases of permanent partial disability, the compensation shall be sixty-six and two-thirds percent of the differ-ence between the injured employee's average weekly wages and his or her wage-earning capacity thereafter in the same employment or otherwise. Compensation under this paragraph shall be payable dur-ing the continuance of such permanent partial disability, but subject to reconsideration of the degree of such impairment by the board on its own motion or upon application of any party in interest however,

> all compensation payable under this paragraph shall not exceed (i) five   hundred twenty-five weeks in cases in which the loss of wage-earning capacity is greater than ninety-five percent; . . . and (xii) two hundred twenty-five weeks in cases in which the loss of wage-earning capacity is fifteen percent or less.

> For those claimants classified as permanently partially disabled who no longer receive indemnity payments because they have surpassed their   number of maximum benefit weeks, the following provisions will apply: (1) There will be a presumption that medical services shall continue notwithstanding the completion of the time period for   com-pensation set forth in this section and the burden of going forward and the burden of proof will lie with the carrier, self-insured em-ployer or state insurance fund in any application before the board to discontinue or suspend such services. Medical services will con-tinue during the pendency of any such application and any appeals thereto. (2) The board is directed to promulgate regulations that

establish an independent review and appeal by an outside agent or entity of the board's choosing of any administrative law judge's determination to discontinue or suspend medical services before a final determination of the board.

Here are the implications of the statutory caps, in simple table form. Take note that for disabilities at or below 15%, there is a minimum number of weeks: 225.

LWEC (%)	Maximum Weeks of PPD Benefit
> 0 - 15%	225 Weeks
> 15 - 30%	250 Weeks
> 30 - 40%	275 Weeks
> 40 - 50%	300 Weeks
> 50 - 60%	350 Weeks
> 60 - 70%	375 Weeks
> 70 - 75%	400 Weeks
> 75 - 80%	425 Weeks
> 80 - 85%	450 Weeks
> 85 - 90%	475 Weeks
> 90 - 95%	500 Weeks
> 95 - 99%	525 Weeks

For disabilities of 95% or higher, there is a maximum number of weeks: 525 weeks.

The number of weeks is based on the LWEC percentage.

§15.07   The Case Law: Buffalo and Longley

The case law instructs us that there is no distinction between working and non-working claimants when calculating LWEC.

[1]   Buffalo Auto Recovery (2009)

The *Buffalo* decision essentially agrees with the long line of cases that interpreted WCL § 15(a) to say that if the claimant is working, her actual wages determine the wage earning capacity.[223] What *Buffalo* did address was the fact that "loss of wage earning capacity" is not defined anywhere in the Statute, and might be a different thing than "wage earning capacity."

The *Buffalo* panel addressed this lapse in definition by stating that "Loss of Wage Earning Capacity" is the inverse of "Wage Earning Capacity." This is essentially the same as a four-year-old child explaining what pizza tastes like by describing all the foods that pizza does not taste like. In other words, not very helpful.

Even though *Buffalo* didn't bother to define "Loss of Wage Earning Capacity" any better than a four-year old would, at least Buffalo explained how the benefits are to be issued.

First, when a claimant has returned to work, the money benefits can fluctuate, but the weeks won't.

Next, when a claimant has post-injury earnings equal to or greater than her pre-injury average weekly wage, benefits stop, and the number of weeks stops running. The unpaid future weeks are "held in reserve."[224]

[2]   Longley (2012)

In *Longley,* a Full Board Panel reviewed a Workers' Compensation Law Judge's determination of Loss of Wage Earning Capacity.[225] The Board took the opportunity to re-write the rules and throw out any conceptual consistency that may have existed under Buffalo.

The facts in *Longley* are simple: the claimant sustained an injury amenable to a finding of permanent partial disability (classification). Because the claimant was working, and his post-injury wages were known (calculated at 75% of the

---

[223] Matter of Buffalo Auto Recovery, 2009 NY Wrk Comp 80703905, as modified by Matter of Longley Jones Management Corp., 2012 NY Wrk Comp 60704882, remains the legal standard for determining LWEC.

[224] There are significant limitations to *Buffalo*: this case does not explore the "impairment, function, vocation" mantra that was introduced in the 2012 Disability Duration Guidelines - it was decided under the 1996 Guidelines, which are no longer applicable to "new" cases.

[225] Matter of Longley Jones Management Corp., 2012 NY Wrk Comp 60704882.

pre-injury wage) the employer argued this should be the basis of the LWEC determination (25% Loss of Wage Earning Capacity).

The Law Judge declined to find the LWEC solely on the earnings information; instead, the Judge ordered that vocational information be provided for consideration.

In *Longley,* the Board Panel found this approach was reasonable and would harmonize the benefits available to working- and non-working claimants. It also means that the simple expedient of looking at actual wages will not be the sole factor in considering LWEC for the working claimant.

[3]   Buffalo and Longley Made Simple

Every case involving a permanent partial disability requires an analysis of "impairment, function, and vocation" - even if the claimant has returned to work and is making his prior wage.

§15.08   Reclassification

Nothing in the 2012 Guidelines prevents an application for reclassification if a worker's medical condition worsens. Of course, this literally renders the concerns of the Board in *Longley* absolutely moot as the Panel seemed obsessed with the possibility that a worker who is actually fine enough to return to work in an absolutely unimpaired fashion - and is actually earning or exceeding his pre-injury wages - is somehow "worse off" in regards to collecting arbitrary sums of money from his employer than the worker who does not return. If sometime in the future the worker who came back to work, earning his full pre-injury wage is somehow unable to work down the road and it is attributable to his underlying (workers compensation) injury, then he can simply seek reclassification to address his (reduced, in comparison to the worker who never returned) capped number of weeks.

PART III: IMPAIRMENT

§15.09   Determining Impairment

Impairment is a purely medical determination made by a physician. Impairment is defined as an anatomic or functional abnormality or loss ("handicap"). Impairment requires a complete medical examination and accurate objective assessment. Impairment is not supposed to be taken at face value and converted into a "percentage" of disability.

The 2012 Disability Duration Guidelines attempt to provide a uniform process for evaluating impairment resulting from a medically documented work-related injury or illness.

An impairment is considered permanent when MMI has been reached and there is a remaining impairment.

§15.10   Finding Maximum Medical Improvement

Before an impairment rating is considered, the injured worker must reach maximum medical improvement (MMI). Classification should not occur until MMI has been reached.

For the purposes of the 2012 Guidelines, if a case does not involve surgery or fractures, MMI cannot be determined prior to 6 months from the date of injury or disablement, unless otherwise agreed upon by the parties.

According to the 2012 Guidelines, the definition of maximum medical improvement (MMI) is:

> A finding of maximum medical improvement is based on medical judgment that (a) the worker has recovered from the work injury to the greatest extent that is expected and (b) no further improvement in his/her condition is reasonably expected. The need for palliative or symptomatic treatment does not preclude a finding of MMI. In cases that do not involve surgery or fractures, MMI cannot be determined prior to 6 months from the date of injury or disablement, unless otherwise agreed to by the parties.

In May 2013 the Board updated the definition of Maximum Medical Improvement:

Injured workers generally reach MMI within two years of the injury. Special circumstances may require additional time to reach MMI, but these circumstances must be documented. If a treating provider or independent medical examiner (IME) is asked to provide a permanency evaluation and believes that the injured worker has not yet reached MMI, the provider must document the treatment the claimant is receiving, specific improvements that are expected, and a timeframe by which the claimant is expected to reach MMI. As clearly stated in the regulatory definition, palliative or symptomatic treatment does not preclude an MMI finding.

The mere assertion of the possibility of future surgery is not a bar to MMI. The appropriateness of surgical intervention should be evaluated in light of applicable Medical Treatment Guidelines. A claimant must not only qualify for surgery but also have specific plans for surgery, including an active request for pre-authorization, if required. Judges may evaluate the credibility of the claimant or provider who asserts the possibility of future surgery, based on such factors as history of treatment, prior requests for surgery, etc. If MMI is deferred because of surgery, the claim will be followed to ensure that surgery occurs, and the claim is reconsidered following post-surgical rehabilitation.

This updated definition of MMI is beneficial to employers and carriers.

Section D of Form C-4.3 poses questions regarding maximum medical improvement (MMI). A provider should indicate if the patient has reached MMI. If the answer is "yes," the doctor must indicate the date the patient reached MMI.

D. Maximum Medical Improvement

1. Has the patient reached Maximum Medical Improvement? ☐ Yes ☐ No If yes, provide the date patient reached MMI: ____/____/____
If No, describe why the patient has not reached MMI and the proposed treatment plan (attach additional documentation, if necessary).

---

§15.11   Preparing the Physician's Report

The doctor's report must find two things (after MMI): a specific medical impairment and a severity ranking for that impairment. To prepare a report, the physician is expected to review the relevant sections of the 2012 Guidelines, Chapters 11 - 17, the claimant's medical records, and perform a thorough history and physical examination.

The physician's report must include:

- Relevant medical history.
- Physical exam findings.
- Test results.
- Work-related medical diagnosis(es) based on the relevant medical history, exam, and test results.
- Body part affected.
- Impairment ranking, based on the 2012 Guidelines' criteria.
- Impact of the impairment(s) on the worker's functional and exertional abilities.

The physician should fully complete Form C-4.3 which has been modified to accommodate the new medical impairment and functional assessment information. Section "E" (part "b") of the form must be completed.

§15.12   Medical Impairment and Severity Rankings

The first step is to determine if there is a permanent medical impairment and if so, the severity of that medical impairment. As per WCL §15(3)(w), the impairment must be permanent and not subject to a schedule award.

A doctor assesses and quantifies the severity of the permanent medical impairment using the 2012 Guidelines. Each impairment class is assigned a severity ranking from A to Z.

If there are multiple permanent medical impairments, the 2012 Guidelines do not provide a mathematical formula for combining them into one number (percentage). In that case, the doctor is supposed to take the multiple impairments into account when performing the functional assessment (next step, below).

In each chapter of the Guidelines there are tables providing specific instructions for classifying medical impairment and establishing severity rankings. Each table includes two parts:

[1]   Explanatory Boxes.

An **Explanatory Box** which provides general considerations for determining the medical impairment class and severity ranking; and

---

Table 11.1: Soft Tissue Spine Conditions - Non Surgically Treated

1. Table 11.1 requires a minimum duration of six months of symptoms from the time of the injury to the impairment rating and no surgical intervention.

2. The appropriate spine injury table (Table 11.1: Soft Tissue Spine Conditions - Non-Surgically Treated, or Table 11.2: Surgically Treated Spine Conditions, or Table 11.3: Vertebral Fractures) should be chosen for determining impairment to a given spinal region.

3. All references to symptoms and findings must be related to and consistent with the specific documented workplace injury. A history of workplace injury encompasses acute, repetitive or episodic events.

4. Severity rankings are from "A" (the least severe medical impairment) to "Z" (the most severe medical impairment) for the Medical Impairment Classes within a Table.

5. The severity ranking is generally predictive of the functional outcome for each Class relative to the other Classes within a Table.

6. Please state diagnosis(es) at time of impairment rating:

7. **The medical impairment ranking is not to be used as a direct translation to loss of wage earning capacity.**

---

[2]   Severity Table

A Severity Table (excerpt below) contains detailed criteria for establishing the medical impairment class and the associated severity ranking.

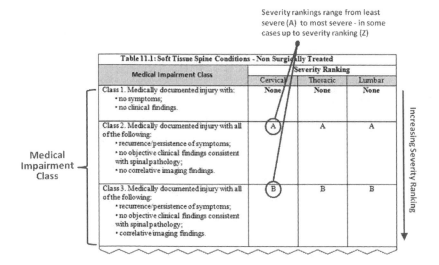

Severity rankings range from least severe (A) to most severe - in some cases up to severity ranking (Z)

Table 11.1: Soft Tissue Spine Conditions - Non Surgically Treated			
Medical Impairment Class	Severity Ranking		
	Cervical	Thoracic	Lumbar
Class 1. Medically documented injury with: • no symptoms; • no clinical findings.	None	None	None
Class 2. Medically documented injury with all of the following: • recurrence/persistence of symptoms; • no objective clinical findings consistent with spinal pathology; • no correlative imaging findings.	(A)	A	A
Class 3. Medically documented injury with all of the following: • recurrence/persistence of symptoms; • no objective clinical findings consistent with spinal pathology; • correlative imaging findings.	(B)	B	B

Medical Impairment Class

Increasing Severity Ranking

[3]   Supplemental Tables

Supplemental tables (noted by an "S" in the table number) are used in conjunction with the primary tables to determine the medical impairment class and severity ranking. The supplemental tables cannot be used alone to determine the medical impairment and severity ranking.

The supplemental tables provide details for determining a specific radiculopathy ranking within a range. Excerpts of the relevant supplemental tables are included below:

[5]   Example: Supplemental Table S11.4

Table S11.4: Radiculopathy Criteria		
Residual radicular pain >6 months after surgery is usually investigated with post-operative imaging.		
Table S11.4: Radiculopathy Criteria		
Objective Testing	**Documented Objective Findings at the Time of Rating**	**Score**
Imaging	Findings of: • significant disc abnormalities that displace nerve tissue **and/or** • bony/mechanical nerve root encroachment evident on imaging. These imaging findings must correlate with the clinical picture.	Yes/No Yes = 16 No=0
EMG Abnormalities	Findings of: • fibrillation potentials **and/or** • positive sharp waves • seen in at least 2 muscles in the distribution of the involved nerve root(s).*	Yes/No Yes = 6 No=0
Muscle Involvement	Findings of: • objective muscle weakness **and/or** • muscle atrophy.	Yes/No *Yes* = 6-20. See Table 11.4(a) to determine

[6]   Example: Supplemental Table S11.5

Table S11.5: Spinal Nerve Root Impairment Affecting the Upper Extremity		
Nerve Root Impaired	**Sensory Deficit**	**Weakness**
C5	0	10
C6	6	10
C7	6	10
C8	4	12
T1	0	12

[7]   Example: Supplemental Table S11.7

Table S11.7: Radiculopathy Severity Rankings

To determine placement within the range of severity rankings for radiculopathy, follow these steps:

1. Determine the number of points from Tables S11.4(a), S11.4(b), S11.5 and S11.6, as applicable.
   a. Cervical: Tables S11.4(a), S11.4(b) and S11.5
   b. Thoracic: Tables S11.4(a) and S11.4(b)
   c. Lumbar: Tables S11.4(a), S11.4(b) and S11.6

2. From either Table S11.7(a) (for cervical or thoracic injury) or Table S11.7(b) (for lumbar injury) below, determine the letter that corresponds to the number of points. This letter is the severity ranking.

Table S11.7(a): Points for Cervical and Thoracic Radiculopathy

Severity Ranking	Cervical	Thoracic
C	0	0
D	4-16	4-16
E	17-32	17-32
F	33-48	33-48
G	49-64	49-64
H	65-80	-

Table S11.7(b): Points for Lumbar Radiculopathy

Severity Ranking	Lumbar	Severity Ranking
D	0	D
E	4-16	E
F	17-32	F
G	33-48	G
H	49-64	H
I	65-80	I
J	81-92	J

[8]   Medical Impairment Class

The following is an excerpt of Table 11.1 showing the Medical Impairment Class and Severity Ranking table for non-surgically treated soft tissue spine conditions.

Non-surgically treated soft tissue spine conditions

Table 11.1: Soft Tissue Spine Conditions - Non Surgically Treated			
Medical Impairment Class	**Severity Ranking**		
	Cervical	Thoracic	Lumbar
Class 4. Medically documented injury with: • recurrence/persistence of symptoms; **and** • (a) weakness in myotomal distribution and/or sensory changes in dermatomal distribution; **or** • (b) tension/compression signs; **or** • (c) objective clinical findings*. The symptoms and findings must be consistent with: • spinal pathology **and** • correlative imaging findings **or** • correlative electro-diagnostic findings as described in the radiculopathy chart (Table 11.4)	C-H See Tables S11.4, S11.5, and S11.7 for determining placement within range.** (This excludes adjustments for multiple roots and root avulsion.)	C-G See Tables S11.4 and S11.7 for determining placement within range.** (This excludes adjustments for multiple roots and root avulsion.)	D-J See Tables S11.4, S11.6 and S11.7 for determining placement within range.** (This excludes adjustments for multiple roots and root avulsion.)
* *Objective clinical findings* mean atrophy or reflex changes. ** Use Tables S11.4, S11.5 and S11.6 as appropriate to determine the number of points associated with the identified radiculopathy. Then use Table S11.7 to determine the letter that corresponds to the number of points. This letter is the Severity Ranking within the radiculopathy range.			

Medical Impairment Class 4

[9]   Severity Ranking Range

For Class 4 non-surgically treated soft tissue spine impairment, the severity ranking for cervical spine injuries is provided as a range from C to H. To determine the appropriate severity ranking within the range, use the supplemental tables as directed (S11.4, S11.5, and S11.7).

Non-surgically treated soft tissue spine conditions

Table 11.1: Soft Tissue Spine Conditions - Non Surgically Treated			
Medical Impairment Class	**Severity Ranking**		
	Cervical	Thoracic	Lumbar

Medical Impairment Class 4

The severity range is C – H.

To determine the specific rating refer to supplemental Tables:

- S11.4
- S11.5
- S11.7

as described in the radiculopathy chart (Table 11.4)

	C-H	C-G	D-J
	See Tables S11.4, S11.5, and S11.7 for determining placement within range.** (This excludes adjustments for multiple roots and root avulsion.)	See Tables S11.4 and S11.7 for determining placement within range.** (This excludes adjustments for multiple roots and root avulsion.)	See Tables S11.4, S11.6 and S11.7 for determining placement within range.** (This excludes adjustments for multiple roots and root avulsion.)

* *Objective clinical findings* mean atrophy or reflex changes.
** Use Tables S11.4, S11.5 and S11.6 as appropriate to determine the number of points associated with the identified radiculopathy. Then use Table S11.7 to determine the letter that corresponds to the number of points. This letter is the Severity Ranking within the radiculopathy range.

PART IV: FUNCTIONAL ABILITY

§15.13   Functional Assessment

Functional assessment includes a medical evaluation of residual functional ability/loss. This takes place at MMI, and at the same time as the medical impairment evaluation.

In general, permanent medical impairment reduces earning capacity because it restricts a worker's ability to perform certain work-related activities or tasks. The treating physician should measure and document the following on Form C-4.3:

- The worker's ability to perform work-related activities such as sitting, standing, walking, overhead reaching.

- Whether there are any restrictions as to how long and/or frequently these activities may be performed.

- The worker's residual exertional capacity such as the ability to lift or carry weights, based on a standard classification of physical demand requirements (Sedentary to Very Heavy).

- Any other limitations such as environmental restrictions that preclude work in a particular occupation or certain work environment.

The physician's functional assessment should be recorded on the Doctor's Report of MMI / Permanent Impairment, Form C-4.3.

§15.14   How the Guidelines Address Functional Abilities/Losses

The 2012 Guidelines contain a functional assessment component (Chapter 9.3) which should be performed along with the medical impairment evaluation and complete Form C-4.3 (part "F"), Doctor's Report of MMI/Permanent Impairment.

F. Functional Capabilities/Exertional Abilities

1. Please describe patient's residual functional capacities for any work at this time (not limited to the at-injury job activities):

	Never	Occasionally	Frequently	Constantly	
Lifting/carrying		lbs.	lbs.	lbs.	Patient's Residual Functional Capacities
Pulling/pushing		lbs	lbs.	lbs.	■ **Occasionally**: can perform activity up to 1/3 of the time.
Sitting					■ **Frequently**: can perform activity from 1/3 to 2/3 of the time.
Standing					■ **Constantly**: can perform activity more than 2/3 of the time.
Walking					
Climbing					
Kneeling					
Bending/stooping/squatting					
Simple grasping					
Fine manipulation					
Reaching overhead					
Reaching at/or below shoulder level					
Driving a vehicle					
Operating machinery					
Temp extremes/high humidity					
Environmental					

Specify:

Psychiatric/neuro-behavioral (attach documentation describing functional limitations)

The provider should rate whether the patient can perform each of the 15 functional abilities (a) never, (b) occasionally, (c) frequently, or (d) constantly.

The provider should also note the specific weight tolerances for the categories lifting/carrying and pulling/pushing. There is also room to describe any functional limitations in connection with environmental conditions (e.g. occupational asthma). If there are any psychiatric/neuro-behavioral functional limitations, attach documentation describing such.

The functional assessment should address the worker's:

[1]   On the Job Activities

The physician should first document whether the injured worker can perform the work activities of the at-injury job.

To understand the major work requirements of the at-injury job, the physician should request a job description or other similar documentation from the employer and speak with the worker about the job requirements. Does the treating physician ever request this? This suggestion is found NOWHERE in the guidelines.

If the employer maintains that the injured worker can perform the at-injury job, the employer must provide appropriate detail about the physical job requirements.

The physician should document whether the worker can perform the at-injury job requirements based on the best information available to the physician about the job requirements at the time of evaluation

[2]   Functional Ability/Loss

On examination, the physician should measure and record the injured worker's performance and restrictions across a range of functional abilities on the form C-4.3, including:

- dynamic abilities (lifting, carrying, pushing, pulling, and grasping).
- general tolerances (walking, sitting, and standing).
- specific tolerances (climbing, bending/stooping, kneeling, and reaching).

Alternatively, the physician may refer the injured worker to a physical or occupational therapist for completion of the functional measurements and, after the physician's review, incorporate them into the Form C-4.3.

[3]   Exertional Capacity

The physician should rate the worker's residual exertional capacity according to the standard classification system of Sedentary to Very Heavy on the Form C-4.3 (Part "F"):

The provider should rate the patient's exertional ability according to the Federal Standards set forth by the Department of Labor:

2. Please check the applicable category for the patient's exertional ability:

- [ ] **Very Heavy Work** - Exerting in excess of 100 pounds of force occasionally, and/or in excess of 50 pounds of force frequently, and/or in excess of 20 pounds of force constantly to move objects. Physical demand requirements are in excess of those for Heavy Work.
- [ ] **Heavy Work** - Exerting 50 to 100 pounds of force occasionally, and/or 25 to 50 pounds of force frequently, and/or 10 to 20 pounds of force constantly to move objects. Physical demand requirements are in excess of those for Medium Work.
- [ ] **Medium Work** - Exerting 20 to 50 pounds of force occasionally, and/or 10 to 25 pounds of force frequently, and/or greater than negligible up to 10 pounds of force constantly to move objects. Physical demand requirements are in excess of those for Light Work.
- [ ] **Light Work** - Exerting up to 20 pounds of force occasionally, and/or up to 10 pounds of force frequently and/or negligible amount of force constantly to move objects. Physical demand requirements are in excess of those for Sedentary Work. Even though the weight lifted may only be a negligible amount, a job should be rated Light Work: (1) when it requires walking or standing to a significant degree; or (2) when it requires sitting most of the time but entails pushing and/or pulling of arm or leg controls; and/or (3) when the job requires working at a production rate pace entailing the constant pushing and/or pulling of materials even though the weight of those materials is negligible. NOTE: The constant stress of maintaining a production rate pace, especially in an industrial setting, can be and is physically demanding of a worker even though the amount of force exerted is negligible.
- [ ] **Sedentary Work** - Exerting up to 10 pounds of force occasionally and/or a negligible amount of force frequently to lift, carry, push, pull or otherwise move objects, including the human body. Sedentary work involves sitting most of the time, but may involve walking or standing for brief periods of time. Jobs are sedentary if walking and standing are required only occasionally and all other sedentary criteria are met.
- [ ] **Less than Sedentary Work** - Unable to meet the requirement of Sedentary Work.

Exertional capacity relates to activities requiring lifting and pushing and/or pulling objects. The definitions, derived from the Dictionary of Occupational Titles and used by the Social Security System, are as follows:

Sedentary: Exerting up to 10 pounds of force occasionally and/or a negligible amount of force frequently to lift, carry, push, pull or otherwise move objects, including the human body. Sedentary work involves sitting most of the time but may involve walking or standing for brief periods of time. Jobs are sedentary if walking and standing are required only occasionally and all other sedentary criteria are met.

Light: Exerting up to 20 pounds of force occasionally, and/or up to 10 pounds of force frequently and/or negligible amount of force constantly to move objects. Physical requirements are more than those for sedentary work. Even though the weight lifted may only be a negligible amount, a job should be rated light work: (1) when it requires walking or standing to a significant degree; or (2) when it requires sitting most of the time but entails pushing and/or pulling of arm or leg controls; and/or (3) when the job requires working at a production rate pace entailing the constant pushing and/or pulling of materials even though the weight of those materials is negligible.

> **NOTE:** The constant stress of maintaining a production rate pace, especially in an industrial setting, can be and is physically demanding of a worker even though the amount of force exerted is negligible.

Medium: Exerting 20 to 50 pounds of force occasionally, and/or 10 to 25 pounds of force frequently, and/or greater than negligible up to 10 pounds of force constantly to move objects. Physical demand requirements are more than those for light work.

Heavy: Exerting 50 to 100 pounds of force occasionally, and/or 25 to 50 pounds of force frequently, and/or 10 to 20 pounds of force constantly to move objects. Physical demand requirements are more than those for medium work.

Very Heavy: Exerting more than 100 pounds of force occasionally, and/or more than 50 pounds of force frequently, and/or more than 20 pounds of force constantly to move objects. Physical demand requirements are more than those for heavy work

[4]   *Psychiatric Limitations*

For claims involving an established, permanent psychiatric impairment, the physician should document the impact of the psychiatric impairment on the worker's ability to function in the workplace including activities relevant to obtaining, performing, and maintaining employment. Examples include personal hygiene, grooming, interpersonal relations, etc.

The physician should also document other limitations caused by the perma-nent impairment(s) that impact the worker's ability to function in the work-place. This includes any limitations caused by the medical condition or treat-ment, including prescription medication, that impact the worker's ability to work.

§15.15   Medical Impairment, Functional Loss, and LWEC

Medical impairment is generally predictive of residual functional ability/loss. Severity ranking within a specific impairment table is generally predictive of the expected functional loss from the medical impairment. Medical impair-ment cannot be directly translated to loss of wage earning capacity (LWEC).

[1]   Assistive Devices

Assistive devices such as canes, crutches, wheelchairs, etc. are not considered in determining medical impairment (remember this on cross-examination of a treating doctor!) but may be considered in the assessment of residual func-tional ability and/or loss.

[2]   Comparing Letter Severity Grades Between Body Parts

In principle, the severity rankings for the classes of one chapter should not be compared to the rankings in other chapters. For example, a "D" ranking in the spine & pelvis is not intended to imply a "D" ranking in the respiratory chapter is of equal severity.

HOWEVER, for purposes of qualitative comparison the Guidelines contain an "IMPAIRMENT SEVERITY CROSS WALK (Table 18.1)" which is intended to allow for some degree of comparison between rankings of different classes and chapters.

PART V: VOCATIONAL FACTORS

§15.16   Measuring Vocational Ability

The 2012 Disability Duration Guidelines are 124 pages long. Add in the associated cases (*Buffalo, Longley*) and the Workers' Compensation Law, and you are
talking about hundreds of pages of reading. Tens of thousands of words. And
in all of that writing, the Board spares just seven paragraphs - *less than a complete page* - to vocational factors. Counsel should view this failure of the Board
to set clear standards as an opportunity to challenge the disability in light of
other factors.

Into this void has emerged venders providing Labor Market Surveys and offering placement services. This is also a fertile ground for challenging the disability
by demonstrating employability, transferable skills, and education.

In considering the litigation of vocational factors, the claimant's pre-injury average weekly wage will be key: low AWW is a disincentive to challenge Loss of
Wage Earning Capacity. For high-earners with transferable skills, vocational
testimony should be obtained.

Here is what the Guidelines say about "vocational factors":

[1]   Education and Training

Education plays a significant role in a worker's ability to qualify for different
occupations and level of income. The relationship between education and loss
of wage earning capacity is complicated by the fact that the impact of education is also generally reflected in workers' pre-injury wages. Those with more
education generally earn more than those with less education, both pre-injury
and post-injury. Thus, in determining loss of wage earning capacity, it is important to evaluate the degree that educational achievement buffers or inten-
sifies the impact of a medical impairment on a worker's earning capacity.

For example, an injured worker whose education and training qualifies him to
perform work that, despite his disability, he is physically capable of doing, and
that pays similarly to his pre-injury work, will have a smaller LWEC. In contrast,
an injured worker whose injury prevents him from doing his former occupation
and does not have the education or training to perform any comparably paid
work will have a higher LWEC.

[2]   Skills

Prior work skills are often as important as formal education in an individual's qualification for employment. Someone who has only performed unskilled or semi-skilled work in the past is unlikely to qualify for skilled work post-injury. A worker who has performed skilled work may be able to find other skilled work within his functional limitations, though this depends on the nature of the worker's job skills.

A key consideration is whether the worker's skills are readily transferable to alternative employment. The transferability of skills from a prior occupation generally depends on the similarity of occupationally significant work activities among different jobs. The similarity can be measured by the level of similarity in the degree of skill involved, the tools and machines used, and the materials, products, processes or services involved.3

[3]   Age

The impact of age on wage earning capacity is complex. Age should be considered in the context of residual function, education, and work experience. Generally, advancing age may adversely impact a person's ability to obtain employment that involves work that is different from one's prior work experience or requires developing new skills.

[4]   Literacy and English Proficiency

The ability to read, write, and speak English fluently is a requirement for many occupations in New York. Those who have limited or no ability to read, write or speak English fluently may still qualify to perform manual labor and other work that does not require interaction with the public or involvement with written documents. Workers who are illiterate or have limited or no English proficiency and, by virtue of their impairment, are rendered unable to perform manual work may have a significant loss of earning capacity.

[5]   Other Considerations

Other factors may be considered in determining an injured worker's loss of earning capacity. The key consideration is whether the factor impacts the injured worker's ability to perform paid employment.

CHAPTER 16: SETTLING CLAIMS

PART I: SETTLEMENT BASICS

§16.01   Putting the Settlement on the Record - WISK

The Board has a program called *WISK* (Walk-In Stipulation Calendar. When interested parties wish to settle matters quickly and equitably, the WISK program allows them to stipulate to certain findings and resolve claims. Upon reaching agreements, the parties may request time on the WISK to seek approval of the agreed upon terms from a Judge.

There are State-wide contact numbers for getting a WISK hearing scheduled.

§16.02   Protracted Healing Period Effects on Settlements

Every "scheduled" body part has a maximum value - expressed in terms of weeks - set forth by the Legislature at WCL § 15. By common usage, injuries to the "ankle" are compensated in terms of the statutory foot and injuries to the wrist are compensated in terms of the statutory "hand." Knee injuries are compensated in terms of the statutory "leg."[226]

[1]   When "Protracted Healing Period" Comes into Play.

New York defines the "normal healing period" for scheduled injuries. In cases where that claimant remained totally disabled for a period of time in excess of the established healing period, additional compensation payments are required.

The Law provides as follows at WCL §15(4-a):

> In case of temporary total disability and permanent partial disability both resulting from the same injury, if the temporary total disability continues for a longer period than the number of weeks set forth in the following schedule, the period of temporary total disability in excess of such number of weeks shall be added to the compensation period provided in subdivision three of this section: Arm, thirty-two weeks; leg, forty weeks; hand, thirty-two weeks; foot, thirty-two weeks; ear, twenty-five weeks; eye, twenty weeks; thumb, twenty-four weeks; first finger, eighteen weeks; great toe, twelve weeks; second finger, twelve

---

[226] There is an easy to read "chart" of scheduled losses provided at the end of this book.

weeks; third finger, eight weeks; fourth finger, eight weeks; toe other than great toe, eight weeks.

So, where the claimant remained totally disabled after the periods of time set forth by the Legislature, the employer/carrier is exposed for additional compensation under the Law.

[2]   Example: SLU Award Applying "Protracted Healing" Calculation

If an injured worker made $200 per week and lost her thumb, according to the Scheduled Loss of Use chart, she would be entitled to 100% loss of the thumb – 75 weeks of compensation. This would be paid at a rate equivalent to 2/3rds (66.6%) of her average weekly wage – or approximately $133.34 per week (two thirds of $200 per week). So in this example, the loss of the thumb would give rise to an award of $10,000 for permanent disability. The other benefit the injured worker would receive is medical treatment for life in regard to the lost thumb.

However, what if the claimant actually lost more than 75 weeks from work? For example, if the claimant lost 90 weeks from work? In that case, the added weeks of lost time would be "Added" to the scheduled award that exceed the "normal healing period." as set forth by the statute. In the case of the thumb, the "normal" healing period is set at 24 weeks.[227]

So, instead of getting nothing as would be due under the Statute without the "protracted healing provision" this claimant would be due the difference between the "normal healing period" for the thumb (24 weeks) and the actual lost time (90 weeks) or an 76 additional weeks of compensation: $10,133.84 in "new" money.

---

[227] WCL § 15(4-a).

PART II: LUMP SUM CLOSURES

§16.03   Section 32 Settlements

New York Workers Compensation Law Section 32(a) permits the claimant and employer to join in an agreement to settle the claim for benefits. The parties can settle all of the issues relating to the claim. The agreement must be submitted to the WCB for approval on a prescribed form or a document which describe the agreement fully. If approved by the Board, the settlement is binding on all the parties and not subject to appeal. Section 32 agreements can expedite the adjudication of issues or entire claims, while assuring the rights of the claimant and all other parties.

The Section 32 settlement is submitted at the time of the hearing. The agreement may also contain a 'reasonable fee' for the claimant's attorney.

After the Section 32 agreement is submitted, the WCB reviews the matter before rendering a decision. This review takes at least 10 days.[228] During this review period, all proceedings in the matter are stayed.

[1]   Reasons for Choosing a Section 32 Settlement

A Section 32 agreement can close all of the claimant's future rights – and that includes compensation and medical benefits. Or, the parties can choose a more limited agreement – one closing the right to just future medical treatment, for example. It is possible to have more than one Section 32 settlement in a case.

[2]   Requirements for a Section 32 Settlement

The Section 32 agreement will be approved as long as:

- It is not unfair;
- It is not unconscionable;
- It is not improper as a matter of law; and
- Both parties wish the Board to approve the agreement (no objections by either side).

Once the agreement is approved by the WCB, it has the same binding effect as an award in an arbitration – it is conclusive and not subject to review or appeal. It is possible that a Section 32 agreement could be challenged for intentional

---

[228] WCL § 32(b)(3).

misrepresentation of a material fact – for example the fraud of a claimant. However, an employer challenging the legitimacy of the agreement *post hoc* will have difficulty recovering moneys already paid to the claimant.

§16.04   Non-Schedule Adjustments

A third option of settling a claim is through a non-schedule adjustment which is a lump-sum settlement. The non-schedule adjustment allows the parties to agree to a lump-sum amount to be paid to the claimant.[229] A lump-sum settlement is considered closed unless there is a change in the claimant's condition that was not contemplated at the time of the agreement.

[1]   When a non-schedule adjustment can be re-opened.

Lump-sum settlements may only be reopened where there is a finding that there was a change in condition of the injury or illness that was not contemplated at the time of the settlement. This is a two-factor test for re-opening:

· The condition has changed; AND
· The change in condition could not have been contemplated at the time of the original settlement.

If the case is re-opened, the employer gets a credit for the amount paid in the settlement.

[2]   When a non-schedule adjustment should be considered.

Examples include:

- Where a working claimant receives an award for permanent disability, but had periods of illness which kept him from work but no compensation was paid to him because his yearly earnings were too high.[230]
- Where are employer, found liable for compensation (directly) due to an illegal employment of a minor, who wishes to close the case with finality.[231]

---

[229] WCL § 15(5)(b) and 12 NYCRR 300.24.

[230] *Badler v. Krakoff*, 297 N.Y. 834, 78 N.E.2d 860 (1948)

[231] *Krefta v. Protective Closures Co.*, 23 A.D.2d 897, 258 N.Y.S.2d 889 (App. Div. 1965)

CHAPTER 17: REOPENING CLOSED PERMANENT PARTIAL DISABILITY CASES

PART I: INTRODUCTION

§17.01 Impact of 2017 Legislation

A closed PPD case can be reopened, and the prior award can be increased or decreased. However, since the Legislature removed the requirement that a permanently partially disabled claimant remain attached to the workforce in April 2017, there is little to be gained by reopening an old case on behalf of the employer/carrier.

§17.02 Vocabulary

We will use the terms "reopening" or "rehearing" interchangeably with "modification." The relevant Statutes and Regulations use these terms without distinction, and so will we.[232]

The reader should be aware that not all sources of law are equal: The Statutes, Regulations, and decisions of the Court of Appeals are granted the most deference, and then the rulings of the Appellate Division (3rd Department). Less reliable are the decisions of the Full Board. Least reliable and the worst source of guidance: published decisions of the Board, and any reserved decisions issued by a workers' compensation law judge.

§17.03 The Law of Reopening

A "closed" PPD case can be reopened. Workers' Compensation Law § 22 states:

> Upon its own motion or the application of any party in interest, on the ground of a change in condition or proof of erroneous wage rate, the board may [subject to limitations] review any award, decision or order and, on such review, make an award ending, diminishing, or increasing the compensation previously awarded.

Under the relevant section, the review will not affect moneys already paid, but if the revised award increases the rate, then it may be made effective from the

---

[232] *See* §§ 22, 123, 142 and 12 N.Y.C.R.R. 300.14, 12 N.Y.C.R.R. 300.23.

date of injury. If the award decreases the rate, the payments already made in excess of the revised rate are deducted from the unpaid compensation.

There is also reference in §142 ("General Powers and Duties of the Workmen's Compensation Board") stating that the Board "shall have power . . . to modify or rescind awards."

PART II: REQUIREMENTS FOR REOPENER

§17.04   Time Limit on Modification

As per §123, the Board has continuing jurisdiction over a closed PPD case. There are two different statutes of limitation that apply, depending on how the case was closed.

[1]   Time limit where "No payments made"

According to the first half of §123 if the case was closed "on the merits" (meaning after trial or hearing and for cause shown) it can be reopened within seven (7) years from the date of injury or death. If the case was "otherwise disposed of without an award after the parties in interest have been given due notice of hearing or hearings and opportunity to be heard and for which no determination was made on the merits." In that case, a closed case can be reopened within seven (7) years from the date of injury or death.

[2] Time limit where payment was made.

The application to reopen must be filed within 18 years of the date of injury and eight (8) years of the date of the last payment of compensation.

§17.05   How a Claimant gets a Rehearing – Medical Change

As per 12 N.Y.C.R.R. 300.14 ("Application of Rehearing") any party in interest may make a request for rehearing or reopening.

The Application must state that a rehearing is necessary because:
- Material evidence was not available at the time of the hearing;
- Material proof of a change in condition; or
- It would be in the interest of justice.

A "change in condition" must be in the form of a verified medical report - signed by a treating physician. This report must come from after the case was closed and contain "objective" medical findings.

The Board has promulgated two forms[233] for use by a claimant in asking for modification of an old claim. Form C-27 is to be used when the request for modification is made within seven (7) years from the date of injury or death. Form C-25 is to be used when more than seven years has elapsed. These forms require that a doctor's report be filed at the same time.

---

[233] Form C-25 & Form C-27.

If the Board grants a rehearing, the case will be returned to the trial calendar.

§17.06   How the Employer gets a Rehearing – Request for Further Action

An employer/carrier seeking to suspend or modify benefits where the Board has made an award for permanent partial disability, the following steps must take place:

1.   An application must be made;
2.   Accompanied by supporting evidence;
3.   along with filed proof of service on the claimant, his representative, and his doctor; and
4.   the Board has ruled on the application (i.e., following a hearing).[234]

There is no "self-help" - the stopping of ordered benefits without court inter-vention - unless one of the following two conditions are met (1) where supporting evidence demonstrating proof of incarceration upon conviction for a felony; or (2) when the claimant has reached the maximum number of weeks under WCL §15(3)(w).[235]

§17.07   Voluntary Withdrawal is no Longer a Defense

Following statutory changes made to the New York Workers' Compensation Law in April 2017, a claimant no longer must demonstrate attachment to the labor market by looking for work within their medical restrictions. This limits the ability of employers to reopen closed PPD awards.

---

[234] 12 N.Y.C.R.R. 300.23(c)(1).
[235] 12 N.Y.C.R.R. 300.23(c)(2).

CHAPTER 18: LIENS, THIRD-PARTY SETTLEMENTS, SPECIAL FUND RE-IMBURSEMENT, AND LOSS TRANS-FER LITIGATION

PART I: LIENS AND THIRD-PARTY ACTIONS

§18.01 Introduction

Under the New York Workers' Compensation Law, a worker injured by the negligence of another can collect workers' compensation benefits and then recover in a civil suit against the actual tortfeasor.[236] An injured worker can pursue both his New York workers' compensation claim and his claim against the actual tortfeasor at the same time. Pursuant to New York Workers' Compensation Law § 29, the employer or carrier responsible for providing workers' compensation benefits is deemed to have a lien against the proceeds of the third-party action. The lien is simple to calculate: it is the sum of the medical benefits issued and indemnity payments made, including future benefits.

The insurance carrier that paid benefits has a lien on the proceeds of the third-party settlement "after the deduction of the reasonable and necessary expenditures, including attorney's fees, incurred in effecting such recovery."[237] The employee may ask the court for an order apportioning the "reasonable and necessary expenditures."

The carrier paying workers' compensation benefits also has the right to sue the actual tortfeasor in court (subrogation). However, the employer/carrier cannot bring this action unless

- one year has passed from the accident or six months from the compensation award (whichever comes first); and
- the employee has been notified in writing (certified mail or personal service) and 30 days has elapsed.[238]

§18.02 Vocabulary

---

[236] WCL § 29.
[237] Id.
[238] WCL § 29(1).

Discussing subrogation rights in New York is a journey into a land of bizarre vocabulary. To begin, let's review some key terms:

· **"Third-party"** refers to the "negligent third-party" or the civil action itself. In the workers' compensation context there are always two parties: the employer and the injured worker. The "third party" (the negligent party - not the employer) is how practitioners refer to the "not comp" action.

· A permanent total disability award, scheduled loss of use award, or death benefits (dependency benefits) are for a **"fixed"** amount of compensation and the present-day values of those awards is readily ascertainable.

· New York Workers' Compensation Law allows for **"reduced earnings benefits"** and permanent partial disability benefits. The value of those benefits may fluctuate (and even cease completely) during the lifetime of the claimant. Reducing those benefits to a "present day value" is not as easily ascertainable as in the case of a death, total disability, or scheduled loss of use benefit.

§18.03   Limitations on Reimbursement: Motor Vehicle Claims

WCL § 29(1-a) states that the employer's reimbursement right does **not** extend to any recovery the claimant may have made under § 5104(a) of the insurance law. That insurance law section (§ 5104(a)) states that a person injured in a motor-vehicle accident is **not** entitled to recovery for "non-economic loss" or for "basic economic loss" except in certain cases (where there has been "serious injury").[239]

Section 5102 of the New York State Insurance Law defines "Basic Economic Loss as up to $50,000 in medical expenses, lost wages and other reasonable and necessary expenses (up to $25 per day) arising from a motor vehicle accident. Because these expenses are paid by the injured party's own insurer, they are not recoverable in a personal injury lawsuit. As a result, a person injured in car accident who incurs less than $50,000 in expenses cannot proceed with a personal injury lawsuit unless he or she has otherwise suffered a serious injury.

The prohibition against allowing the comp carrier to get reimbursement from this first $50,000 in "first party" benefits makes sense in a roundabout way: an employee who is injured (while working) in a car accident collects $50,000 in lost wages and medical expenses from her own insurance policy, so granting

---

[239] NY No-Fault Law § 5102 & WCL § 29(1-a).

the compensation carrier the right to reimbursement from that money is kind of like letting the comp carrier get away with having the claimant self-fund the first $50,000 of her own workers' compensation losses.

§18.04   Limitations on Reimbursement: Kelly

The decision in *Kelly v. State Insurance Fund* is simple: it stands for the proposition that the carrier's reimbursement is reduced **as a percentage** of what the claimant expended on securing the third-party recovery.[240] It does not matter if, as in the *Kelly* case, the claimant recovers $315,000 and the workers' compensation carrier had paid out only $54,127.56 in benefits. The $54,127.56 was reduced by the *percentage* of the claimant's litigation expenses ("reasonable and necessary expenditures, including attorney's fees", see WCL § 29) which was determined to be 34.27% of the total recovery (for how this percentage is calculated, read on).

The Court in *Kelly* ruled that the carrier had also received a second benefit from the claimant's recovery against the third-party: not having to pay an ongoing dependency award (remember that dependency awards can be estimated by taking the claimant's life expectancy in weeks and multiplying it by the weekly award).[241] The *Kelly* Court ruled that the carrier's lien should not only be reduced by the amount paid by the claimant to obtain her award (attorney's fees and "reasonable" costs) but also by the amount of future payments *avoided* by the carrier.

[1]   Applying Kelly Math

Figuring out the impact of a third-party settlement on a carrier's exposure involves knowing the following facts:
1.   The settlement amount.
1.   Total of disbursements made to get the settlement (legal costs such as filing, expert witness fees, exhibits fees, etc.).
2.   The attorney's fee paid (either dollar figure or percentage).
3.   Amount paid by the compensation carrier for medical and indemnity benefits.
4.   Present value of future benefits due to the claimant.

Then, the following formula can be applied:
(Carrier's lien amount) * (cost of collection percentage) = net lien recovery

---

[240] *Kelly v. State Ins. Fund*, 60 N.Y.2d 131 (1983).
[241] *Id.*

197

To make it easy, use round numbers for an example:
1.   The settlement amount: $400,000.
1.   Total of disbursements made to get the settlement: $10,000.
2.   The attorney's fee: 33% ($130,000)
3.   Amount paid by the compensation carrier for medical and indemnity benefits: $90,0000.
4.   Present value of future benefits due to the claimant: Presume nothing.

In this formula, the lien amount is the total value of the *past* medical and indemnity paid. Here it is, as a math formula:

$130,000 attorney's fee + $10,000 in costs = $140,000 paid to get the settlement.
$140,000 cost of collection / total settlement ($400,000) = 35% of total recovery

Under this example, the carrier's lien would be reduced by 35% (percentage costs of recovery).

$90,000 lien * .35% = $31,500.

So, the carrier would recover $58,500.

After the carrier's reimbursement, the formula for calculating the claimant's net is:
   $400,000 - costs and fee $140,000 - carrier's lien = $201,500 net to claimant.

What about where the carrier's obligation to pay continues, but is reduced or extinguished by the amount of the third-party settlement? (This was the case in *Kelly*).

In that circumstance, the carrier didn't just get repaid for benefits already issued - but got to defer payment on future benefits **which would have been paid out if the third party had not settled.** In that case, the carrier's second benefit is reduced too.

Presume that the claimant would be entitled to a fixed benefit for either a scheduled loss of use, permanent disability or a dependency benefit (the claimant is *Kelly* was entitled to a dependency benefit.) In that case, the carrier is getting the second benefit - not having to pay all those weeks of compensation that the claimant would have had coming to her.

For example, if the claimant was getting a benefit of $300 a week, it would take 671.66 weeks or approximately 13 years to use up the remaining "net settlement"" (see above example, where the claimant "netted" $201,500, and dividing that figure by the $300 weekly rate to arrive at a number of weeks). In such a case, the future benefit is reduced to present value. Assume for the sake of this example that the present value of $201,500 is $136,188. Then, the **real** amount that the carrier recovered is **the total amount already paid in indemnity and medical benefits** *plus* **the current value of the future benefits avoided ($136,188).**

This benefit ($90,000 + $136,188 = $226,188) would be reduced by the percentage cost of procurement (35%) and then subtracted from the carrier's lien for benefits already paid ($90,000). In our example, the $90,000 lien (current value of medical and indemnity already paid) would be reduced by the *future* benefit (payment avoidance) so the carrier's net lien is reduced by $79,166 to just $10,834.

In this example, where the claimant recovered $400,000 in a third-party claim, where the carrier expended $90,000 in medical and indemnity benefits during the case, and has an ongoing obligation to pay benefits, the impact of the third-party case is that the carrier recovers $10,834 from the third-party action and then takes a break from having to pay *anything* until 13 years passes.

The formula for this would be:
$Current lien - (($Current lien + $future benefit) * cost of recovery%)

[2] ˋ "Fresh Money"

As is shown above, the amount the workers' compensation carrier pays is the function of two things: the amount already paid at the time of settlement (medical and indemnity benefits) *plus* the future payments avoided. In our example above, this "total" amount is then multiplied by the "equitable share" percentage (the costs of procuring the recovery divided by the recovery) to arrive at the new, total (lower) lien reimbursement (but remember, the carrier then gets a holiday until the proceeds are exhausted).

When the amount already paid is much smaller than the future benefits avoided, the carrier may have to pay "fresh money" to the claimant as its equitable share for the recovery.

Here is an example where "fresh money" would have to be paid, using the same settlement in our example above, but *reducing* the already-incurred medical and indemnity component (the present lien) to show how fresh money would be payable.

To use easy, round numbers for an **example**:
1.   The settlement amount: $400,000.
1.   Total of disbursements made to get the settlement: $10,000.
2.   The attorney's fee: 33% ($130,000)
3.   Amount paid by the compensation carrier for medical and indemnity benefits: **$20,0000.**[242]
4.   Present value of future benefits due to the claimant: $138,188.

In this formula, the lien amount is the total value of the *past* medical and indemnity paid. Here it is, as a math formula:
$130,000 attorney's fee + $10,000 in costs = $140,000 paid to get the settlement.
$140,000 cost of collection / total settlement ($400,000) = 35% of total recovery

Under this example, the carrier's lien would be reduced by 35% (percentage costs of recovery).

$20,000 lien + $138,188 * .35% = $55,365.80.
This would be **subtracted** from what the carrier has already paid to get to the net lien: $20,000 - $55,365 = $35,365 in fresh money moving to the claimant.

After the carrier's reimbursement, the formula for calculating the claimant's net is:
$400,000 - costs and fee $140,000 - carrier's lien (add $35,365) = $236,865 net to claimant.

§18.05   PPD and Reduced Earnings Awards: Burns

In *Burns v. Varriale, 9 N.Y. 3d 207 (2007),* the Court of Appeals reviewed a case in which the claimant was receiving "reduced earnings" benefits of $400 per

---

[242] *Note bene*: this is the only figure we will change for this "fresh money example" versus our prior example, above.

week. This represented the difference between the claimant's pre-injury and post-injury wage (after his condition had reached a state of partial permanent disability.) This case is interesting because under the *Kelly* calculations, considering the "future exposures" avoided by the workers' compensation carrier by the claimant, the claimant would have been due **fresh money** from the compensation carrier.

The compensation carrier argued that the future benefits was essentially unknowable - that the reduced earning benefit would change during periods of higher and perhaps lesser earnings. Therefore, the compensation carrier (Travelers) argued that it was unfair for the claimant to get the benefit of the carrier's contribution for benefits which may never have been realized by the claimant.

The Court in *Burns* stated that, "if a claimant does not receive benefits for death, total disability or schedule loss of use, the carrier's future benefit cannot be quantified by actuarial or other means."[243]

The Court found it unfair to have the carrier pay an "equitable share" of attorney's fees and costs for future benefits whose future value could not be ascertained at the time of the third-party recovery. Instead, the Court ruled that the trial court, in the exercise of its discretion, can fashion a means of apportioning litigation costs as they accrue and monitoring (e.g., by court order or stipulation of the parties) how the carrier's payments to the claimant are made.

§18.06   Future Medicals: Bissel

In Bissell v. Town of Amherst, 18 N.Y.3d 697 (3rd Dept. 2012), the claimant received a third-party award that included an amount awarded by a jury for "future medical expenses" ($4,260,000). Under a Kelly calculation, the carrier would have had to pay $1,399.734 in "fresh money" representing its equitable portion of the fees and costs necessary to obtain the verdict that would ultimately allow the compensation carrier to avoid those future medical expenses.

The Court in *Bissell* ruled that future medical expenses

---

[243] *Burns v Varriale,* 9 N.Y.3d 207 at 146 (2007)(*citing McKee v. Sith Indepen. Power Partners*, 281 A.D.2d 891 (4th Dep't 2001) and *Briggs v. Kan.s Fire & Marine Ins. Co.,* 121 A.D.2d 810, 812 (3d Dep't 1986).)

cannot reliably be calculated in a manner similar to [benefits for death, total disability or schedule loss of use] because it is impossible to reliably predict the future medical care the claimant will need, when the expenses from such care will accrue and how much it will cost when it does.

Instead, the compensation carrier offered to pay its equitable portion of the cost when Bissell actually incurred each medical expense. The *Bissell* Court expressly agreed with this approach.

§18.07   Permission to Settle Third-Party Cases

Workers' Compensation Law § 29(5) requires either the carrier's written consent or a compromise order from the court in which a third-party settlement is pending for a claimant to settle a third-party case and continue to receive compensation benefits. If an employer or carrier refuses to consent to a settlement, a claimant may move in the trial court for judicial approval of the settlement, as well as an equitable apportionment of the litigation costs. When an employer/carrier consents to a third-party settlement, the right to future offset should be set forth - otherwise the Board can decide.

The employer/carrier should reserve the right to future offsets in writing, at the time the third-party settlement is approved. Remember - if the claimant fails to seek the approval of the employer/carrier for the third-party settlement or abandons that third-party claim without providing notice to the employer/carrier, her right to compensation benefits is extinguished!

§18.08   Time Limits

The employer by statute has an opportunity to separately pursue reimbursement of workers' compensation benefits paid and payable if the injured worker has not done so within one year from when the action accrued or six months after the awarding of compensation whichever comes first, but only 30 days after the injured worker has been notified in writing by personal service or by certified mail that the failure to commence an action within 30 days will operate as an assignment of the claim to the employer.[244]

§18.09   Practical Guidance: Getting Reimbursed

---

[244] WCL § 29(1).

The workers' compensation law provides two separate ways for a compensation carrier to obtain reimbursement from the proceeds of a claimant's third-party settlement:

1.   Assert a lien against the recovery for the amount of benefits already disbursed by the carrier[245]; or

2.   Offset the claimant's future compensation benefits by the amount of the claimant's net recovery in the third-party action.[246]

§18.10   Asserting a Lien for Past Benefits Conferred

The workers compensation carrier "shall have a lien on the proceeds of any recovery from" a third-party settlement less reasonable and necessary expenditures, such as attorney's fees.[247] The employee may apply on notice to the lienor to the court for an order apportioning reasonable and necessary expenditures including attorney's fees. The court shall apportion such expenditures equitably between the employee and the lienor.[248]

§18.11   Offsetting Future Compensation Benefits

The carrier must affirmatively preserve its right to offsets, or it may involuntarily waive such right.[249] The claimant's third-party settlement recovery less the carrier's lien is credited by the carrier against future compensation payments. The net amount the claimant receives offsets future compensation payments, and no future payments will be made until the credit is exhausted. The carrier may waive the lien or the offset.[250]

§18.12   New York's "Grave Injury" Exception

The New York Workers' Compensation Law prevents an employee from directly suing their employer in civil court for injuries arising out of and in the course of employment. Instead, the employer's liability to the employee is limited to the benefits allowed under the Workers' Compensation Law.

---

[245] WCL § 29(1).

[246] WCL § 29(4).

[247] WCL § 29(1).

[248] *Id.*

[249] *Hilton v. Truss Sys., Inc.*, 82 A.D.2d 771 (3d Dep't 1981), *order aff'd*, 56 N.Y.2d 877 (1982).

[250] WCL § 29(1).

Of course, an injured worker can always sue the "actual tortfeasor" (the person who injured them) in civil court - if that person is not their employer. This section discusses what happens when a defendant sued by the employee files a civil claim against the injured workers' employer by alleging the employer contributed to the injury or should indemnify the defendant. That "third-party" claim is a civil claim made by a defendant within an existing legal proceeding which seeks to enjoin a person not party to the original action, to enforce a related duty.

Even though the employee cannot sue their employer directly in civil court, New York provides an exception to this immunity if employee has sustained a "grave injury." If the employee sustains a "grave injury" an employer may be liable for contribution when they are third-partied in. In those situations, the employer may defend a workers' compensation claim and then be brought into a civil suit as a third-party defendant.

New York's Workers' Compensation Law, § 10, defines "grave injury" as follows:

> death, permanent and total loss of use or amputation of an arm, leg, hand or foot, loss of multiple fingers, loss of multiple toes, paraplegia or quadriplegia, total and permanent blindness, total and permanent deafness, loss of nose, loss of ear, permanent and severe facial disfigurement, loss of an index finger or an acquired injury to the brain caused by an external physical force resulting in permanent total disability.

§18.13   Making the Third-Party Claim

A third-party claim is begun by filing a Third-Party Summons and Complaint with the Court. CPLR §1007. Although the third-party plaintiff pays an index number fee ($210), the entire action retains the same index number as the underlying/pre-existing case. The party filing the third-party complaint must serve copies of all the prior pleadings filed in the case within 120 days of the filing. Best practice is to attach the prior pleadings to the third-party complaint.

In addition to serving copies of all prior pleadings on the third-party defendant, the third-party plaintiff must also simultaneously serve the Summons and Complaint on plaintiff's counsel and all other parties who have appeared in the action.[251]

---

[251] CPLR §§ 1007, 2103(e).

[1]   Who can Make a Third-Party Claim?

Third-party claims (impleaders) are limited to causes of action for contribution and/or indemnification only. As per CPLR § 1007, third-party practice is only allowed when the claim of the defendant is against "a person not a party [to the original action] who is or may be liable to that defendant for all or part of the plaintiff's claim against that defendant." The employer is usually third-partied in by the actual tortfeasor when the injured employee files a civil lawsuit against the party that actually harmed her.

[2]   Statute-of-Limitations for a Third-Party Claim

The Statute of Limitations for an action for contribution or indemnification is six years from the date of accrual. The clock starts running not on the date of loss for which the party seeking indemnification may be held liable, but from the time payment is made on the underlying claim.

§18.14 Defending Third-Party Claims

The same attorney defending the workers' compensation matter can defend the associated third-party claim, as long as the following conditions are met to ensure there is no conflict of interest:

- The carrier is defending both matters (*Part A coverage* and *Part B coverage*) without challenging entitlement to coverage;

- There are no adverse interests.

As the cases will involve the same proofs, and the carrier is asserting the right to reimbursement from the proceeds of any third-party suit (as per Workers' Compensation Law §29) having one attorney handle both matters could result in a better outcome and cost savings.

§18.15   Answers and Defenses

Depending on how and where the Summons and Complaint is served, the third-party defendant has either 20 or 30 days to answer.[252] Generally speaking, domestic or "authorized foreign" corporations have 30 days to file answering pleadings once service has been affected.

Answers to Complaints and Third-party complaints are not filed with the Court, they are simply served upon plaintiff's counsel.[253] Answers must be served within 20 days, with exceptions to this general rule.

---

[252] CPLR §§320(a), 3012(a) and (c), Bus. Corp Law §306(b)1.

[253] CPLR § 3012(a)

PART II: NEW YORK LABOR LAW

§18.16   Claims Arising Under New York's Labor Law

New York's Scaffold Law (Labor Law § 240) imposes a liability for damages to workers injured as a result of an "elevation related hazard" during the course of employment in the building trades. This Law allows workers to sue their employer for injuries arising out of and in the course of employment when the injury arises from a fall from height or something falling onto the worker. These claims are not barred by the Workers' Compensation Act.

[1]   The Interplay Between Scaffold Law Cases and Workers' Compensation

Under the New York Workers' Compensation Law, an employer is immune for suit from an employee except for four specific circumstances:

- The employer is uninsured;
- the injury to the employee is intentional;
- where the employee sustains "grave injury;" and
- Scaffold Law claims.

[2]   Scaffold Law Claims

The Scaffold law specifically states that it applies to

> All contractors and owners and their agents . . . in the erection, demolition, repairing, altering, painting, cleaning or pointing of a building or structure.

Case law has made it clear that even "inspecting" a work site, if the inspection was incidental to the actual work tasks being performed there, could bring a worker under the Scaffold Act.

[3]   Plaintiff's Proofs in a Labor Law Claim

To prevail in such a claim, which pierces the immunity offered employers under the Workers' Compensation Law the plaintiff must show

> he was subjected to an elevation-related risk which the statute was designed to obviate and that there was a causal connection between a violation of the statute and the injury sustained.

Failure to provide safety devices to prevent falls is prime facie evidence of violation and the strict liability standard will apply.[254]

[4]   Defending Labor Law Claims

To defend these claims, most employers have separate law firms representing them in the workers' compensation case and the Labor Law case. Meanwhile, the claimant in both cases is the same, and uses the workers' compensation claim to "fund" and prepare the civil action, usually by seeking unnecessary medical care and seeking to extend time lost from work in order to "build up" the third-party (civil) claim.

Coordination between the defense counsel defending the workers' compensation claim and the civil claim can be an enormous advantage in defending these claims. However, there is no collateral estoppel effect to decision in the workers' compensation court unless the issues and proofs are shown to be identical.[255]

For large self-insured employers and construction entities with choice of counsel, coordination between counsel in the workers' compensation the civil proceedings is recommended.

---

[254] *Zimmer v. Chemung Cty. Performing Arts*, 65 N.Y.2d 513 (1985).

[255] Aqui v Seven Thirty One Limited and the Court of Appeals decision of December 13, 2013.

PART III: SPECIAL FUNDS REIMBURSEMENT

§18.17   Shifting Exposure to Special Funds

New York has a Special Fund for Reopened Cases to assume liability for re-opener workers' compensation claims. When a claimant moves to reopen a closed case, the employer/carrier requests relief from the Special Fund for Reopened Cases. By shifting cases over to the Special Fund, the carrier/employer shifts the burden for paying compensation to the Special Fund.

The Business Relief Act, adopted as part of the 2013-2014 New York State Budget, closed Special Funds to new claims for reimbursement.

As of January 1, 2014, new applications for the transfer of liability to the 25-a Fund were not accepted.

On October 24, 2017, the Court of Appeals ruled that retroactive closure of the Fund for Reopened Cases was constitutional.

§18.18   Filing Requirements

An employee seeking to reopen a closed claim can file Form C-25.[256] A new medical record can be sufficient to reopen the case if it provides notice to the Board of the change in condition; in that case, Form C-27 (Medical Proof of Change in Condition in Support of Application for Reopening) should be used.[257] The medical report must demonstrate a new condition and not merely the continuing effects of the original disability or injury.

§18.19   Time Factors

There are time limitations for the shift of exposure to the Special Fund. These rules are as follows:

- More than seven years from the date of a compensable injury or death and the claim has been disposed of without a compensation award being issued;

---

[256] http://www.wcb.ny.gov/content/main/forms/c25.pdf
[257] http://www.wcb.ny.gov/content/main/forms/c27.pdf

- More than seven years has elapsed from the compensable injury or death which was compensated, and more than three years has elapsed from the last date of payment of compensation;

- After death, occurring more than seven years from a compensable injury and either more than three years unless payment of compensation or from acclaimed disposed of without an award.

Payment for continuing medical care does not bar the transfer of liability under Section 25.[258]

This is important factor to consider; as the Worker's Compensation Board does not consider payments for medical services "compensation." Oftentimes in a reopener case, the claimant has been receiving ongoing medical care and in-demnity benefits have ceased.

§18.20   Closed Status – Not as Simple as it Could be

In the past few years the issue of whether a case was "closed" has been exten-sively litigated. In 2011 alone, there were at least nine reported decisions on whether the workers compensation claim had been "truly closed" by the Board and the requisite amount of time had elapsed, thereby creating a viable claim for relief from the Special Fund for Reopened Cases.

Since 2001 the Board has been marking cases as "No Further Action" rather than stating a case is closed. This "No Further Action" marking confuses the issue as to whether a case is truly closed at the time of adjudication.

In *Hosey v Central New York DDSO*, decided January 5, 2012, the Appellate Di-vision found that the underlying case had not been "truly closed" and therefore the employer could not get the benefit of reimbursement from Special Funds for what they were calling a reopener claim.[259] In the *Hosey* decision, the claim-ant had a 2000 back injury and returned to work in 2002. The claimant contin-ued to work with no additional lost time but had some work restrictions and received ongoing payments for medical treatment. Although his treating phy-sician in 2002 indicated the claimant had a permanent disability referable to the work injury, the issue of permanency was never formally addressed.

---

[258] *Beder v Big Apple Circus*, 84 A.D.3d 1653 (3d Dep't 2011).
[259] *Hosey v. Cent. N.Y. DDSO*, 91 A.D.3d 993 (3d Dep't 2012).

Although seven years elapsed, and the claimant returned to work, the Special Fund argued that the issue of permanent residual disability had remained unresolved and therefore the case was still "open." Even though no lost time benefits were issued for the prior seven years, after three years of litigation on this issue, the Appellate Division upheld the denial of reimbursement for reopener benefits to the employer.

The Appellate Division considered whether the case of a claimant who had already pled guilty for fraudulently collecting workers comp benefits while working was "truly closed."[260] In that case, the claimant made an argument that her condition had worsened and that she was due further benefits. The claimant had a ready been disqualified from obtaining further indemnity (wage replacement benefits) as *she had been deemed a fraud* after trial pursuant to § 114a of the Worker's Compensation Act. In this interesting case, the Appellate Division found because the claimant was a fraud and therefore not due any lost wage benefits the claim was truly closed at that time and that the only payments ongoing were for consequential medical treatment. Therefore, the employer in this case was able to shift responsibility for the alleged reopener or worsening of the claimant's underlying medical condition to the Special Fund for reopener cases.

§18.21   Practice Tips for Adjusters

First, identify claims where significant time has elapsed from last payment of lost time or permanency benefits. The passage of time is critical to establishing Special Fund exposure.

Next, confirm the case was "truly closed" at a prior proceeding by settlement or by Order of the Workers' Compensation Law Judge. This will usually involve reviewing old EC-23's (decisions) in the electronic case file. Knowledge of these reopening rules in the instances where cases been "truly closed" can significantly reduce exposure for New York employers and carriers.

As this issue continues to be raised before the Board and continues to be a steady source of Appellate Division review, it is clear that the rules concerning whether or not cases "truly closed" are nuanced and require a close analysis of the facts and the applicable law in your case.

---

[260] *Palermo v Primo Coat Corp.*, 88 A.D.3d 1042 (3d Dep't 2011).

PART IV: LOSS TRANSFER LITIGATION

§18.22   Understanding Loss Transfer Litigation

A person injured in a motor vehicle accident, has the right to recovery under the New York No Fault Statute.[261] If the person was in the course of their employment at the time of the motor vehicle accident, the Workers' Compensation insurer becomes the "primary" insurance which is responsible for paying out the lost wages and medical benefits which normally would be the responsibility of the No Fault carrier.[262]

The Workers' Compensation carrier can recover benefits issued to the claimant in this situation.[263] There is a right to recovery through the process of **inter-company loss transfer arbitration** for payment of medical and lost wage benefits made by a Workers' Compensation insurer authorized under § 5105(a) of the Insurance Law.

[1]   The Law

The statutory basis for recovery under Insurance Law Section 5105 is explained in § 5102(l), which defines a "compensation provider" to include

> the person, association, corporation or insurance carrier or statutory fund liable under state or federal laws for the payment of workers' compensation benefits or disability benefits under article nine of the Workers' Compensation law.

When Workers' Compensation insurance provides primary coverage for a motor vehicle accident that occurs in the course of employment, the compensation provider is authorized to pursue recovery for payments made in lieu of No-Fault benefits when authorized under the limited circumstances set forth in Insurance Law § 5105(a). The payments may include medical and health expenses and loss of wages, which are reimbursable as No-Fault benefits under Insurance Law § 5102(a)(1) and (2).

A claimant injured in the course of his employment is entitled to receive Workers' Compensation benefits. The obligation of the No-Fault carrier to pay No Fault benefits is reduced accordingly. When the total benefits payable by both

---

[261] This section ("Loss Transfer Litigation") contributed by Steven Bedoya, Esq.
[262] § 5102(1) of the New York Insurance Law
[263] §5105.

the Workers' Compensation and the No Fault carrier reach New York's basic minimum first party no fault level of $50,000, the injured individual is considered to have maxed out his or her no fault benefits and different rights of the subrogating carrier will attach. The Workers' Compensation insurer can then look to the No-Fault carrier to recover the "reduced" amount which it paid out to the claimant in benefits.

When the total between the two carriers reaches $50,000 the Workers' Compensation benefits paid thereafter are no longer in lieu of PIP but are considered "straight" Workers' Compensation. The Workers' Compensation insurance carrier is no longer reducing the amount that the No-Fault carrier would be responsible to pay for. Therefore, it follows that $50,000 is the maximum amount recoverable through loss transfer since that is the maximum amount that the No-Fault carrier would be responsible for in a motor vehicle accident.

[2]   Where Loss Transfer is Litigated

As discussed above, New York Insurance Law § 5105(a) governs loss transfer in New York State. That statute provides a mechanism for an insurer who has paid first party No- Fault benefits to recover those same payments from the insurer of the at-fault party.

The proceeding to recover loss transfer benefits does not occur in the Workers' Compensation courts. When you have a matter that qualifies for loss transfer subrogation, the only recourse available pursuant to § 5105 is intercompany arbitration. All carriers and legal self-insureds in New York are required to submit to this arbitration. In pertinent part, New York Insurance Law § 5105(b) states:

> the sole remedy of any insurer or compensation provider to recover on a claim arising pursuant to subsection(a) hereof, shall be the submission of the controversy to mandatory arbitration pursuant to procedures promulgated or approved by the superintendent. Such procedures shall also be utilized to resolve all disputes arising between insurers concerning their responsibility for the payment of first party benefits.

[3]   Requirements for Loss Transfer Recovery

The first and most important factor is the time limitation involved. The statute of limitations for loss transfer claims is 3 years from the date of each payment. Once the statute of limitations has expired the Workers' Compensation insurer will have been deemed to waive their right to recover the amount in question.

If the claim is submitted in a timely fashion, the next factor to consider is whether one of the vehicles involved in the accident weighs more than 6500 pounds (the **weight requirement**) or if one of the vehicles involved is a vehicle used principally for the transportation of persons for hire (the **livery requirement**). Although these may seem like straightforward requirements, there are important nuances worth noting when assessing whether a claim will qualify for loss transfer recovery.

[4]   The Weight Requirement

If any of the vehicles involved in the accident is over 6500 pounds unladen, the accident qualifies for loss transfer. The weight requirement is commonly accepted to mean the actual weight of the vehicle excluding any item that is made a part of the vehicle and excludes anything being carried or towed. Therefore, the weight of a trailer towed by the vehicle cannot be used to meet the weight requirement. Evidence which can be submitted to prove the vehicle's weight includes the vehicle VIN information from the DMV, a certificate of title, certificate of origin; a weight certificate from an official weighing station or Red Book/Blue Book information. Furthermore, in a situation involving more than two vehicles, a third vehicle involved in the accident which meets the weight requirement can be used as a basis for asserting loss transfer jurisdiction and the third vehicle does not even have to be named in the claim! As long as the pleadings set forth that this third vehicle is the basis for bringing the loss transfer claim, that will be deemed sufficient.

[5]   The Livery Requirement

The **transportation of persons for hire** requirement refers to whether the vehicle was used as a livery vehicle. This includes vehicles hired to transport people, such as taxis and buses, and vehicles hired to transport property, such as a tow truck. The vehicle must be shown to be used primarily as a livery vehicle and not simply on the date of the accident. If the vehicle is registered as a regular passenger vehicle but was used as a livery vehicle on the date of loss that must be taken into consideration when applying for loss transfer.

§18.23   Recovering Benefits Issued

A Workers' Compensation carrier can be an applicant for loss transfer and seek recovery of its payments in an arbitration forum, but a Workers' Compensation provider cannot be a respondent in the mandatory No-Fault Inter Company

Arbitration program! If a claimant is eligible for a workers' compensation, then said compensation provider shall serve as the sole provider of benefits.[264]

If a claimant in a workers' compensation claim has received medical and/or indemnity benefits and the accident involved a vehicle over 6,500 pounds or a livery vehicle, the compensation carrier may have a viable claim for loss transfer reimbursement for the first $50,000 of benefits issued.

§18.24   When SLU Awards are Subject to Recovery

A Schedule Loss of Use (SLU) award is compensation for loss of wage earning ability and may be recoverable.[265] A SLU is an award for permanent partial disability made pursuant to N.Y. Workers' Comp. Law § 15(3) which constitutes compensation for the loss of a claimant's earning ability that are made in lieu of No-Fault benefits for loss of earnings for work, and are covered No-Fault benefits under Insurance Law § 5102(a)(2). Therefore, SLU awards paid by a workers' compensation provider may be recoverable in loss-transfer arbitrations when warranted pursuant to Insurance Law § 5105(a).

---

[264] New York State Insurance Law Regulation 68 Section 65-3.5; 11 NYCRR 65.
[265] *See* General Counsel Informal Opinion #07-06-09 http://www.dfs.ny.gov/insurance/ogco2007/rg070609.htm

CHAPTER 19: PENALTIES

PART I: EMPLOYER AND CARRIER PENALTIES

§19.01 Background

The New York Workers' Compensation Board collects $3 Million per year in *procedural* penalties alone. This is a staggering figure - amounting to approximately $300 in penalties for each new case accepted by the WCB. New York is a form-driven jurisdiction, and most common penalties arise from the late filing of required boilerplate forms.

The Workers' Compensation Law is a minefield of penalties, fines, and criminal complications for the unwary. There are different penalty considerations for employers, claimants, insurers, and even attorneys. This section discusses the most common penalties from the perspective of each participant.

§19.02 Employer Penalties

Employers face penalties for

- failing to obtain insurance and
- cheating their insurer by misclassifying or concealing employees.

[1]   When an Employer Fails to Obtain Insurance

An employer failing to provide worker's compensation insurance coverage for her employees is subject to a penalty of $1,000 for every 10 days without coverage.[266] The employer is also responsible for paying all medical and wage benefits awarded.[267]

In addition, there are criminal penalties for failure to carry workers' compensation coverage: For employers with fewer than five employees, the criminal penalties could be conviction of a misdemeanor, and a fine (between $1,000 and $5,000). For employers with more than five employees, the potential criminal penalties could be conviction of a Class E felony, subject to a fine (between $5,000 and $50,000) or prison from one to four years, or both.[268]

---

[266] Workers' Compensation Law § 52(1).
[267] WCL § 26.
[268] WCL § 52(1)(b).

Furthermore, the law prohibits business owners that fail to comply with workers' compensation from bidding on public works contracts.[269] It creates a one year ban on a business owner (or a substantially owned entity of such person) from bidding on a public contract if he or she was (1) fined, (2) served with a stop work order, or (3) convicted of a misdemeanor violation for failing to comply. It prohibits any owner (or a substantially owned entity of such person) from bidding on public contacts for five years if he was convicted of a workers' compensation (1) felony or (2) a Class A misdemeanor for discriminating against an injured veteran.

The law authorizes the Workers' Compensation Board to issue stop-work orders and immediately shut down a business that is not complying with workers' compensation requirements.[270] In 2010 (the most recent year for which statistics are available) the Board issued more than 1,600 stop work orders. Such orders can be made for failing to (1) maintain workers' compensation coverage for employees and (2) pay penalties related to previous failures. These violations are deemed a sufficient danger to public health and safety to justify the stop-work order. The issuance of the "stop work" order does not terminate the employer's responsibility for placing coverage or paying benefits.[271]

It is an affirmative defense to a criminal prosecution under this provision that the employer took reasonable steps to secure compensation coverage.[272]

[2]   Payroll Fraud by Misclassification or Concealment

The law provides a penalty where an employer is found to "intentionally and materially misclassifying employees as independent contractors" or misrepresenting employees' duties. The penalty for misclassification is $1,000 for every 10 days.[273]

For intentionally and materially understating or concealing payroll, the penalty is $1,000 for every 10 days.[274] In additional, there is a criminal penalty of "not less than $5,000 nor more than $10,000." Subsequent violations are class E felonies subject to a fine of "not less than $10,000 nor more than $25,000."

---

[269] WCL § 141B.
[270] WCL § 141a.
[271] WCL § 52(1)(e).
[272] WCL § 52.
[273] WCL § 131.
[274] WCL § 131.

The Board may collect these penalties from both the real and personal property of the employer - which includes the corporate officers - who are personally liable for any debt to the Board.[275]

§19.03   Carrier Penalties

[1]   Failure to Pay Award.

For failure of employer or carrier to pay compensation installment within 25 days of it being due, there is a mandatory penalty of 20% of compensation then due and an assessment of $300 - which is payable to claimant.[276]

[2]   Failure to File Controversy.

(In a denied case) The WCL requires a penalty of $300 - payable to claimant - when a carrier fails to file Form C-7, Notice of Controversy within 18 days after disability or within 10 days after knowledge or within 10 days after receipt of notice (Form C-2) by carrier, whichever period is greater.[277]

[3]   Failure to Begin Payments.

(In an accepted case) For failure of carrier to begin compensation payments within 18 days after disability or within 10 days after knowledge or within 10 days after receipt of notice (Form C-2) by carrier, whichever period is greater, the penalty is $300 - payable to claimant.[278]

[4]   For Frivolous Controversy.

Where the Board finds that the employer or carrier has objected to an award without just cause, a penalty $300 payable to the claimant may be ordered.[279]

[5]   For Unnecessary Adjournment.

Under WCL § 25-3(c) a carrier can be penalized for causing an unnecessary adjournment. The penalty is $25 to Special Funds and $75 paid directly to the claimant. The law defines what could be considered "behavior causing an unnecessary adjournment." WCL § 25-3(c) states as follows: Dilatory tactics may include but shall not be limited to: failing to subpoena medical witnesses or to secure an order to show cause as directed by the referee, failing to bring proper files, failing to appear, failing to produce witnesses or documents after they have been requested by the referee or examiner or as directed by the hearing

---

[275] WCL § 141-a(6).
[276] WCL § 25-2(c).
[277] WCL § 25-2(c).
[278] WCL § 25-2(c).
[279] WCL § 25-2(c).

notice, unnecessarily protracting the production of evidence, or engaging in a pattern of delay which unduly delays resolution.

[6]   Failing to File Employer's Report of Injury.

For refusing (or neglecting) to file Form C-2F, "Notice of Injury," or to keep proper records, a penalty of "not more than $1,000."[280]

[7]   Failing to File Requested Record.

A carrier can be penalized $50 for every report or requested filing that is not filed within time. The Board is especially aggressive in applying this penalty, which grants the WCB power to penalize where the carrier:... failed to file a notice or report requested or required by the board or chair or otherwise required within the specified time period or within ten days if no time period is specified, the board may impose a penalty in the amount of fifty dollars unless the employer or carrier produces evidence sufficient to excuse its conduct to the satisfaction of the board.[281]

[8]   For Frivolous Appeal.

Section 114-a —for filing an appeal "without reasonable ground - the costs of "such proceedings" may be payable to the Board as a penalty, including attorney's fees.

[9]   Failing to File IME Report or Provide Notice.

NYCRR § 300.2(3) (WCB rules and regulations) provides that if the employer/carrier fails to file an independent medical report or notice same properly (within the time requirement and using forms promulgated by the Board) the IME report will be precluded.[282]

[10]   For Failure to Proceed in Expedited Case.

As per WCL § 25-3(d), a carrier is subject to a penalty of $1,000 for "frivolous adjournment of an expedited case." This penalty is payable to Chair, for deposit in WCB Special Revenue Account. This penalty may be payable by the carrier or by carrier's attorney if the attorney is not an employee of carrier.

§19.04   Attorney Penalties

The WCL allows for penalties to be assessed against attorney - not just their clients - who request frivolous adjournments. The law states that the penalty

---

[280] WCL § 100-4.
[281] WCL § 25-3(e)
[282] WCL § 137.

is payable by the attorney - not their client. The penalty for an employer's attorney who requests a "frivolous" adjournment of an expedited hearing is $1,000, payable to the Board.[283] The penalty for a claimant's attorney who makes such a frivolous request is $500. Unrepresented claimants are not subject to any penalty.

---

[283] WCL § 25(3)(d).

PART II: CLAIMANT PENALTIES

§19.05   Claimant Penalties

As per Section 25-3(d) a claimant's attorney - not the claimant - is subject to a penalty of $500 for a "frivolous request for an adjournment" of a special part/expedited hearing. These penalties are rarely, if ever, applied.

Any person who knowingly intends to defraud the workers' compensation system by presenting (or assisting in presenting) an application for benefits, which contains a misrepresentation of a material fact.[284] The penalty: Class E Felony charges. In addition to a Class E Felony conviction, the claimant who is convicted loses the right to all past and future compensation benefits. Fraudsters must return any money they got through their fraud. This is contrary to the general rule of law that claimants do not have to pay back money fraudulently obtained.

---

[284] WCL § 114-a

CHAPTER 20: WORLD TRADE CEN-TER HEALTH FUND

PART I: CHAPTER OVERVIEW

§20.01 Background

The World Trade Center (WTC) Health Program provides medical monitoring and treatment for responders at the WTC and related sites in New York City, Pentagon, and Shanksville, PA, and survivors who were in the New York City disaster area.

When a claimant has medical conditions treated under the World Trade Center Health Program and is later entitled to a worker's compensation award or establishment of a case, the workers' compensation employer/carrier must consider exposure for reimbursement to the World Trade Center Health Fund. In all cases, workers' compensation benefits are to be primary to the WTCHF.

§20.02 Section 32 Settlements with a WTC Health Fund Beneficiary

[1]   If WC Carrier was Primary Payer from Beginning

The way that these interactions are supposed to go when there is a WC carrier and the claimant can utilize the WTC Health Program, is that the claimant and carrier should develop a Section 32 settlement with a set aside for future medical costs that is approved by the WTC Health Program. This way, the WTC Health Program is providing treatment and the carrier should be paying in accordance with how much they would typically be paying in a WC claim.

[2]   The Reality of Lump-Sum Settlements

When a claimant who is a member of the WTC Health Program accepts a lump-sum settlement for a WC claim relating to conditions for which treatment is provided by the WTC Health Program, and that settlement releases the carrier from responsibility for future medical expenses, the WTC Health Program will seek to recoup its costs of providing health care, including pharmacy benefits, either from the individual/entity designated to administer any set-aside established   to   pay   future   medical   expenses. https://www.cdc.gov/wtc/pdfs/WTCHP-PP-Lump-Sum-WC-Settlements-01042015.pdf at (III. Policy).

When creating the lump-sum settlements, there is a duty to protect the interests of the WTC Health Program by creating the future set asides, but there is no duty to protect the interest of the WTC Health Program if the settlement does not release the carrier from the duty to pay future medical benefits. Id. at (IV)(C)(1)(b). The WTC Health Program and NYS WCB will notify the parties of their duty to ensure that the interests of the WTC Health Program are protected in settlement. Id. at (IV)(C)(1)(f). To help parties gauge how much money should be set aside, either party may request information from the WTC Health Program about the amount of the Program's expenditures for medical treatment and prescription medications since July 2011. Id. at (V)(A).

§20.03   WTC Health Program Seeking Recoupment

The WTC Health Program will only seek to recoup up to the amount approved as set-aside. Id. at (IV)(C)(1)(c). The WTC Health Program will pay all medical expenses incurred for treatment above the amount of the approved set-aside. Id. Because WC insurance pays for treatment at a lower rate, the WTC Health Program will recoup treatment costs at the WC insurance rate. Id. at (IV)(C)(1)(d).

Contracts between the World Trade Center Health Program and the Clinical Centers of Excellence (CCEs) and the Nationwide Provider Network (NPN) require the CCEs and NPN to seek recoupment from Workers' Compensation carriers when they have been identified by the CCE and the NPN. https://www.cdc.gov/wtc/pdfs/WTCHP_PP_Recoupment_Work_Comp_rev_10012013.pdf at (II)(A). The WTC Health Program relies on the Health Insurers' Match Program (HIMP), authorized under New York State law to recover payments from carriers. Id. The "WTC Health Program has entered into a contract to recover money retrospectively" from NY WC carriers. Id.

The Zadroga Act, which governs the WTC Health Program, grants the WTC Health Program Administrator the authority to reduce or recoup payments for treatment of an individual's WTC-related certified health condition that is work-related "to the extent that...the Administrator determines that payment has been made, or can reasonably expected to be made, under a workers' compensation law...". Id. at (III)(A)(1). The WTC Health Program will seek to recoup from carriers that have the primary responsibility to pay. Id. at (III)(B)(1). The Administrator may file a recoupment action against a primary payer, if the primary payer tries to shift cost onto the WTC Health Program or if the Program can't recover WC payments under HIMP. Id. at (III)(B)(2).

§20.04   Who is Primary Payer, When?

The WTC Health Program is the primary payer when the claimant is a WTC Health Program member with a WTC-related health condition and is eligible for WC or another illness or injury benefit plan to which New York City is obligated to pay. Id. at (IV)(A)(1). But, when a WTC Health Program member has filed a WC claim for a WTC-related health condition and has a WC plan to which New York City is not obligated to pay, the WC carrier is the primary payer. Id. at (IV)(B)(1). When coverage is available for a certified WTC-related health condition from a WC plan, those plans must pay for treatment services rendered by the WTC Health Program consistent with applicable laws. Id. at (VII).

The WTC Health Program is the primary payer when a WTC Health Program member has filed a WC claim for a WTC-related health condition and the claim is pending, but if the claim is ultimately accepted by the WCB, the WC carrier is responsible for reimbursing the WTC Health Program for any treatment provided during the pendency of the claim. Id. at (IV)(A)(2). WTC Health Program is the secondary payer. Id. at (IV)(B)(1).

§20.05   Disputing Claims

A carrier may dispute a claim under the rules and regulations applicable to HIMP. Id. at (IV)(B)(2). The WTC Health Program will defer to the final WCB decisions to determine whether, and if so how much, a carrier must pay for a claim. Id.

Because the WCB has a fee schedule for the payment of claims, the WTC Health Program will seek recoupment only of fees payable under the WCB fee schedule. Id. at (IV)(B)(3). "The health insurer shall be responsible for initiating claims for reimbursement of amounts paid by them which may be the responsibility of the carrier, as provided in Workers' Compensation Law section 13(d)." HIMP Rules and Regulations § 325-6.2(a).

§20.06   Practice Tips

There is no presumption set forth in Article 8-A or anywhere else in the Workers' Compensation Law that a claimant's alleged medical conditions are causally related, merely because they have been certified by NIOSH for treatment under the World Trade Center Health program.[285] Unless the WCB has already accepted the claim of leukemia as work related, then just treatment from the

---

[285] N.Y.C. Dept. of Bldgs, 2015 WL 5711254 (N.Y. Work. Comp. Bd. Sept. 29, 2015.)

WTC Health Program would not be enough, there would have to be an IME performed.

Under the Zadroga Act and the federal regulations which implement it, the costs of providing medically necessary treatment, services and outpatient prescription pharmaceuticals for a WTC-related health condition or a health condition medically associated with a WTC-related health condition are payable by the WTC Program Administrator (see 42 CFR 88.16). Under 42 USC § 300mm-41(b)(1), those payments made are to be reduced or recouped if the WTC Program Administrator determines that payment has been made, or can reasonably be expected to be made, under a workers' compensation law, or under other benefit plans for such treatment specified in the statute.[286]

---

[286] Pinnacle Envtl., 2016 WL 411597 (N.Y. Work. Comp. Bd. Feb. 2, 2016.)

^Same issue as the cite above it

PART II: PERTINENT SECTIONS OF THE HIMP RULES AND REGULATIONS

§20.07   HIMP Rules and Regulations § 325-6.3

(A)(2) A health insurer must serve a HIMP-1 form on the carrier, in accordance with subdivision (a) of section 325-6.15 of this Subpart, within one year of the latest date of the following:

i. the acceptance of the claim or the establishment of ANCR to the particular body part or disease in question;

ii. the date the Board notifies the health insurer of the full match pursuant to Subpart 325-5 of this Part;

iii. the date of payment for services; or

iv. the effective date of this regulation.

C) The health insurer must complete all information required on the HIMP-1 form and must serve the completed form on the carrier, together with copies of all provider bills and/or other documents which form the basis for the request for reimbursement. The provider bills and/or other documents shall include the name of the person for whom treatment was rendered, a diagnosis with applicable ICD code(s), the date(s) of treatment or hospitalization, an itemization of the services rendered and the corresponding charges with standardized billing codes, and in the case of hospital bills, the nature of the treatment for which the claimant was hospitalized. The bills or supplemental documentation must also identify the diagnosis and/or treatment codes, including CPT codes or DRG codes where applicable, utilized by the health insurer to determine the amount of payment to the provider. All requests for reimbursement served on the carrier after establishment of ANCR must contain a form C-23, C-18, C-67 or any other notice of decision issued by the Board establishing ANCR to the part of the body or for the condition for which the health insurer made payment to the provider, if such form was available to the health insurer at the time form HIMP-1 is served. The name of the claimant (or, in the case of death, the decedent) on the notice of decision must be the same as that of the person on whose behalf the health insurer made the payments for which reimbursement is being sought. All requests for reimbursement served on the carrier before establishment of ANCR must contain documentation indicating acceptance of the claim. The name of the claimant (or, in the case of death, the decedent) on such document must be the same as that of the person on whose behalf the health insurer made the payments for which reimbursement is being sought.

D) Medical records.

227

1.   A carrier, through its attorney, may request from the treating health care provider such medical records associated with the treatment paid by the health insurer and submitted for reimbursement under this Subpart that are necessary for the carrier to manage the related workers' compensation claim. The **treating health care provider shall provide such records to the carrier, within fourteen days of the request.** Failure to comply with such request may be grounds for action pursuant to section 13(d) of the Workers' Compensation Law.

2.   A carrier may issue a subpoena duces tecum to the treating health care provider in accordance with Workers' Compensation Law section 119 to compel production of medical records set forth in section 325-6.3(f)(1) of this Subpart.

3.   The health insurer and carrier shall not unreasonably refuse to modify filing deadlines to allow time for a carrier to receive medical records, where necessary for resolution of a reimbursement request, as provided in section 325-6.16 of this Subpart. Requests for medical records shall not be used by a carrier solely to delay reimbursement or arbitration of a request for reimbursement.

§20.08   HIMP Rules and Regulations § 325-6.4

1.   The following issues may be interposed by a carrier as objections to requests for reimbursement, in whole or in part, by a health insurer:

i.   The fee was in excess of the workers' compensation fee schedule or, in the case of inpatient hospital bills, in excess of the rate of payment for inpatient hospital services established pursuant to the provisions of the Public Health Law, or the proper fee schedule amount or rate of payment for inpatient hospital services cannot be determined. In any case in which this objection is interposed, the carrier must explain why the fee was in excess of the fee schedule or rate of payment or why the proper amount cannot be determined. If this is the sole objection to the request for reimbursement, the carrier must state the amount which it believes to be the proper amount and must pay the undisputed amount to the health insurer.

ii.   The bill should have been pro-rated with another physician or health provider.

iii.   The carrier cannot determine from the documentation served whether it is responsible for payment.

CHAPTER 21: MEDICARE SECOND-ARY PAYER ACT

PART I: BACKGROUND AND BASICS

§21.01   Medicare Secondary Payer Act

Medicare is a federally sponsored health care plan that is available to individuals who are 65 or over and to individuals who have received Social Security Disability Insurance (SSDI) benefits for more than two years. This includes a significant number of workers' compensation claimants. Since the mid-1980s, the Medicare Secondary Payer Act[287] has made clear that if medical expenses could be covered under either workers' compensation or Medicare, workers' compensation, and not Medicare, should pay. Workers' compensation is primary, and Medicare is secondary. The position of Medicare was further strengthened by amendments to the Act in December of 2003. Medicare is administered by the Centers for Medicare and Medicaid Services (CMS). This agency was previously known as the Health Care Finance Administration. CMS delegates some of its work, especially work dealing with the collection of overpayments, to private contractors that vary by region and state.

In the past, workers, their attorneys, employers, and even insurance companies have ignored or attempted to evade the fact that workers' compensation is primary to Medicare. There were undoubtedly some instances in which a worker would go into a hospital for treatment of a work-related problem and show a Medicare card, and the hospital would bill Medicare. No one on behalf of the employer or its insurer went out of the way to tell the hospital that the bill should have been sent to workers' compensation or to reimburse Medicare after it had paid the bill. There were also, undoubtedly, situations in which a worker and an employer agreed to settle a workers' compensation claim and the worker asked, "What about my future medical expenses?" The employer, insurer, attorney or even judge responded by saying, "Just charge them to Medicare."

Medicare expenditures represent about 25 percent of the total budget of the federal government. There is tremendous pressure to reduce Medicare expenses. On several occasions in the last few years, Medicare has, for example,

---

[287] 42 U.S.C. § 1395y(b).

arbitrarily reduced the amount it pays doctors by four percent or more. Medicare has been searching for every way it can to control its costs. In 2000 and 2001, studies by the General Accounting Office pointed out that Medicare was losing money by paying for certain services that should have been covered under workers' compensation. At about the same time (perhaps in response to the GAO), CMS began to more aggressively enforce its right to have workers' compensation insurers pay Medicare back when required.

§21.02   Lump-Sum Settlements and the Medicare Secondary Payer Act

Lump-sum payments to close claims are attractive as a speedy alternative to protracted litigation and trial. A recent interest on the part of the Federal government in the enforcement of the Medicare Secondary Payer Act requires the parties to consider Medicare's potential interest in resolving disputes in which future medical costs may become the responsibility of Medicare. This is especially important in § 32 settlements (lump-sum dismissals).

With regard to ongoing care when a worker is currently entitled to workers' compensation, the situation is fairly straightforward: Workers' compensation should pay, and Medicare should not.

The situation becomes much more complicated with regard to settlements. When a worker receives a lump sum and an employer is relieved of its liability for future benefits, in most cases, some of the lump sum is for the payment of future medical benefits. Until that amount is exhausted Medicare should not be expected to pay for medical expenses for the covered condition. When that amount is gone, Medicare should begin paying. The problems concern how we will determine how much of a settlement should be allocated for future medical expenses and how we will know when that amount has been exhausted.

§21.03   Considering Medicare's Interest

In July 2001 CMS issued a memo[288] to its regional offices. It suggests that under certain circumstances parties to workers' compensation claims should not settle those cases until after CMS has had an opportunity to review the settlement and approve the allocation to future medical expenses. The memo discussed the circumstances under which the regional offices will "pre-approve" such an allocation. It discusses pre-approval in two categories of cases:

---

[288] [All citations to the "Manual" are to the Medicare Secondary Payer (MSP) Manual (revision 34, released September 7, 2005) or specific Medicare Memorandums.]

1. Cases in which the workers' compensation claimant is currently entitled to Medicare benefits.
2. Cases in which the injured individual has a "reasonable expectation" of Medicare entitlement within 30 months of the settlement date and the settlement is over $250,000.[289]

Medicare announced that the 'threshold' for reviewing cases was to be set at $25,000. Medicare refuses to provide a pre-approval of set-aside unless the lump-sum payment to the claimant exceeds $25,000.

[1]   When Medicare's Interest Must be Considered

Medicare's interest must always be considered whenever:
(A) Medicare has paid for treatment for a disability/injury alleged in the claim petition; and/or
(B) In the closure of a workers' compensation case the petitioner is Medicare entitled and future medicals for a disability/injury maintained in the claim petition are being foreclosed.

[2]   Failure to Obtain Approval for Section 32 Settlements

An insurance company who fails to make certain that CMS approval has been obtained is on the hook for double the amount of the settlement.

---

[289] Patel 2001, Question 1.

^No idea what this is referring to

§21.04   How to Know if CMS/Medicare Review is Necessary

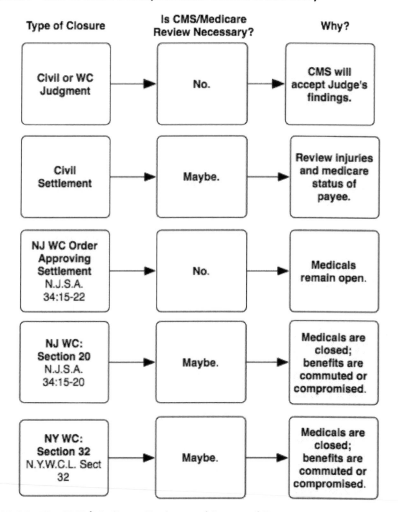

Type of Closure	Is CMS/Medicare Review Necessary?	Why?
Civil or WC Judgment	No.	CMS will accept Judge's findings.
Civil Settlement	Maybe.	Review injuries and medicare status of payee.
NJ WC Order Approving Settlement N.J.S.A. 34:15-22	No.	Medicals remain open.
NJ WC: Section 20 N.J.S.A. 34:15-20	Maybe.	Medicals are closed; benefits are commuted or compromised.
NY WC: Section 32 N.Y.W.C.L. Sect 32	Maybe.	Medicals are closed; benefits are commuted or compromised.

§21.05   The CMS/Medicare Review and Approval Process

CMS has emphasized that there are two separate and distinct tracks or processes involved in MSPS cases (the "Past Payment" track and the "Future Consideration" track). Both tracks must be considered and appropriately managed
when applicable to adequately deal with Medicare's interests.

[1]   The "Past Payment" Track

This track involves repayment (or obtaining a waiver) for any conditional payments made by Medicare on behalf of the petitioner for injuries or disabilities alleged in the claim petition pending the closure of the workers' compensation case. To initiate this "past payment" process, one should first call the "MSP Claims Investigation Project" with the file and case information. CMS will take the necessary information, provide a bar code number, and send the necessary consent form.

Once the claim is reported, a fiscal intermediary is assigned by CMS, and one will then need to deal directly with the fiscal intermediary for resolution of any past payment issues.

Medicare providers have up to eighteen (18) months to file for Medicare payment when Medicare is being utilized. Counsel should therefore advise a petitioner who is Medicare entitled not to utilize Medicare for disabilities or injuries alleged in the claim petition. Additionally, it would be prudent for petitioner's counsel to obtain information on all medical treatment petitioner received in the two years prior to the anticipated case closure to avoid Medicare paid bills after the case is closed. An appropriate Motion for Medical Treatment is the proper mechanism to resolve treatment issues arising from alleged work-connected injuries or medical conditions.

FAQ: Is repaying Medicare for conditional payments (or obtaining a waiver), always required when the petitioner has received Medicare benefits? - Yes.

[2]   The "Future Consideration" Track

According to CMS, a Workers' Compensation Medicare Set-aside Arrangement (WCMSA) is appropriate whenever future medical benefits are foreclosed in the resolution of a workers' compensation case. Specifically, a CMS/Medicare approved WCMSA is required whenever future medicals are being foreclosed and:

(A) Petitioner is Medicare entitled (regardless of the settlement amount); or

(B) Petitioner has a reasonable expectation of becoming a Medicare beneficiary within 30 months of the settlement date and the settlement totals more than $250,000.00.

Note: Since very few §32 workers' compensation settlements in New York are over $250,000, situations under this section would not be a common occurrence. A "reasonable expectation of becoming a Medicare beneficiary within 30 months of the settlement date" would likely include those situations where the petitioner: (1) has applied for Social Security Disability (SSD); (2) has been denied SSD, but is appealing or anticipates appealing the denial; (3) is 62 years and 6 month old (and thus would be eligible for Medicare within 30 months); or (4) has End Stage Renal Disease but does not yet qualify for Medicare based upon ESRD.

This track involves obtaining CMS/Medicare review and approval of any WCMSA whenever liability for future medical benefits is being foreclosed for an injury or disability maintained in the claim petition. (Situations where no monies need to be withheld are referred to as "$0.00 WCMSA" situations.)

Note: The parties to the workers' compensation case must agree on how this two-track process will be handled and how the costs involved will be allocated. Options for obtaining Medicare approval may include: Claimant's attorney doing the work; employer/carriers' attorney doing the work; or hiring specialized legal counsel or a vendor to do the work. In practice, the allocation and approval are almost always done by a vendor.

PART II: COMPLIANCE VIA SET ASIDE AND REIMBURSEMENT

§21.06   Set-Asides

After a case is settled, CMS encourages the parties to create some form of "set-aside" arrangement in which the funds for future medical expenses that would be covered under Medicare are placed in a trust or deposited in a separate account. Medicare will begin paying medical bills for the work-related condition only when the set-aside is depleted, and the funds are accounted for. If Medicare determines that no set-aside is necessary, then a waiver will be issued.

This has caused considerable difficulty for the workers' compensation system. If a case is settled for more than $250,000, it is reasonable to devote the time and resources necessary to obtain pre-approval and create some form of set-aside agreement. However, the vast majority of workers' compensation claims are settled for much smaller amounts.

Medicare continually issues guidance as to how Set-Aside proposals "could" be submitted to Medicare. These recommendations are "best practices" for dealing with Set-Aside arrangements.

§21.07   What you Should Expect your Defense Attorney to do

- Review the medical situation and prepare a defensible estimate of how much of a lump-sum settlement should be allocated to future medical expenses. This is sometimes called a "life care plan." More frequently, defense counsel simply reviews what is prepared by a Medicare Set Aside vendor.
- Obtain pre-approval from CMS of the amount of the settlement that will be allocated to future medical expenses.
- Create a Medicare set-aside arrangement. These are sometimes formal trusts, and sometimes less formal agreements, that pay or keep track of the expenditure of the portion of the settlement that is allocated to future medical expenses. Vendors have played a significant role in creating and administering these arrangements

Often, a defense attorney will merely monitor the claimant's counsel's progress or the progress of the chosen vendor in achieving the milestones discussed above.

§21.08   Conditional Payments

The status of conditional payments or payments for medical treatment by Medicare which should have been paid for by the workers' compensation insurer remain the province of Medicare in every case.

The Medicare statute does not allow Medicare to make a payment if a workers' compensation policy should be the proper primary payer. In the case of a denied claim, the workers' compensation carrier will not pay for medical treatment. In such cases Medicare pays for the medical treatment conditioned on the premise that the workers' compensation carrier must reimburse Medicare if the workers' compensation carrier has or had the responsibility to make primary payment.

If Medicare has provided treatment, then Medicare's interest must be considered. If Medicare has not paid for treatment for the disability/injury alleged in the claim petition, then the type of closure must be considered.

As Medicare will treat the judgment of a workers' compensation judge as final as to compensability and causal relationship, closure by way of Judgment with dismissal does not trigger a Medicare interest.

§21.09   Defining "Medicare Eligible"

"Medicare eligible" identifies any claimant who could receive Medicare benefits **currently**.

§21.10   Determining a "Reasonable Expectation" for Entitlement to Medicare

A workers' compensation carrier has a "reasonable expectation" that a claimant will become entitled to Medicare when (1) the claimant has already applied for SSDI, (2) the claimant was denied SSDI but may appeal that decision of denial, (3) Is currently appealing a decision of denial for SSDI, (4) has end-stage renal disease, and (5) is 62.5 years old (and therefore will be entitled to Medicare in 30 months).

This set of fact prerequisites establishing a "reasonable expectation" is not likely to be known by the employer/carrier in a pending workers' compensation case. Defense counsel should be expected affirmatively ask these questions of claimant's attorney during the settlement process.

§21.11   When a Petitioner is Considered "Medicare Entitled"

A petitioner is Medicare entitled if he or she is:

- 65 years or older (assuming sufficient work quarters); or
- On Social Security Disability (SSD) for 24 months or longer; or
- Suffering from End Stage Renal Disease (ESRD).

§21.12   Updated Forms (September 2009 and March 2013)

Medicare has issued a reference guide with a checklist including sample forms that it 'recommends' submitters utilize. According to CMS, "cases using this or similar format can generally be processed more quickly with fewer errors - resulting in faster determinations at less cost to submitters and the government." The 'recommended' submission form is divided into numbered sections to correspond to the electronic folders in which CMS scans and files documents for review. For submissions by CD-ROM, grouping and naming documents by the CMS conventions is the preferred method of delivery.[290]

CMS recommends the following numbered sections:

Section 05 - Cover Letter;
Section 10 - Consent Form;
Section 15 - Rated Ages;
Section 20 - Life Care/Treatment Plan;
Section 25 - Court/WC Board Documents;
Section 30 - WCMSA Administration Agreement;
Section 35 - Medical Records;
Section 40 - Payment Information;
Section 50 - Supplemental - Additional Information.

---

[290] http://www.cms.gov/Medicare/Coordination-of-Benefits-and-Recovery/Workers-Compensation-Medicare-Set-Aside-Arrangements/Downloads/March-29-2013-WCMSA-Reference-Guide-Version-13-copy.pdf

237

For more on these submissions, see the Workers' Compensation Set Aside Reference Guide published March, 2013.

§21.13   Avoiding MSP Complications – Our Checklist

Each carrier and self-insured must establish protocols to comply with the Medicare reporting requirements imposed by the "Medicare, Medicaid and SCHIP Extension Action of 2007" ('MMSEA'). Each carrier and self-insured is left to its own devices to come up with these protocols. We have seen many of our clients turn to vendors to review claims and communicate with Medicare.

[1]   Our Checklist:

•   Carriers must determine which claimants are Medicare beneficiaries and those non-Medicare beneficiaries who have a reasonable expectation of entitlement within 30 months of the settlement date.

•   A claims representative should determine entitlement to Social Security and Medicare as early as possible in the file's life. **Warning flags** include:

(a) Has the claimant been out of work more than six months (SSD);

(b) Has the claimant been off work for 30 months or longer (Medicare);

(c) Was it a catastrophic injury?

(d) Is the settlement value over $250,000 (including the cost of medicals paid)?

(e) Does the claimant admit to applying for SSD and getting denied or is the SSD denial on appeal?

(f) Is the claimant aged 62 and six months old or older?; and

(g) Does the claimant have end-stage renal disease?

•   Our rule of thumb is that where the parties negotiate a settlement that terminates the obligation of the self-insured or carrier to pay for future medicals, even if the claimant denies being on Social Security Disability, independent verification should be obtained. A vendor can be used to identify Social Security recipients.

•   If the claimant is on Medicare but the settlement is less than $25,000 (and forecloses the possibility of the carrier/self-insured being responsible for future medicals) CMS will not review the settlement and either 'approve' a proposed set-aside or 'waive' Medicare's set-aside requirement. In such an instance, the carrier/self-insured can prepare their own set aside agreement with the claimant. At settlement, appropriate consent and/or testimony should be obtained from the payee, making sure they understand that the payee must spend down the allocable amount with medical bills prior to submitting bills to the compensated injury to Medicare.

- One way of verifying that a payee is not on Medicare is to ask for copies of recent pay stubs. If the pay stubs are less than six months old, they cannot be a Medicare beneficiary.

§21.14   MSP Act and Third-Party Liability Cases

The MSP has been in effect since 1980, and there has been little effort to enforce its provisions in third-party liability cases. Moreover, there has been no indication from CMS that they would seek to exercise their MSP rights retroactively. Indeed, the workers' compensation example has shown that CMS is not interested in looking back to impose MSP responsibility.

Since the passage of the MMSEA, Medicare has required reporting of claims and indicated that where medical treatment continues, the plaintiff who obtained a civil recovery must use their settlement monies first for the payment of medical before they can obtain benefits from Medicare. CMS said "(w)here future medicals are a consideration in arriving at a settlement, then appropriate arrangements should be made for appropriate exhaustion of the settlement before Medicare is billed for related services."

CHAPTER 22: OSHA – DEVELOPING A COMPREHENSIVE PREVENTION STRATEGY FOR WORKPLACE INJURIES

PART I: CHAPTER OVERVIEW

§22.01   The NY Workers' Compensation Act and The OSH Act

The New York Workers' Compensation Act was devised and adopted to provide speedy assistance, both medical and compensatory, to an employee injured in the course and scope of his employment.

From a macroeconomic perspective, the New York Workers' Compensation Act was also envisioned to internalize the true costs of production, which necessarily include employee injury and illness, into the products and services delivered. In this way, the New York Workers' Compensation Act passes on the costs of employee injuries from the producers of products to consumers of products and allows the "invisible hand" of the marketplace to reduce or tolerate (as the case may be) the effects of workplace accidental injury and occupational illness.

The Occupational Safety and Health Act (OSH Act) has a similar purpose to the New York Workers' Compensation Act when viewed through our macroeconomic lens. The OSH Act is intended to pass on costs to consumers of products for safety and health-related exposures. Contrary to the macroeconomic effect of the New York Workers' Compensation Act, the OSH Act passes along costs to consumers regardless of whether or not there has been an actual employee injury related to the regulated occupational hazard.

Also, unlike the New York Workers' Compensation Act, the OSH Act seeks to reduce the incidence of workplace injuries through a penalty-only scheme. That is to say, an employer may be penalized for failure to comply with an OSHA regulation. The fine exacted is passed along to the consumer of a product, serving the macroeconomic function. However, the fine or penalty collected by OSHA is not used to compensate the injured party (as typically, there is no "injured" party). The OSH Act authorizes the use of collected fines and penalties (over $85M in 2004) to fund OSHA. In the New Jersey Workers'

Compensation System, liabilities created by workplace injuries and the costs passed along to consumers are derivative of the costs to compensate the injured or ill worker.

The issuance of fines and penalties is important to OSHA. OSHA's budget has grown from $303M in 1996 to $483M in 2006. OSHA's budget has grown 5.9% per year. At the same time, the United States economy has grown only 2.1% per year. The regulatory mechanism has grown faster than the market it regulates. An analysis of OSHA's budget for FY2007 indicates that 37.1% of all resources are used to finance inspection and enforcement activities. In 2007, OSHA expects to fund approximately 17% of its operating costs through its inspection and enforcement actions.

OSHA performs one function which is not envisioned by the New York Workers' Compensation Act: OSHA educates and trains employers and employees to recognize and abate safety and health risks. This function will be discussed below, infra.

§22.02   What the OSH Act Covers

The OSHA standards include safety and health standards. Figuring out exactly what is a 'safety' hazard and what is a 'health' hazard is somewhat unscientific. Most people would agree that a traumatic injury caused by a machine or electrical discharge is a 'safety' hazard. Chemical exposures causing burns or illness are classified as 'health' hazards. Noise is characterized as a 'health' hazard, even though a hearing loss can be traumatic in origin and result from a single noise exposure.

The following is a general overview of the OSHA requirements that apply to most general industry employers.

[1]   Hazard Communication

OSHA requires chemical manufacturers and importers to convey hazard information to downstream employers by means of labels on containers and material safety data sheets (MSDS's). In addition, all covered employers must have a hazard communication program to get this information to their employees through labels on containers, MSDS's, and training.

All employers in addition to those in manufacturing and importing are responsible for informing and training workers about the hazards in their workplaces, retaining warning labels, and making available MSDS's with hazardous chemicals.

[2]   Emergency Action Plans

An emergency action plan may be mandatory (if required by an OSHA Standard). The general rule is that if an employer is required to maintain fire extinguishers on site, then an emergency action plan is required.

[3]   Fire Safety Plans

A fire safety plan may be required if an employer handles certain chemicals and/or is otherwise required by OSHA regulations.

[4]   Exit Routes

All workplaces must have at least two exit routes for prompt evacuation. More than two exits may be required based upon the size of the workplace, number of employees, etc.

[5]   Walking/Working Surfaces

OSHA recognizes that "floors, aisles, platforms, ladders, stairways, and other walking/working surfaces are present, to some extent, in all general industry workplaces." Because these surfaces exist, and may pose a threat to employees, OSHA has issued more than a dozen standards relating to them, including guidance on housekeeping ("keep floors clean") and maintenance ("no protruding nails" on walking surfaces" and "floors should be free of holes.")

[6]   Medical and First Aid

Employers are required to provide first aid and medical supplies appropriate to the hazards of the workplace. Several directives and interpretations are available as to the requirements for specific situations. Industry and job-specific guidance have been issued regarding the medical equipment required for various work-duties. For example, stations where car batteries are being charged require an eye-wash station, ventilation equipment, etc.

[7]   Machine Guarding

Machine parts which have the potential for causing injuries, such as crushed fingers or hands, amputations, burns, or blindness must be safeguarded. When the operation of a machine or accidental contact with it can injure the operator or others in the vicinity, the hazards must be either eliminated or controlled. OSHA has distributed a Machine Guarding Checklist for use by employers which is useful in determining if safeguards are required.[291] OSHA has published a manual entitled "Concepts and Techniques in Machine Safeguarding" OSHA Publication 3067, (1992), which is available to download.[292]

---

[291] http://www.osha.gov/Publications/Mach_SafeGuard/checklist.html.
[292] http://www.osha.gov/Publications/osha3067.pdf.

[8]   Lockout/Tagout

"Lockout/Tagout" refers to the process in which electrical, mechanical, pneu-matic, or "other" machinery is 'de-energized' to prevent sudden start-up while an employee is cleaning or maintaining the machinery. The procedures require the development of systems to ensure that lockout/tagout procedures are in place to curtail injuries. OSHA has published an example of actual lockout pro-cedures as an appendix to the regulations.

[9]   Electrical Hazards

OSHA has promulgated electrical standards designed to protect employees ex-posed to dangers such as electric shock, electrocution, fires, and explosions.

[10]   Personal Protective Equipment (PPE)

OSHA requires the use of PPE to reduce employee exposure to hazards when engineering and administrative controls are not feasible or effective in reduc-ing these exposures to acceptable levels. OSHA prefers the implementation of engineering (or environmental) controls to abate hazards rather than personal protective devices issued to employees. OSHA prefers a facility undergo re-modeling or re-tooling to abate noise rather than issue personal protective hearing devices to employee and mandate their use.

[11]   Respirators

OSHA has issued standards for the use of respirators in specific industries: mar-itime, construction, and general industries. Further, OSHA has delineated the use of respirators in relation to specific chemicals, such as asbestos, benzene, and methylene chloride, among others.[293]

[12]   Noise

If employees are exposed to "excessive noise" a hearing conservation program is required to be implemented. Standards for the methods of computing noise exposures are promulgated by OSHA. A comparison of various hearing protec-tion equipment, with noise reduction ratings, is maintained by the Mine Safety and Health Administration.[294]

[13]   Confined Spaces

A workplace may be "confined" because their configurations limit the activities of any employees who must enter, work in, and exit them.[295]

---

[293] For a listing, see 29 C.F.R. 1910.1000-1910.1052.
[294] http://www.msha.gov/1999noise/hearingprotect.htm.
[295] Confined spaces are regulated at 29 C.F.R. 1910.

[14]   *Blood or Bodily Fluids*

Employers are required to maintain reporting logs and implement work con-trols to reduce needlestick injuries and other sharps-related injuries. Further, employees must consider and implement technologies to reduce occupational exposure to bloodborne pathogens. Bloodborne pathogens include: hepatitis B, hepatitis C, and human immunodeficiency virus (HIV).

[15]   *Forklifts*

Forklifts are regulated as "powered industrial trucks."

[16]   *Recordkeeping*

OSHA requires recordkeeping of workplace injuries and illnesses for certain employers. Exemption from reporting requirements is provided for employers with less than ten employees and for certain low-hazard retail and service in-dustries. All employers must report work-related deaths and any hospitaliza-tions of three or more employees. Further, all employers must exhibit the OSHA poster in a prominent location. Further, employers must provide em-ployees, their designated representatives, and OSHA with access to employee exposure and medical records. Employers generally must maintain employee exposure records for 30 years and medical records for the duration of the em-ployee's employment plus 30 years.

[17]   *And this was just a taste.*

The listed regulations (1)-(16), infra, are provided for illustrative purposes only. Over a thousand individual subpart regulations exist, covering injuries as rare as scalping injuries from farm equipment to the costumes worn by employees at Disney World.

§22.03 Those Covered by the OSH Act

In general, coverage of the act extends to all employers and their employees in the fifty states and all territories under federal government jurisdiction. The definition of employer is: any "person engaged in a business affecting com-merce who has employees but does not include the United States or any State or political subdivision of a State."

The OSH Act excludes the following from coverage:
1.   Employees of the United States and of state and political subdivisions.
1.   Self-employed persons.
2.   Family members co-operating a farm.
3.   Domestic household employees.

4. Workplaces already protected by other federal agencies.
5. Workplaces employing ten or fewer employees are partially exempted from coverage: these employers are still subject to accident investigations, worker complaint investigations, and hazard complaint requirements.

PART II: KEEPING IN COMPLIANCE WITH OSHA STANDARDS

§22.04   Identifying Workplace Hazards and Assessing Risk

Historical data provides insight into the employment accidents associated with specific industries.

[1]   Fatalities

In 2004, 236 fatal work-injuries were reported in the New York-New Jersey metropolitan area. Twenty-two of the fatalities were on-the-job suicides. Forty-five of the work-deaths were attributed to homicides. In 58 deaths workers were killed by a vehicle or while on a roadway. Forty-six deaths were caused by falls.

Most of the 2004 fatalities in the New York metropolitan area were in the construction sector (22% of all deaths). The second highest sector for worker fatality was the warehousing and trucking industry, where most of the deaths were related to fatal truck crashes. Most interesting, the retail industry reported 20 deaths in 2004 with more than half (13) being attributed to homicide.

[2]   Injuries

A total of 4.3 million injuries and illnesses were reported in private industry workplaces during 2004. Nationally, this equates to 4.8 cases per 100 full-time workers. Nearly half of all injuries reported to OSHA in 2004 were "sprains, strains, bruises, and contusions." Cuts, lacerations, and fractures, the next most common forms of injury, comprised 17% of the reported injuries.

§22.05   Self-Audit

Self-audit implies a common-sense approach to identifying and abating hazards in the workplace.

OSHA publishes an excellent checklist which is helpful in conducting a workplace audit. In September 1999 OSHA published "Hazard Adviser, Version 1.0" software package which generates a report based upon workplace-specific input that identifies common occupational and safety hazards in a particular workspace. This software can be downloaded, for free, from OSHA.[296]

---

[296] https://www.osha.gov/dts/osta/oshasoft/

§22.06   Inspection

In 2001, OSHA conducted over 30,000 inspections and proposed penalties of approximately $90M. 50% of the inspections were in the construction area, and 25% were in manufacturing.

In 2004 Federal OSHA inspectors performed nearly 40,000 inspections and found 86,708 violations. Penalties amounting to $85,192,000 were proposed. 57% of the inspections were conducted in the construction sector. 22.4% of the inspections were conducted in the manufacturing sector. 19% of the inspections were conducted in what OSHA classifies "other industries."

In 2004, nearly 58,000 state OSHA inspections took place, with $74M being proposed in penalties.

Under the OSH Act, the Secretary, through her "Compliance Safety and Health Officers" ("CSHOS") is authorized to enter workplaces to conduct safety and health inspections. Usually, an inspector focuses on safety hazards (and is therefore a "safety officer" or "safety inspector") or health hazards (and is a "industrial hygiene officer" or "health inspector"). There are far more safety inspectors than health inspectors.

OSHA inspectors, whatever the breed ("safety" or "health"), will inspect the workplace, gather up evidence of non-compliance, write up citations to be issued to their area directors, participate in informal settlement conferences, and testify for the Secretary (if the case is contested).

OSHA inspections are either (1) programmed in advance or (2) un-programmed. Un-programmed inspections are usually done in response to a complaint by a union or employee, following an accident, based upon a referral (often by competitors), or otherwise 'tickled' by a non-routine stimulus. Programmed inspections are supposedly scheduled based upon "industry hazard rankings" classification schemes and an "inspection register" maintained by local area offices of OSHA.

In 2004, 55% of the inspections were programmed. In the same year, 23% of the inspections were conducted following an accident or complaint. 21.5% of 2004 inspections were conducted in response to a referral or in 'follow-up.'

OSHA has the authority to enter premises to inspect workplaces, as provided by the OSH ACT at Sect 8(a), 29 U.S.C. Sect. 657 (A):

[T]o enter without delay and at reasonable times any factory, plant, establishment, construction site, or other area, workplace, or environment where work is performed by an employee of an employer; and

to inspect and investigate during regular working hours and at other reasonable times, and within reasonable limits and in a reasonable manner, any such place of employment and all pertinent conditions, structures, machines, apparatus, devices, equipment, and materials therein, and to question privately and such employer, owner, operator, agent, or employee.

While this grant of authority to make inspections does not mention a need for a warrant, the Supreme Court has held that the Fourth Amendment guarantees a businessperson the constitutional right to go about his business free from unreasonable official entries upon his private commercial property.

OSHA therefore cannot enter private premises for an inspection unless the employer's consent is first obtained or a warrant is issued by a court authorizes the inspection.

[1]   Voluntary (Consent to Enter Premises)

Most companies allow warrantless searches of their premises by OSHA inspectors. The reasons for this are largely socio-political: many companies feel that forcing OSHA to obtain a warrant, or even challenging the constitutionality of the warrant, will antagonize OSHA.

A consensual search may be preferable to a search authorized by a warrant. Why? Because the 'boilerplate' warrant usually presented by OSHA to the magistrate gives OSHA much more investigative power than an employer would permit during a consensual search.

[2]   Involuntary (Uninvited OSHA Inspection, Without Consent)

If an employer does not consent to the inspection, OSHA cannot enter to conduct an inspection unless a warrant is issued by the U.S. District Court authorizes the inspection. Warrants are typically obtained *ex parte*. The application for the warrant must state the reasons why the business was selected for inspection and must be sworn to under oath. To issue a warrant, the magistrate must make a finding of 'probable cause.'

Probable cause for a warrant to inspect can come in the form of specific evidence, such as an employee complaint that a specific violation is alleged to exist. Specific evidence can come in many forms: including newspaper articles, referral, or follow-up.

In the alternative, OSHA can show probable cause by demonstrating to the magistrate that the criteria used to select the employer was based upon a 'neutral administrative selection plan.'

Warrants to perform an involuntary inspection typically contain limitations as to the time, scope, and manner of the inspection.

[3]   Why Object to an Inspection?

To buy time to address and immediate violations that require 'sprucing up' or to assemble the inspection team.

[4]   Downsides to Challenging a Warrant for Inspection

The Secretary has brought contempt proceedings, civil and criminal, against employers for refusing warrant inspections. If an employer is found to be in contempt of court, fines and costs may be assessed against the employer.

[5]   What to do in the Event of an Inspection

Inspections follow the following format: (1) opening conference, (2) inspection, and (3) closing conference. During the opening conference, the OSHA inspector (safety or health) will provide the reason for the inspection and the scope of the inquiry. The compliance officer will request to review all documentation, including the OSHA 300 (reportable events) log. If the documentation and log are up-to-date, OSHA will likely choose not to investigate further. The documentation typically reviewed at this opening conference includes the hazard communication plan, MSDS sheets, OSHA 300 log, emergency action plane, and safety and health program.

If an inspection takes place, an employer-representative (or assembled compliance team, including legal counsel) should accompany the OSHA inspector at all times. An employer should avoid any admission of guilt or knowing violation of regulations. The compliance officer cannot order employees to do anything, but may ask questions of employees. If the compliance officer takes photographs, make sure an employer representative takes a photograph of the same inspected item.

During the closing conference the inspector will disclose all unsafe or unhealthful conditions observed. The compliance officer should not specify citations or penalties to be issued. Citations and penalties are the province of the OSHA area director. New York is in Area 2, with offices in Albany, Queens, Buffalo, Long Island, Manhattan, Syracuse, and Tarrytown. New Jersey is also in Area 2, with offices in Hasbrouck Heights, Avenel, Parsippany, and Marlton.

CHAPTER 23: HIPAA

PART I: BACKGROUND

§23.01 Background

The Health Insurance Portability and Accountability Act (HIPAA) was created by Congress in 1996. Title I of HIPAA protects health insurance coverage for workers and their families when they change or lose their jobs. Title II of HIPAA, known as the Administrative Simplification (AS) provisions, requires the establishment of national standards for electronic health care transactions and national identifiers for providers, health insurance plans, and employers. It helps people keep their information private.

In a nutshell: The Privacy Rule defines and limits the circumstances in which an individual's protected heath information may be used or disclosed by covered entities. A covered entity may not use or disclose protected health information, except either: (1) as the Privacy Rule permits or requires; or (2) as the individual who is the subject of the information (or the individual's personal representative) authorizes in writing. We will talk about "required disclosures."

The Administration Simplification provisions also address the security and privacy of health data. The standards are meant to improve the efficiency and effectiveness of the nation's health care system by encouraging the widespread use of electronic data interchange in the U.S. health care system. In a nutshell, it hasn't worked as advertised or created the 'intended' health system.

§23.02 A (Very) Brief Look at Title I: Portability and Look Back

Title I of HIPAA regulates the availability of group health plans and certain individual health insurance policies. It amended the Public Health Service Act and the Internal Revenue Code. Title I limits restrictions that a group health *plan can place on benefits for preexisting conditions.*

Group health plans may refuse to provide benefits relating to preexisting conditions for a period of 12 months after enrollment in the plan (or 18 months in the case of late enrollment.) Individuals may reduce this exclusion period if they had group health plan coverage or health insurance prior to enrolling in the plan. Title I allows individuals to reduce the exclusion period by the amount of time that they had "creditable coverage" prior to enrolling in the plan and after any "significant breaks" in coverage. "Creditable coverage" is defined quite broadly and includes nearly all group and individual health plans, Medicare, and Medicaid. A "significant break" in coverage is defined as any 63-day period without any creditable coverage.

Some health care plans are exempted from Title I requirements, such as long-term health plans and limited-scope plans such as dental or vision plans that are offered separately from the general health plan. However, if such benefits are part of the general health plan, then HIPAA still applies to such benefits. For example, if the new plan offers dental benefits, then it must count creditable continuous coverage under the old health plan towards any of its exclusion periods for dental benefits.

However, an alternative method of calculating creditable continuous coverage is available to the health plan under Title I. That is, five categories of health coverage can be considered separately, including dental and vision coverage. Anything not under those five categories must use the general calculation (*e.g.*, the beneficiary may be counted with 18 months of general coverage, but only 6 months of dental coverage, because the beneficiary did not have a general health plan that covered dental until 6 months prior to the application date). Unfortunately, since limited-coverage plans are exempt from HIPAA requirements, the odd case exists in which the applicant to a general group health plan cannot obtain certificates of creditable continuous coverage for independent limited-scope plans such as dental to apply towards exclusion periods of the new plan that does include those coverages.

Hidden exclusion periods are not valid under Title I (e.g., "The accident, to be covered, must have occurred while the beneficiary was covered under this exact same health insurance contract.") Such clauses must not be acted upon by the health plan and must be re-written so that they comply with HIPAA.

For example, suppose someone enrolls in a group health plan on January 1, 2006. This person had previously been insured from January 1, 2004 until February 1, 2005 and from August 1, 2005 until December 31, 2005. To determine how much coverage can be credited against the exclusion period in the new plan, start at the enrollment date and count backwards until you reach a significant break in coverage. So, the five months of coverage between August 1, 2005 and December 31, 2005 clearly counts against the exclusion period. But the period without insurance between February 1, 2005 and August 1, 2005 is greater than 63 days. Thus, this is a significant break in coverage, and any coverage prior to it cannot be deducted from the exclusion period. So, this person could deduct five months from his or her exclusion period, reducing the exclusion period to seven months. Hence, Title I requires that any preexisting condition begin to be covered on August 1, 2006.

Confused yet?

In short, all of this legal verbiage (see above) means that most employees, moving from job to job (with less than six months of "in-between" time) must be covered for "pre-existing conditions" at their new job if the new place of employment offers a similar health care plan. Under HIPAA, a plan can look back only six months for a condition that was present before the start of coverage in a group health plan. (Note: for 'late enrollees' - people who turn down the health coverage at first but then take it later - the "look back period" is 18 months).

Specifically, the law says that a preexisting condition exclusion can be imposed on a condition only if medical advice, diagnosis, care, or treatment was recommended or received during the six months prior to your enrollment date in the plan. As an example, you may have had arthritis for many years before you came to your current job. If you did not have medical advice, diagnosis, care, or treatment – recommended or received – in the six months before you enrolled in the plan, then the prior condition cannot be subject to a preexisting condition exclusion. If you did receive medical advice, diagnosis, care, or treatment within the past six months, then the plan may impose a preexisting condition exclusion for that condition (arthritis). In addition, HIPAA specifically prohibits plans from applying a preexisting condition exclusion to pregnancy, genetic information, and certain children.

If you have a preexisting condition that can be excluded from your plan coverage, then there is a limit to the preexisting condition exclusion period that can be applied. HIPAA limits the preexisting condition exclusion period for most people to 12 months (18 months if you enroll late), although some plans may have a shorter time period or none at all. In addition, some people with a history of prior health coverage will be able to reduce the exclusion period even further using "creditable coverage." Remember, a pre-existing condition exclusion relates only to benefits for your (and your family's) preexisting conditions. If you enroll, you will receive coverage for the plan's other benefits during that time.

Although HIPAA adds protections and makes it easier to switch jobs without fear of losing health coverage for a preexisting condition, the law has limitations. For example, HIPAA: (A) Does not require that employers offer health coverage; (B) Does not guarantee that any conditions you now have (or have had in the past) are covered by your new employer's health plan; and (C) Does not prohibit an employer from imposing a preexisting condition exclusion period if you have been treated for a condition during the past 6 months.

§23.03   "The Privacy Rule"

Title II of HIPAA defines numerous offenses relating to health care and sets of civil and criminal penalties for them. It also creates several programs to control fraud and abuse within the health care system. However, the most significant provisions of Title II are its 'Administrative Simplification' rules. Title II requires the Department of Health and Human Services (HHS) to draft rules aimed at increasing the efficiency of the health care system by creating standards for the use and dissemination of health care information.

These rules apply to "covered entities" as defined by HIPAA and the HHS. Covered entities include health plans, health care clearinghouses, such as billing services and community health information systems, and health care providers that transmit health care data in a way that is regulated by HIPAA.

Per the requirements of Title II, the HHS has promulgated five rules regarding Administrative Simplification: The Privacy Rule, the Transactions and Code Sets Rule, the Security Rule, the Unique Identifiers Rule, and the Enforcement Rule. This presentation focuses on the application of the Privacy Rule.

Is it working? No, of course it isn't.

The HIPAA Privacy Rule in a nutshell is: **Whenever there is doubt, there is no doubt about what to do: err on the side of caution. Don't disclose PHI.** Act as if you are a covered entity. Then, call your attorney.

[1]   Effects on Research

HIPAA restrictions have affected researchers' ability to perform retrospective, chart-based research as well as their ability to prospectively evaluate patients by contacting them for follow-up. A study from the University of Michigan demonstrated that implementation of the HIPAA Privacy rule resulted in a drop from 96% to 34% in the proportion of follow-up surveys completed by study patients being followed after a heart attack. Another study, detailing the effects of HIPAA on recruitment for a study on cancer prevention, demonstrated that HIPAA-mandated changes led to a 73% decrease in patient accrual, a tripling of time spent recruiting patients, and a tripling of mean recruitment costs.

In addition, informed consent forms for research studies now are required to include extensive detail on how the participant's protected health information will be kept private. While such information is important, the addition of a lengthy, legalistic section on privacy may make these already complex documents even less user-friendly for patients who are asked to read and sign them.

These data suggest that the HIPAA privacy rule, as currently implemented, may be having negative impacts on the cost and quality of medical research. Dr. Kim Eagle, professor of internal medicine at the University of Michigan, was quoted in the Annals article as saying, "Privacy is important, but research is also important for improving care. We hope that we will figure this out and do it right."

[2]   Effects on Clinical Care

The complexity of HIPAA, combined with potentially stiff penalties for violators, can lead physicians and medical centers to withhold information from those who may have a right to it. A review of the implementation of the HIPAA Privacy Rule by the U.S. Government Accountability Office found that health care providers were "uncertain about their [legal] privacy responsibilities and often responded with an overly guarded approach to disclosing information...than necessary to ensure compliance with the Privacy rule." This uncertainty continues, as evidenced by a New York Times article in July 2007. "Keeping Patients' Details Private, Even From Kin," New York Times, July 3, 2007.

[3]   Effects on Privacy

Unlike the effects describe above, it is safe to say that the HIPAA law and the Privacy Rule has had an effect on increasing the privacy of our health information. Notable "celebrity" examples aside (Octomom, cough cough), the privacy rule is working as intended.

[4]   Cost of Implementation

In the period immediately prior to the enactment of the HIPAA Privacy and Security Acts, medical centers and medical practices were charged with getting "into compliance." With an early emphasis on the potentially severe penalties associated with violation, many practices and centers turned to private, for-profit "HIPAA consultants" who were intimately familiar with the details of the legislation and offered their services to ensure that physicians and medical centers were fully "in compliance." In addition to the costs of developing and revamping systems and practices, the increase in paperwork and staff time necessary to meet the legal requirements of HIPAA may impact the finances of medical centers and practices at a time when insurance company and Medicare reimbursement are also declining.

The fact that attorneys are still explaining the implementation of the rules to covered entities 13 years after the passing of this series of regulations is proof that the HIPAA rules have over-complicated an already complex interaction between patients, covered entities, and other parties with an interest in the medical care an individual has received.

[5]   Dates & Deadlines

The Privacy Rule took effect on April 14, 2003, with a one-year extension for certain "small plans." The HIPAA Privacy Rule regulates the use and disclosure of certain information held by "covered entities" (generally, health care clearinghouses, employer sponsored health plans, health insurers, and medical service providers that engage in certain transactions.) It establishes regulations for the use and disclosure of Protected Health Information (PHI). PHI is any information held by a covered entity which concerns health status, provision of health care, or payment for health care that can be linked to an individual. This is interpreted rather broadly and includes any part of an individual's medical record or payment history.

Covered entities must disclose PHI to the individual within 30 days upon request. They also must disclose PHI when required to do so by law, such as reporting suspected child abuse to state child welfare agencies.

A covered entity may disclose PHI to facilitate treatment, payment, or health care operations or if the covered entity has obtained authorization from the individual. However, when a covered entity discloses any PHI, it must make a reasonable effort to disclose only the minimum necessary information required to achieve its purpose.

The Privacy Rule gives individuals the right to request that a covered entity correct any inaccurate PHI. It also requires covered entities to take reasonable steps to ensure the confidentiality of communications with individuals. For example, an individual can ask to be called at his or her work number, instead of home or cell phone number.

[6]   Notification & Enforcement

The Privacy Rule requires covered entities to notify individuals of uses of their PHI. Covered entities must also keep track of disclosures of PHI and document privacy policies and procedures. They must appoint a Privacy Official and a contact person responsible for receiving complaints and train all members of their workforce in procedures regarding PHI.

An individual who believes that the Privacy Rule is not being upheld can file a complaint with the Department of Health and Human Services through the Office for Civil Rights (OCR).

§23.04   Covered Entities

The Privacy Rule, as well as all the Administrative Simplification rules, apply to health plans, health care clearinghouses, and to any health care provider who transmits health information in electronic form in connection with transactions for which the Secretary of HHS has adopted standards under HIPAA (the "covered entities").

[1]   Health Plans

Individual and group plans that provide or pay the cost of medical care are covered entities. Health plans include health, dental, vision, and prescription drug insurers, health maintenance organizations ("HMOs"), Medicare, Medicaid, Medicare+Choice and Medicare supplement insurers, and long-term care insurers (excluding nursing home fixed-indemnity policies). Health plans also include employer-sponsored group health plans, government and church-sponsored health plans, and multi-employer health plans.

There are exceptions—a group health plan with less than 50 participants that is administered solely by the employer that established and maintains the plan is not a covered entity. Two types of government-funded programs are not health plans: (1) those whose principal purpose is not providing or paying the cost of health care, such as the food stamps program; and (2) those programs whose principal activity is directly providing health care, such as a community health center, or the making of grants to fund the direct provision of health care. Certain types of insurance entities are also not health plans, including entities providing only workers' compensation, automobile insurance, and property and casualty insurance.

[2]   Health Care Providers

Every health care provider who electronically transmits health information in connection with certain transactions, is a covered entity. These transactions include claims, benefit eligibility inquiries, referral authorization requests, or other transactions for which HHS has established standards under the HIPAA Transactions Rule. Using electronic technology, such as email, does not mean a health care provider is a covered entity; the transmission must be in connection with a standard transaction. The Privacy Rule covers a health care provider whether it electronically transmits these transactions directly or uses a billing service or other third party to do so on its behalf. Health care providers include all "providers of services" (e.g., institutional providers such as hospitals) and "providers of medical or health services" (e.g., non-institutional providers such as physicians, dentists and other practitioners) as defined by Medicare, and any other person or organization that furnishes, bills, or is paid for health care.

[3]   Health Care Clearinghouses

Health care clearinghouses are entities that process nonstandard information they receive from another entity into a standard (i.e., standard format or data content), or vice versa. In most instances, health care clearinghouses will receive individually identifiable health information only when they are providing these processing services to a health plan or health care provider as a business associate. In such instances, only certain provisions of the Privacy Rule are applicable to the health care clearinghouse's uses and disclosures of protected health information. Health care clearinghouses include billing services, repricing companies, community health management information systems, and value-added networks and switches if these entities perform clearinghouse functions.

[4]   Business Associates

In general, a business associate is a person or organization, other than a member of a covered entity's workforce, that performs certain functions or activities on behalf of, or provides certain services to, a covered entity that involves the use or disclosure of individually identifiable health information. Business associate functions or activities on behalf of a covered entity include claims processing, data analysis, utilization review, and billing. Business associate services to a covered entity are limited to legal, actuarial, accounting, consulting, data aggregation, management, administrative, accreditation, or financial services. However, persons or organizations are not considered business associates if their functions or services do not involve the use or disclosure of protected health information, and where any access to protected health information by such persons would be incidental, if at all. A covered entity can be the business associate of another covered entity.

PART II: WHEN HIPAA APPLIES

§23.05   What Information is Covered?

The Privacy Rule protects all "individually identifiable health information" held or transmitted by a covered entity or its business associate, in any form or media, whether electronic, paper, or oral. The Privacy Rule calls this information "protected health information (PHI)."

"Individually identifiable health information" is information, including demographic data, that relates to:

- the individual's past, present, or future physical or mental health or condition,

- the provision of health care to the individual, or

- the past, present, or future payment for the provision of health care to the individual, and that identifies the individual or for which there is a reasonable basis to believe can be used to identify the individual. Individually identifiable health information includes many common identifiers (e.g., name, address, birth date, Social Security Number).

- The Privacy Rule excludes from protected health information employment records that a covered entity maintains in its capacity as an employer and education and certain other records subject to, or defined in, the Family Educational Rights and Privacy Act, 20 U.S.C. §1232g.

[1]   When you CAN Disclose PHI

I.   When you have an authorization (written release) from the patient. What constitutes a 'valid authorization' for release of records?

    A.   A covered entity must obtain the individual's written authorization for any use or disclosure of protected health information that is not for treatment, payment or health care operations or otherwise permitted or required by the Privacy Rule. [Note: as we will discuss later, according to the law, a workers' comp carrier or attorney does not need to get a release to get PHI on a claimant. The practice, of course, is far different.]

261

B.   A covered entity may not condition treatment, payment, enrollment, or benefits eligibility on an individual granting an authorization, except in limited circumstances.

C.   An authorization must be written in specific terms. It may allow use
and disclosure of protected health information by the covered entity seeking the authorization, or by a third party. Examples of disclosures that would require an individual's authorization include
disclosures to a life insurer for coverage purposes, disclosures to an
employer of the results of a pre-employment physical or lab test, or
disclosures to a pharmaceutical firm for their own marketing purposes.

D.   All authorizations must be in plain language and contain specific information regarding the information to be disclosed or used, the
person(s) disclosing and receiving the information, expiration, right
to revoke in writing, and other data. The Privacy Rule contains tran-
sition provisions applicable to authorizations and other express legal permissions obtained prior to April 14, 2003

II.   To the individual (unless required for access or accounting of disclosures);

III.   To further treatment, payment, and health care operations;

IV.   When the patient has had an opportunity to agree or object (even informally . . .);

V.   For an otherwise permitted use and disclosure (this is one we care
about);

VI.   For Public Interest and Benefit Activities (specifically: in response to a
subpoena or by other Order of Court, or as authorized by statute or
regulation); or

VII.   As part of a Limited Data Set for the purposes of research, public
health or health care operations.

[2]   When you MUST Disclose PHI

A covered entity <u>must</u> disclose protected health information (without the conditions described above being met) in only two situations:

- to individuals (or their personal representatives) specifically when they request access to, or an accounting of disclosures of, their protected health information; and

- to HHS when it is undertaking a compliance investigation or review or enforcement action.

§23.06   De-Identified Health Information

There are no restrictions on the use or disclosure of de-identified health information. De-identified health information neither identifies nor provides a reasonable basis to identify an individual. There are two ways to de-identify information; either: 1) a formal determination by a qualified statistician; or 2) the removal of specified identifiers of the individual and of the individual's relatives, household members, and employers is required, and is adequate only if the covered entity has no actual knowledge that the remaining information could be used to identify the individual.

§23.07   Rules for Carriers

Covered entities must adopt written PHI privacy procedures; designate a privacy officer; require their business associates to sign agreements respecting the confidentiality of PHI; train all of their employees in privacy rule requirements; give patients written notice of the covered entities' privacy practices and access to their medical records; a chance to request modifications to the records; a chance to request restrictions on the use or disclosure of their information; a chance to request an accounting of any use to which the PHI has been put; and a chance to request alternative methods of communicating information. They must also establish a process for patients to use in filing complaints and for dealing with complaints. Finally, they must take any measures necessary to see that PHI is not used for making employment or benefits decisions, marketing, or fundraising.

§23.08   The "Enforcement Rule"

On February 16, 2006, HHS issued the Final Rule regarding HIPAA enforcement. It became effective on March 16, 2006. The Enforcement Rule sets civil money penalties for violating HIPAA rules and establishes procedures for investigations and hearings for HIPAA violations.

Consistent with the principles for achieving compliance provided in the Rule, HHS will seek the cooperation of covered entities and may provide technical assistance to help them comply voluntarily with the Rule. The Rule provides processes for persons to file complaints with HHS, describes the responsibilities of covered entities to provide records and compliance reports and to cooperate with, and permit access to information for, investigations and compliance reviews.

The deterrent effects seem to be negligible with few (if any) prosecutions for violations.

[1]   Civil Money Penalties

HHS may impose civil money penalties on a covered entity of $100 per failure to comply with a Privacy Rule requirement. That penalty may not exceed $25,000 per year for multiple violations of the identical Privacy Rule requirement in a calendar year. HHS may not impose a civil money penalty under specific circumstances, such as when a violation is due to reasonable cause and did not involve willful neglect and the covered entity corrected the violation within 30 days of when it knew or should have known of the violation.

[2]   Criminal Penalties

A person who knowingly obtains or discloses individually identifiable health information in violation of HIPAA faces a fine of $50,000 and up to one-year imprisonment. The criminal penalties increase to $100,000 and up to five years imprisonment if the wrongful conduct involves false pretenses, and to $250,000 and up to ten years imprisonment if the wrongful conduct involves the intent to sell, transfer, or use individually identifiable health information for commercial advantage, personal gain, or malicious harm. Criminal sanctions will be enforced by the Department of Justice.

PART III: THE PRIVACY RULE AND WORKERS' COM-PENSATION

§23.09   Applying the Privacy Rule to Workers' Compensation Claims

What should be considered as PHI? This may surprise you, but the 'Employers' First of Accident or Injury' (FROI-101, or L-101) is considered PHI! Here are some examples of PHI that we are likely to see crossing our desks in relation to a claim:

- Health care claims or health care encounter information, such as documentation of doctor's visits and notes made by physicians and other provider staff;

- Health care payment and remittance advice;

- Coordination of health care benefits;

- Health care claim status - your notes as adjuster;

- Enrollment and disenrollment in a health plan;

- Eligibility for a health plan;

- Health plan premium payments;

- Referral certifications and authorization;

- First report of injury;

- Health claims attachments.

There is no problem with employers, workers' compensation insurance carriers, physicians, and other participants in the workers' compensation system sharing protected health information with each other in connection with workers' compensation claims and appeals. HIPAA specifically allows three exemptions for workers' compensation-related matters:

I. If the disclosure is "[a]s authorized and to the extent necessary to comply with laws relating to workers' compensation or similar programs established by law that provide benefits for work-related injuries or illness without regard to fault."[297]

II. If the disclosure is required by state or other law, in which case the disclosure is limited to whatever the law requires.[298]

III. If the disclosure is for obtaining payment for any health care provided to an injured or ill employee.[299]

So, the employee's written authorization is not necessary for disclosure if one of those exceptions applies, and the employee also would not be able to require the covered entity to withhold the information under 45 CFR § 164.522(a). The bottom line is that if any health-related information is being exchanged in conjunction with a workers' compensation claim or appeal, the HIPAA privacy rule will not stand in the way.

A little more nuanced is the distinction for medical records and other PHI related to prior claims or conditions of the claimant. A covered entity may disclose protected health information regarding previous conditions where the individual's written authorization has been obtained, consistent with the Privacy Rule's requirements at 45 CFR § 164.508. A covered entity would be permitted to make the above disclosure if the individual signed an authorization. For prior records, have your attorney subpoena them with an executed HIPAA-compliant release attached.

§23.10   Other Types of Claims (Non-Workers' Compensation)

Even easier: Apply the general rules on privacy! There is no specific exemption for tort or other civil litigation. The exchange of PHI is subject to state laws and regulations, so standard discovery procedures (with HIPAA-compliant releases) should be observed.

§23.11   For Carriers and their "Business Associates"

---

[297] 45 C.F.R. § 164.512(l).

[298] 45 C.F.R. § 164.512(a).

[299] 45 C.F.R. § 164.502(a)(1)(ii).

Just as covered entities' must implement procedures to make sure they comply with the securitization and privacy rules, their contracts with outside vendors/partners must include a statement that the vender will abide by the rules.

So, carriers (as covered entities or business associates) and their TPAs should adopt written PHI privacy procedures; designate a privacy officer; require their business associates to sign agreements respecting the confidentiality of PHI; train all of their employees in privacy rule requirements; give patients written notice of the covered entities' privacy practices and access to their medical records; a chance to request modifications to the records; a chance to request restrictions on the use or disclosure of their information; a chance to request an accounting of any use to which the PHI has been put; and a chance to request alternative methods of communicating information. They must also establish a process for patients to use in filing complaints and for dealing with complaints. Finally, they must take any measures necessary to see that PHI is not used for making employment or benefits decisions, marketing, or fundraising.

CHAPTER 24: OWNER CONTROLLED INSURANCE POLICIES (OCIP) AND CONTRACTOR CONTROLLED INSUR-ANCE POLICIES (CCIP)

PART I: BACKGROUND

§24.01 Background

In defending workers' compensation claims arising out of an Owner Controlled Insurance Policy (OCIP) or a Contractor Controlled Insurance Policy (CCIP), it is important to understand how these policies work.

OCIP/CCIPs are becoming more and more popular in the construction industry today, especially in large-scale, high-risk projects. OCIP/CCIPs are commonly referred to as "wrap up" policies, a term that is often thrown around in workers' compensation courts when coverage is being denied. An OCIP is one where the policy is sponsored by the owner of the project, and a CCIP is one where the policy is generally sponsored by the construction manager or general contractor. Both types of policies provide coverage for the entire project, that is, all enrolled contractors, subcontractors and sub-subcontractors.

An OCIP is usually dedicated to one particular project (though there are times when an owner has an OCIP for multiple projects), while a construction manager or general contractor can enroll several projects under its CCIP. The determination of whether there will be an OCIP or a CCIP on a project depends on the parties involved, and who is interested in sponsoring the policy. Some factors that are taken into consideration are the cost of the project, the owner's and the construction manager's or general contractor's relationship with its carrier, and who would rather bear the administration responsibilities.

§24.02 Why Employers Choose an OCIP/CCIP

OCIP/CCIPs are beneficial to all parties involved, though some benefit more than others. Some of the major benefits of an OCIP/CCIP are: reduction in insurance costs, reduction in litigation (elimination of cross-litigation), prevention of gaps in coverage, efficient claims handling, and reduced risk through a uniform site safety program.

While an OCIP/CCIP covers an "entire" project, there will be several parties working on the project who will not be covered under the policy. For example, those working less than a certain number of hours, those with a contract value under a certain amount, hazardous materials contractors, architects and vendors. Therefore, an OCIP/CCIP requires that all eligible parties enroll in the program. However, enrollment is not auto-matic, and requires proactive steps by both the eligible party and the sponsor of the OCIP/CCIP. If a party is not eligible, it must have its own insurance policy, and cannot claim coverage under the OCIP/CCIP.

§24.03   Defending OCIP/CCIP Workers' Compensation Claims

Since the overarching premise of an OCIP/CCIP is that it covers the "entire" project, it is not uncommon for one to assume that every claim from that project is a covered claim. This is simply not the case. Coverage may oftentimes be contested under an OCIP/CCIP. As noted above, some parties are ineligible for coverage under an OCIP/CCIP. In addi-tion, the accident may have occurred before or after the policy period. Or, the accident may have arisen from an activity that is outside the scope of the policy. In these scenar-ios, the claim would be denied based on lack of coverage.

In ensuring that the overarching issue of coverage is properly addressed in defending an OCIP/CCIP workers' compensation claim, the following should be available to the defense attorneys:

- The certificate of coverage (proof of coverage) showing that the employer (contractor, subcontractor or sub-subcontractor) is covered under the policy
- The policy manual showing all of the details of the policy
- Any project completion documentation, if coverage is being contested on the basis that insured's job on the project had ended prior to the alleged accident;
- The parameters of the project site that is covered by the policy;
- The scope of work covered under the policy;
- The date, location and exact activity being carried out at the time of the alleged accident;
- The claims handling process, to ensure that all information is obtained through the proper channels, and in a timely manner

Ensuring that the attorneys have all of the above available to them from the inception of a claim will allow for quick closure of claims that are not covered by the OCIP/CCIP, thereby reducing litigation costs for the carrier.

APPENDIX I: GLOSSARY OF TERMS

Abey (a Case)
(WCB Claims) To assign to a claim a future date at which time the claim will be re-examined, to allow time for receipt of information needed to proceed. In the Claims Information System (CIS), claims are abeyed automatically at certain stages of processing.

Accident, Notice and Causal Relationship (ANCR)
(WCB) - Minimal conditions that must be met before financial responsibility can be assigned to a claim for workers' compensation. Specifically, it must be established that (a) a work-related accident covered by the Workers' Compensation Law has occurred; (b) following the accident, the Claimant has notified her/his employer within the time limit required by the Workers' Compensation Law; and (c) a causal relationship exists between the accident and the resulting injury or disability.

Adjourn (a Hearing)
(WCB) - To put off or suspend until a future time, without issuing a decision.

Aggregate Trust Fund
(WCB) - A trust fund established under Section 27 of the Workers' Compensation Law to assure the payment of workers' compensation in claims involving death, permanent total disability, and the loss of major members. In the case types above, a private carrier is required and, under certain circumstances, a self-insured employer is permitted to pay the actuarial value of a claimant's future compensation payments into the fund. Upon such payment, the Carrier and the Self-Insured Employer are discharged from future liability to the Claimant for compensation or death benefits.

Appeal
(WCB) - A legal action taken by one of the parties in the Appellate Division, Third Department, to reverse or amend a decision or direction made by a Board Panel or the Chair of the Workers' Compensation Board.

Apportionment
(WCB) - A proportionate division of all or part of the benefit costs in a case between two or more injury claims for the same claimant, based on an evaluation of the relative contribution that the injuries have made to the claimant's permanent disability.

Arising Out of and In the Course of Employment (ACOE)
(WCB) - Two necessary conditions that must be met to establish a work-connected accidental injury. An injury that "arises out of" is one that results from a hazard of the employment, while an injury "in the course of employment" is one that occurred at a time, place, and under circumstances related to the employment.

Assembled Case
A case which has the minimum required information of: claimant name and address, employer name and address, and an indication of a work-related injury or illness.

Average Weekly Wage (AWW)
(WCB) - Wage used to calculate total disability benefit rates for most claimants defined as 1/52nd of the Injured Worker's average annual earnings (200-300 times average daily wage, depending on work schedule), based on the prior year's payroll data. If the Injured Worker did not work a substantial portion of the immediately preceding year, the average wage of a comparably employed worker is used in the Board's calculations.

C-240
A WCB form titled "Employer's Statement of Wage Earnings (Preceding the Date of Accident)" which includes (in addition to case identification information) a summary of gross weekly earnings for the 52 weeks immediately preceding the date of accident for either the injured Employee or, if the Employee did not work a full year prior to the accident, a worker in the same class as the injured Employee. The C-240 form often is used by the Board in establishing the Claimant's average weekly wage.

C-3
A WCB form titled "Employee Claim" that should be completed by the injured Worker and submitted to the Board within two years of the accident, or within two years after employee knew or should have known that injury or illness was related to employment.

C-4
A WCB form titled "Doctor's Initial Report" that requests information from the physician about the claimant's initial visit/rendering of treatment. The form must be filed by the Doctor within two days of initial treatment.

C-4.2
A WCB form titled "Doctor's Progress Report" that requests information from the physician about follow-up visits and continuing services provided to the claimant. Following the filing of Form C-4, Doctor's Initial Report, this form should be filed at 45 day intervals during continued treatment, unless change in condition necessitates additional reporting.

C-4.3
A WCB form titled "Doctor's Report of MMI/Permanent Impairment" that requests information from the physician when a patient/claimant has reached Maximum Medical Improvement and to render an opinion on permanent impairment, if any.

C-4AUTH
A WCB form titled "Attending Doctor's Request for Authorization" used to confirm a telephone request for written authorization for special service(s) costing over $1,000 in a non-emergency situation.

C-669 (obsolete form - but still referred to often)
A form that was previously utilized by Claim Administrators to indicate they were accepting a claim. The form included: (a) information identifying the claim, injured person, employer and carrier; (b) a brief diagnosis of the injury and town/county/state where injury occurred; (c) a summary of payment start dates and benefit rate, including the basis for computing the latter; and (d) dates for start of disability, first knowledge of injury, receipt of a First Report of Injury from the Employer, mailing of first payment, and payee if different from the injured person. Effective 5/23/14, form C-669 is no longer an acceptable filing and the Claim Administrator must file the appropriate FROI/SROI.

C-7 (obsolete form - superseded by electronic denials, but one we still serve on claimants)
A form that was previously utilized by Claim Administrators to controvert (deny) a claim. The form included (a) information identifying the claim, person (allegedly) injured, employer; and carrier; (b) diagnosis of alleged injury and town/county/state where alleged injury occurred; (c) reasons why right to compensation is controverted; (d) dates for start of alleged disability, employer/carrier first knowledge of injury, receipt of a First Report of Injury from the Employer; and (e) statement concerning whether notification has been given to the disability benefits insurance Carrier, and date of notification. Effective 5/23/14, form C-7 is no longer an acceptable filing and the Claim Administrator must file the appropriate FROI/SROI.

C-8/8.6 (Obsolete Form)
A form that was previously utilized by Claim Administrators to show payments on a claim. The form included: (a) information identifying the claim, injured Person, Employer and Carrier; (b) a summary of total disability benefits, partial disability benefits and disfigurement awards paid; (c) a summary of the Claimant's return-to-work and earnings status; and (d) if appropriate, an explanation of why disability benefits had not been paid in full. Depending on circumstances cited by the Carrier and the Claimant's response, the filing of a C-8/8.6 may or may not have triggered an immediate hearing. Effective 5/23/14, form C-8/8.6 is no longer an acceptable filing and the Claim Administrator must file the appropriate SROI.

C-8.1

A WCB form titled "Notice of Treatment Issue/Disputed Bill" submitted by an Insurance Carrier/Board approved self-insurer within 5 days after terminating medical care (Part A) or refusing authorization or objecting to payment of a bill within 45 days of submission of bill for treatment provided (Part B).

C-8.4

A WCB form titled "Notice to Health Care Provider and Injured Worker of a Carrier's Refusal to Pay All (or a Portion of) a Medical Bill Due to Valuation Objection(s)" submitted by an Insurance Carrier/Self-Insured Employer within 45 days after a bill is submitted. This form was designed specifically to provide carriers with a useful format for the notification of valuation objections. The use of this form is not required but is encouraged.

Carrier

Insurance company that issues policies (for Workers' Compensation or Disability Benefits).

Carrier Code

The ten-character code that identifies a specific insurance carrier. W is always the first character in the code for a carrier of Workers' Compensation policies. The codes for carriers of Disability Benefits insurance always begins with the letter B. Carrier codes are issued by the Finance Office of the WCB.

Case

(WCB) A reported work injury or illness which has been assembled and assigned a case number by the Workers' Compensation Board.

Case Number

(WCB) The case number structure is eight characters beginning with an alpha character, followed by seven numeric characters. For example, G1234567.
- Volunteer ambulance workers' cases begin with AA, followed by six numbers (e.g. AA123456).
- Volunteer firefighters' cases begin with FA, followed by six numbers (e.g. FA123456).

The WCB case number does not designate the district or year the case was created. For eClaims purposes the JCN is the WCB case number.

Claim

(WCB) - A request on a prescribed form C-3 for workers' compensation for work-connected injury, occupational disease disablement, or for death (form C-62) resulting from either cause. A claimant must file a claim within a two-year period from the occurrence of the accidental injury, knowledge of occupational disablement, or death. Failure to file a claim may bar an award for compensation unless the Employer has made advance benefit payment, in which event the claim filing requirement is waived.

Concurrent Employment

Employment of one worker in more than one job during the same period.

Consequential Accident
(WCB) - A second accident resulting from a prior accidental injury which arose out of and in the course of employment; e.g., a claimant who falls down a flight of stairs at home while using crutches because of a leg injury incurred at work.

Continue (a Case)
(WCB) - To complete a hearing on a case without closing the case, leaving additional matters to be resolved at a future hearing.

Controverted Claim
(WCB) - A claim challenged by the Carrier on stated ground. A pre-hearing conference is set by the Board, and the parties are directed to appear and present their case.

Denial
Full denial of a workers' compensation claim by the Claim Administrator. A Claim Administrator may file a FROI 04 or SROI 04 transaction indicating the claim is denied in its entirety. Upon implementation of eClaims for a Claim Administrator this will be the only acceptable full denial of a claim.

Dependent (in a Death Case)
(WCB) A person eligible to receive death benefits in a fatal injury case. The regular receipt of contributions by the alleged dependent upon which s/he relies and needs to sustain her/his customary mode of living constitutes dependency. Surviving spouses and children under age 18 years are eligible for benefits without proving dependency, and other eligible recipients (if dependency is established) may include dependent handicapped children over age 18 years, grandchildren, brothers and sisters under age 18, dependent parents, and grandparents.

Double Compensation - (Also Double Indemnity)
(WCB) - A duplicate award of either compensation or death benefits made on the grounds that the injured Worker, at the time of the accident, was under the age of 18 years and was permitted or suffered to work in violation of the New York Labor Law. The Employer alone and not the Insurance Carrier is liable for the additional compensation.

Earning Capacity
(WCB) - The ability of a claimant (i.e., one who has suffered a work-connected disabling injury) to earn wages in the labor market. A claimant's earning capacity is determined by actual post-accident earning, or, in the absence of such earnings, a theoretic wage-earning capacity may be established by the Workers' Compensation Board.

Electronic Data Interchange (EDI)
EDI is the structured transmission of data between organizations by electronic means. This exchange of data will take place between trading partners and the WCB.

First Report of Injury (FROI)
A record of an event sent to the WCB that completes the first report of an injury requirement

Hearing
(WCB) - The Workers' Compensation Law provides that no case may be closed without notice to all parties interested, with all such parties having an opportunity to be heard. The Workers' Compensation formal "hearings" are held before Workers' Compensation Law Judges who hear and determine claims for compensation, for the purpose of ascertaining the rights of the parties.

Hearing Point
(WCB) - facilities, other than the nine district offices, for which calendars are prepared and at which hearings are held.

Indexed Claim (manually assembled)
A complete case without any of the following present: Acceptance, Denial, or Report of Payment. NOTE: If a C-3 is present and has the prior injury and treatment boxes checked, there must also be a signed C-3.3 present to index.

Licensed Representative
(WCB) - (a) Any person other than an attorney who is authorized by the Workers' Compensation Board to represent claimants before the Board and, in some instances, to receive a fee, fixed by the Board, for such services; also (b) Any person other than an attorney who is authorized by the Workers' Compensation Board to represent self-insureds before the Board.

Lost Time
(WCB) - A period of total wage loss and loss of earning capacity, beyond the waiting period (first 7 days of disability for workers' compensation cases), caused by the claimant's work-connected disability. In workers' compensation cases only, if the disability period exceeds 14 days, compensation will be paid from the first day of disability; there is no waiting period for volunteer ambulance worker or volunteer firefighter cases.

Maintenance Type Code (MTC)
The MTC defines the specific purpose of each FROI/SROI transaction being submitted.

Maximum Medical Improvement
(WCB) - An assessed condition of a claimant based on medical judgment that (a) the claimant has recovered from the work-related injury to the greatest extent that is expected, and (b) no further change in her/his condition is expected. A finding of maximum medical improvement is a normal precondition for determining the permanent disability level of a claimant.

Medical Benefits

Medical treatment provided, under the Workers' Compensation Law, to injured workers as a result of injuries arising out of and in the course of employment.

Medical Fee Schedule
(WCB) - A schedule, established by the Chair of the Workers' Compensation Board, of charges and fees for medical treatment and care furnished to workers' compensation claimants.

No Further Action (NFA)
(WCB) - To remove a case from further consideration on the calendar unless action is taken by Parties of Interest (POI). The decision to change the status of a case to No Further Action (NFA) is based upon the determination that no further rulings by the Board can be made unless action is taken by Parties of Interest (POI). This case status is indicated by a statement on a WCB decision (e.g., "No further action is planned by the Board at this time").

Notice
(WCB) - Written notification from an employee to her/his employer, indicating that a work-connected injury or illness has occurred. For injuries, notice must be given no later than 30 days after the accident. The Board may excuse a failure to give notice on the grounds that (a) for some reason, notice could not have been given; (b) the employer had knowledge of the accident; or (c) the employer's case has not been prejudiced. In cases involving occupational diseases, the time period for notice is two years from the date of disablement or from the date when the employee knew, or should have known, that the disease was due to the nature of employment.

Occupational Disease (OD)
A disease arising from employment conditions for a class of workers, with the disease occurring as a natural incident for particular occupations, distinct from and exceeding the ordinary hazards and risks of employment. To be considered an occupational disease, there must be some recognizable link between the disease and some distinctive feature of the worker's job.

Occupational Disease
(WCB) - Disabling non-accidental injuries and illnesses arising from conditions of employment, including occupational hearing loss and 30 diseases listed under Section 3(2) of the Workers' Compensation Law. A distinguishing characteristic of occupational diseases is the lack of a clear date of accident -- so special rules are needed in OD cases to establish a date of disablement, "timely notice" requirements, etc.

Occupational Disease, Notice and Causal Relationship (ODNCR)
(WCB) Minimal conditions that must be met before financial responsibility can be assigned to a claim for workers' compensation based on occupational disease. Specifically, it must be established that (a) the claimant has an occupational disease recognized by the Workers' Compensation Law; (b) the claimant has, after the onset of the disease, notified her/his employer within the time limit set by the Workers' Compensation Law

for occupational diseases (two years from date of disablement or from date when claimant knew or should have known that the disease was due to the nature of the employment, whichever is greater); and (c) a causal relationship exists between work-related activities and exposure, the development of the occupational disease, and a subsequent disability.

ODNCR
See Occupational Disease, Notice and Causal Relationship

PFME
See Prima Facie Medical Evidence

Prima Facie Medical Evidence (PFME)
A finding by the WCLJ that the medical report in the file is sufficient to proceed further in the hearing process. A finding that the Medical Report or Reports constitute prima facie medical evidence is an evidentiary determination that the case may proceed and is interlocutory and is not reviewable by the Board.

Protracted Healing Period
(WCB) - In cases involving a schedule permanent partial disability, if the WCB finds that the healing period (period of temporary total disability) exceeds the normal healing period allowed for the injury by the Workers' Compensation Law (Section 15(4-a)) than awards for the protracted healing period may be added to the award. {Example: A claimant suffers a 25% permanent loss of use of an arm (.25 x 312 week maximum = 78 weeks schedule award) and the claimant is judged to have been unable to work for 40 weeks, rather than the 32 week normal healing period; the award is for 78 (schedule) + 8 (protracted healing) = 86 weeks}

Reduced Earnings
(WCB) A compensation rate based on the claimant's partial wage loss or partial loss of earning capacity due to a condition related to a compensable work-connected injury.

Scheduled Loss of Use (SLU)
Maximum benefit week schedules in the Workers' Compensation Law generally are used in determining lifetime benefits for permanent partial injuries to an arm (312 weeks), leg (288 weeks), hand (244 weeks), foot (205 weeks), eye (160), finger (25-75 weeks, depending on digit), toe (16-30 weeks), or for hearing loss (60 weeks for one ear, 150 weeks for both). Injuries amounting to less than a 100% functional loss are awarded a percentage of the scheduled weeks, and there are also special provisions for additional weeks required for a protracted healing period.

Self-Insurance
(WCB) - A method by which an employer or group of employers may secure the payment of workers' compensation benefits to employees by depositing securities or a surety bond in an amount required by the Workers' Compensation Board (this

requirement is waived for local government self-insures); the self-insurance method is in lieu of purchasing insurance from an insurance carrier.

Stay
Under WCL section 23, when a party files an application for review from a WCLJ decision, the portion of the award that is under appeal is 'stayed'. For example, if a carrier appeals the WCLJ finding of total disability, but its consultant says moderate disability, then during the appeal the carrier must pay the conceded moderate rate, but need not pay at the total rate. Even if the carrier loses the appeal, it should not be penalized for late payment under sec. 25(3)(f). Awards are, however, subject to interest per section 20. Once the Board Panel issues its Memorandum of Decision (MOD), if the carrier loses, it must pay the award directed by the Board Panel. If the losing party appeals an MOD to the Appellate Division, Third Department, and/or files a request for Full Board Review, there is no stay on the awards rendered in the MOD. For example, if the carrier lost the appeal, and the MOD directed payment at the total rate, and the carrier filed a request for Full Board Review and/or a notice of appeal to the Appellate Division, it is not allowed to withhold payment pending resolution of that/those application(s). There is no stay following an MOD. There is one exception to this rule. If the MOD is not unanimous, in other words if there is a dissenting panel member, then if the losing party seeks Full Board Review, this is called mandatory Full Board Review, and there is probably a stay on awards rendered in that MOD. This is extremely rare. Well over 99% of all MODs are unanimous. In the event of a dissent, and a request for mandatory Full Board Review, OOA will make sure that the claims examiner is properly informed of this in the case note.

Subrogation
(WCB) - The assignment of a cause of action against a third party by the claimant to the carrier. If cause for an action (e.g., a product liability lawsuit) against a third party exists based on a work injury or illness, and the claimant fails to commence such action within the period specified by Section 29 of the Workers' Compensation Law (6 months after the awarding of compensation or 9 months after the enactment of new laws permitting additional remedies), the failure operates as an assignment of the cause of action to the insurance carrier liable for the payment of compensation benefits.

Subsequent Report of Injury (SROI)
A record of an event sent to the WCB that completes a subsequent report of injury requirement.

Third Party Administrator
(WCB) - A person, firm, corporation or insurance carrier licensed by the Workers' Compensation Board to solicit the business of representing self-insurers in dealings before with the Board.

Third Party Settlement
(WCB) - This term refers to lawsuits against equipment manufacturers, facility owners and other non-employer parties whose products or services contributed to the

occurrence of an accident. Under workers' compensation law, a compensation claim is a worker's sole remedy against the employer, but lawsuits may be initiated against third parties for contributory negligence, product defects, etc.

Wage Expectancy

(WCB) - A decision element assigning an artificial wage rate to a young claimant, based on the authority of Section 14(5) of the Workers' Compensation Law: "If it be established that the injured employee was under the age of twenty-five when injured, and that under normal conditions his wages would be expected to increase, that fact may be considered in arriving at his average weekly wage".

Waiting Period

(WCB) - Period covering the first 7 days of disability resulting from a work-connected injury or illness. Workers' compensation indemnity benefits are not allowable for the first 7 days of disability, except that (a) in cases where the disability period exceeds 14 days, indemnity awards are allowed from the date of disability,(b) under a plan or agreement accepted by the Chair, the waiting period may be less than 7 days or eliminated entirely and (c) there is no waiting period for (VAWBL/VFBL) cases covering volunteer ambulance workers or volunteer firefighters.

Walk-In Stipulation Calendar (WISK)

Hearings are not pre-scheduled; parties "walk in" on the designated day and present to the Judge a resolution of the case by stipulation of the parties. Judge hears and rules on the stipulation, and, if appropriate, closes the case.

APPENDIX II: NEW YORK "CHEAT SHEETS."

Deadlines (Chart).

Trigger	Deadline
Claim Denial	25 days after indexing
First Payment	18 days after disability or 10 days after employer's or carrier's knowledge
Compensability Decision	18 days after disability or 10 days after employer's or carrier's knowledge
Intro Packet	within 14 days of C-2/FROI-00
Payment of Award	10 days
Object to Proposed Decision	30 days (but look at PD, because it may have a different date)
Object to bill	45 days
Appeal Law Judge	30 days

Benefits

[1]   TTD Benefits Guidelines.

Waiting Period: 7 non-consecutive calendar days
Retro Period: 14 days

[2]   AWW/TTD Calculation:

52 Weeks before the date or injury or 52 weeks of a similar employee

[3]   Multipliers for calculating wages.

260 for a 5 day a week
300 for a 6 day a week
Between 234-260 days in 52 weeks use 260 multiplier
Between 261-299- use without a multiplier

[4]   Use of multiplier:

Total Wages for 52 weeks worked/ days worked = ADW
ADW x Multiplier = Annual wages
Annual wages/52 = AWW
AWW/1.5 = TTD

[5]   TTD Rates

2017 Minimum weekly TTD- $150.00 (Applies to cases with dates of loss *after* May 1, 2013)
2017 Maximum weekly TTD- $870.61 (Effective July 1, 2017 to June 30, 2018)

[6]   Degree of Disability.

Degree of disability * the TTD rate = the weekly benefit rate.
Mild: 25%
Moderate: 50%
Marked: 75%
Total: 100%

- Work Status expired after 90 days (claimant must produce medical every 90 days).
- Once there is a decision or award you must file a RFA-2 to reduce rate beyond the award.
- If the claimant returns to work you are able to stop TTD without a RFA.

[7]   Permanent Disability Benefits

- There is a credit for the number of weeks TTD paid in SLU cases.
- Protracted Healing Period- If the number of weeks of TTD surpasses the number of weeks for the healing period you must subtract the number of weeks surpassing the healing period from your TTD credit.
- Classification- For body parts that are not covered in schedule loss of use.

Form Deadlines (Chart).

Form Name	Deadline
C4 AUTH	30 days
MG-1	8 days (must have medical evidence)

MG-2 Variance	5 days if not obtaining an IME, 30 days with IME
C-2 Employer's Report of Work-Re-lated	10 days after accident
C-8.1(a) or (b)	45 days after receipt of bill

APPENDIX III: SCHEDULED LOSS OF USE CHART

Percent %	Hand	Arm	Thumb	First Finger	Second	Third	Fourth	Leg	Foot	Big Toe	Toes	Eye	Partial Total	Percent %
Maximum	244	312	75	46	30	25	15	288	205	38	16	160	600	Maximum
1	2.44	3.12	0.75	0.46	0.3	0.25	0.15	2.88	2.05	0.38	0.16	1.6	6	1
2.5	6.1	7.8	1.875	1.15	0.75	0.625	0.375	7.2	5.125	0.95	0.4	4	15	2.5
5	12.2	15.6	3.75	2.3	1.5	1.25	0.75	14.4	10.25	1.9	0.8	8	30	5
7.5	18.3	23.4	5.625	3.45	2.25	1.875	1.125	21.6	15.375	2.85	1.2	45	45	7.5
10	24.4	31.2	7.5	4.6	3	2.5	1.5	28.8	20.5	3.8	1.6	16	60	10
12.5	30.5	39	9.375	5.75	3.75	3.125	1.875	36	25.625	4.75	2	20	75	12.5
15	36.6	46.8	11.25	6.9	4.5	3.75	2.25	43.2	30.75	5.7	2.4	24	90	15
17.5	42.7	54.6	13.125	8.05	5.25	4.375	2.625	50.4	35.875	6.65	2.8	28	105	17.5
20	48.8	62.4	15	9.2	6	5	3	57.6	41	7.6	3.2	32	120	20
22.5	54.9	70.2	16.875	10.35	6.75	5.625	3.375	64.8	46.125	8.55	3.6	36	135	22.5
25	61	78	18.75	11.5	7.5	6.25	3.75	72	51.25	9.5	4	40	150	25
27.5	67.1	85.8	20.625	12.65	8.25	6.875	4.125	79.2	56.375	10.45	4.4	44	165	27.5
30	73.2	93.6	22.5	13.8	9	7.5	4.5	86.4	61.5	11.4	4.8	48	180	30
33.3	81.252	103.896	24.975	15.318	9.99	8.325	4.995	95.904	68.265	12.654	5.328	53.28	199.8	33.3
35	85.4	109.2	26.25	16.1	10.5	8.75	5.25	100.8	71.75	13.3	5.6	56	210	35
37.5	91.5	117	28.125	17.25	11.25	9.375	5.625	108	76.875	14.25	6	60	225	37.5
40	97.6	124.8	30	18.4	12	10	6	115.2	82	15.2	6.4	64	240	40
42.5	103.7	132.6	31.875	19.55	12.75	10.625	6.375	122.4	87.125	16.15	6.8	68	255	42.5
45	109.8	140.4	33.75	20.7	13.5	11.25	6.75	129.6	92.25	17.1	7.2	72	270	45
47.5	115.9	148.2	35.625	21.85	14.25	11.875	7.125	136.8	97.375	18.05	7.6	76	285	47.5
50	122	156	37.5	23	15	12.5	7.5	144	102.5	19	8	80	300	50
55	134.2	171.6	41.25	25.3	16.5	13.75	8.25	158.4	112.75	20.9	8.8	88	330	55
60	146.4	187.2	45	27.6	18	15	9	172.8	123	22.8	9.6	96	360	60
65	158.6	202.8	48.75	29.9	19.5	16.25	9.75	187.2	133.25	24.7	10.4	104	390	65
70	170.8	218.4	52.5	32.2	21	17.5	10.5	201.6	143.5	26.6	11.2	112	420	70
75	183	234	56.25	34.5	22.5	18.75	11.25	216	153.75	28.5	12	120	450	75
80	195.2	249.6	60	36.8	24	20	12	230.4	164	30.4	12.8	128	480	80
85	207.4	265.2	63.75	39.1	25.5	21.25	12.75	244.8	174.25	32.3	13.6	136	510	85
90	219.6	280.8	67.5	41.4	27	22.5	13.5	259.2	184.5	34.2	14.4	144	540	90
95	231.8	296.4	71.25	43.7	28.5	23.75	14.25	273.6	194.75	36.1	15.2	152	570	95
100	244	312	75	46	30	25	15	288	205	38	16	160	600	100

Normal healing periods

As per WCL § 15(4-a):

* Arm, thirty-two weeks;
* leg, forty weeks;
* hand, thirty-two weeks;
* foot, thirty-two weeks;
* ear, twenty-five weeks;
* eye, twenty weeks;
* thumb, twenty-four weeks;
* first finger, eighteen weeks;
* great toe, twelve weeks;
* second finger, twelve weeks;
* third finger, eight weeks;
* fourth finger, eight weeks;
* toe other than great toe, eight weeks.

APPENDIX IV: LWEC WEEKS CHART

LWEC (%)	Maximum Weeks of PPD Benefits
> 0 - 15%	225 Weeks
> 15 - 30%	250 Weeks
> 30 - 40%	275 Weeks
> 40 - 50%	300 Weeks
> 50 - 60%	350 Weeks
> 60 - 70%	375 Weeks
> 70 - 75%	400 Weeks
> 75 - 80%	425 Weeks
> 80 - 85%	450 Weeks
> 85 - 90%	475 Weeks
> 90 - 95%	500 Weeks
> 95 - 99%	525 Weeks

For a discussion of Loss of Wage Earning Capacity ("LWEC") and how to use this chart, *see* Chapter 15, "Understanding LWEC."

APPENDIX V: MAXIMUM RATES BY YEAR

Maximum rates in effect by year (1986 to 2017).

Date of Accident	Weekly Maximum (Total/Partial)
July 1, 1985 - June 30, 1990	$300 / $150
July 1, 1990 - June 30, 1991	$340 / $280
July 1, 1991 - June 30, 1992	$350 / $350
July 1, 1992 - June 30, 2007	$400 / $400
July 1, 2007 – June 30, 2008	$500 / $500
July 1, 2008 – June 30, 2009	$550 / $550
July 1, 2009 – June 30, 2010	$600 / $600
July 1, 2010 - June 30, 2011	$739.83
July 1, 2011 - June 30, 2012	$772.96
July 1, 2012 - June 30, 2013	$792.07
July 1, 2013 - June 30, 2014	$803.21
July 1, 2014 - June 30, 2015	$808.65
July 1, 2015 - June 30, 2016	$844.29
July 1, 2016 - June 30, 2017	$864.32
July 1, 2017 - June 30, 2018	$870.61
July 1, 2018 – June 30, 2019	$904.74

For a discussion of temporary disability benefits and how to use this chart, *see* Chapter 7; for the application of these maximums in permanent disability awards, *see* Chapter 15, "Understanding LWEC."

INDEX

ABOUT LOIS LLC

Lois LLC is 22 lawyers defending employers in New York, New Jersey, and Federal Longshore cases.

Our focus is on defending employers and carriers in workers' compensation claims in New York, New Jersey, and Longshore. We offer general litigation services defending carriers and self-insureds in civil actions and pursue reimbursement claims under New York's WCL § 29 and New Jersey's § 40 (N.J.S.A. 34:15-40).

New York
We represent insurance carriers, self-insured employers, third party claim administrators, and employers before the New York State Workers' Compensation Board. We handle cases from cradle-to-grave. We want to be by your side, moving cases aggressively to closure from the start of litigation all the way through to settlement.

We handle cases throughout New York State.

New Jersey
In New Jersey we represent insurance carriers, self-insured employers, third party claim administrators, and employers before the New Jersey's Division of Workers' Compensation. Our founding partner, Gregory Lois, is the co-author of Lexis-Nexis New Jersey Workers' Compensation Practice Guide (2016 & 2017) and served as Law Clerk to Hon. Joan Mott, Administrative Supervisor of Workers Compensation.

We regularly appear in all New Jersey courts.

- Atlantic City
- Bridgeton
- Camden
- Elizabeth
- Freehold
- Hackensack
- Lebanon
- Jersey City
- Mount Holly
- Mount Arlington
- Newark
- New Brunswick
- Paterson
- Toms River
- Trenton

Longshore and Harbor Workers' Compensation Act | Defense Base Act.

- New York District Office
- OAL – Cherry Hill, NJ
- 2nd & 3rd Cir.

General Litigation.

Lois LLC counts among its clients several general liability, premises liability and automobile liability insurance carriers and third party administrators. We regularly represent these clients' insureds in defense of personal injury matters filed in all counties in Metropolitan New York, all counties in New Jersey and in the federal courts.

The author of this handbook is the managing partner at *Lois LLC*.

For more about *Lois LLC*: https://www.loisllc.com

Neither the use of this book or any linked site nor the transfer of information to or from any linked site shall create or constitute an attorney-client relationship between Gregory Lois or *Lois Law Firm LLC* and any person.

Please see *Disclaimer,* beginning of this book

ABOUT THE AUTHOR

Gregory Lois's practice involves representation of employers, self-insured companies, third party administrators, and insurance carriers in workers' compensation matters. Greg has served as lead attorney on more than 100 trials involving workplace discrimination, workers' compensation, and civil claims. Greg is the author of the prior editions of this book ("New York Workers' Compensation Law.") Greg is the co-author of the LexisNexis "Practice Guide to Workers' Compensation in New Jersey" (2016 & 2017).

Gregory Lois is the Managing Partner at Lois LLC. Greg supervises the Firm's Workers' Compensation Department. Greg regularly appears in New York and New Jersey workers' compensation courts and in Federal courts on Longshore and Harbors' Workers Compensation matters (including claims under the Defense Base Act).

Before founding Lois LLC in 2015, Greg was a partner at a mid-size law firm (125 attorneys) where he managed the New York office. Formerly Law Clerk to the New Jersey Division of Workers' Compensation, Greg is active in the Justice James H. Coleman Jr., Workers' Compensation Inn of Court.

Greg is admitted to practice law in New Jersey, New York; and Massachusetts.

Greg can be contacted at *Lois Law Firm LLC,* The Chrysler Building, 405 Lexington Ave, 26th Floor, New York, NY 10174; 201-880-7213 x 115 and via email to glois@lois-llc.com

For in-depth case law discussions: https://www.loisllc.com

Follow Greg on Twitter: @gregorylois

Newsletter signup: Email to glois@loisllc.com or on the web at https://www.loisllc.com/newsletter

Made in the USA
Columbia, SC
26 November 2018